Decorative Painting Techniques for
WILDFLOWERS & BERRIES

23 STEP-BY-STEP PROJECTS IN THE TRADITIONAL STYLE

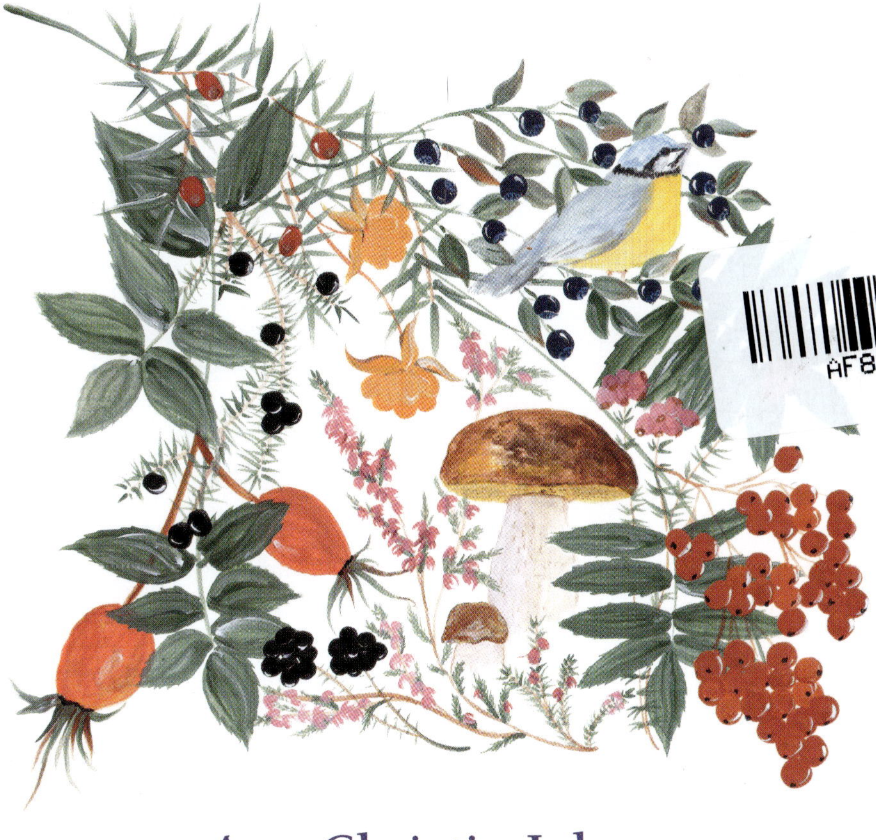

Ann Christin Johansen

Hand Books Press

Contents

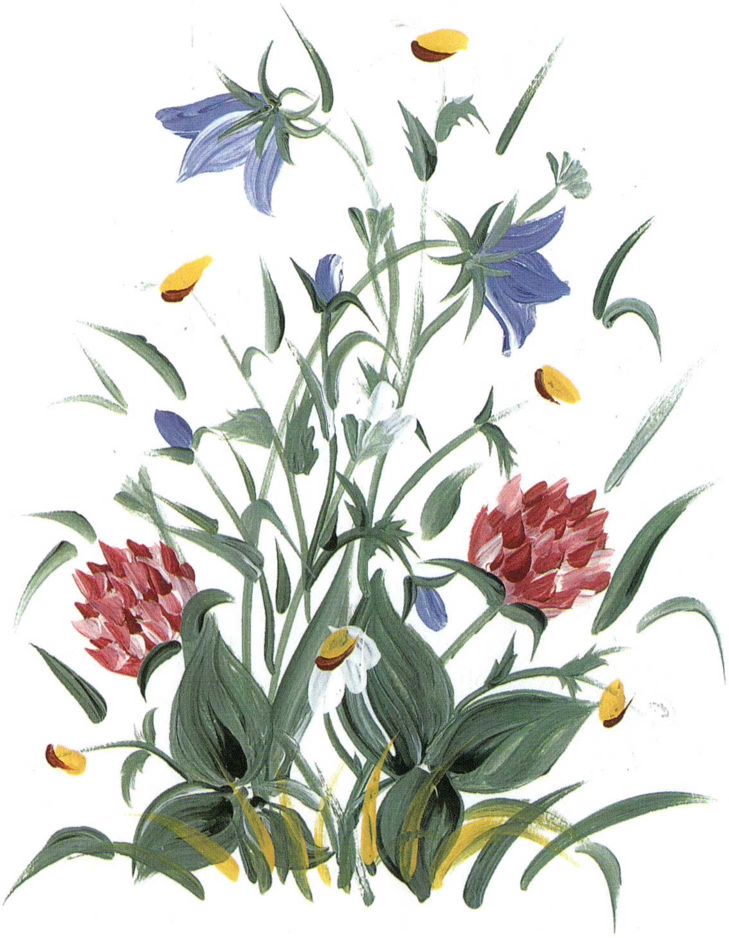

Decorative Painting Techniques for Wildflowers & Berries
By Ann Christin Johansen

First published in the U.S.A.
by Hand Books Press
931 East Main Street #106
Madison, WI 53703–2955 U.S.A.

ISBN 0-9658248-6-1

02 01 00 99 98 5 4 3 2 1

Distributed to the book trade and art trade in the U.S.A. by
North Light Books,
an imprint of F&W Publications
1507 Dana Avenue,
Cincinnati, Ohio 45207
Telephone: (800) 289-0963,
Fax: (513) 531-4082

English language edition produced by Design Books International.
English text translation by Vera Hart.
English language edition edited by Nicole Skelly.
Indexing by Ann Fleury.

Printed and bound in Denmark

Introduction

Let's take a journey into the world of wildflowers, berries and mushrooms. You'll see your creations come to life as you learn to paint these elements of nature through step-by-step instruction. The next time you take a nature walk, you will look at the fields and forests with "new eyes" and inspiration, knowing that you can paint this natural beauty. With the aid of step-by-step instructions, you'll find that this is not a difficult task. Take along some drawing paper and be patient, as you watch your brush creating the most beautiful floral and wildlife motifs. What could be more therapeutic and adventurous than a beautiful walk in fields or wooded areas?

You'll also learn how to paint leaves, stems, berries and mushrooms, as well as a small titmouse and a bullfinch. Look around as you wonder into the woods with a self-painted basket that is ready to be filled with wildflowers, berries and mushrooms, or perhaps you have already filled it before your walk with a picnic lunch.

I hope you will find joy in this book and that it inspires you to get out your paint brush, because you will find that when using my method, the flowers are easy to paint. Soon you will be a master at painting wildflowers. Perhaps you have a friend who would also like to learn painting from nature. This book is a great gift for the flower lover.

I got inspired to write this book by my students after many years of teaching workshops. The book is based on basic ground rules that I have developed and tested in classes, and that I know my students have been satisfied with. Your painting skills will improve as you practice. Every time you pick up your brush and use this book for guidance, you'll notice your improvement. You will become more daring with shading after a while, and feel more confident as you develop your skills.

What's great about this technique is that it can be used with all types of painting, such as oil paint, watercolor, glass paint and painting on china. Get inspired to paint on everyday objects — baskets, trays, mailboxes, furniture, doors and cabinets — the possibilities are endless. You will also find sources of inspiration inside your home, such as flower arrangements, napkins, wallpaper, curtains, greeting cards, etc. And remember that your technique improves the more you practice.

I wish you luck painting everything that our beautiful fields, gardens and wooded areas have to offer.

A nature greeting from Ann Christin

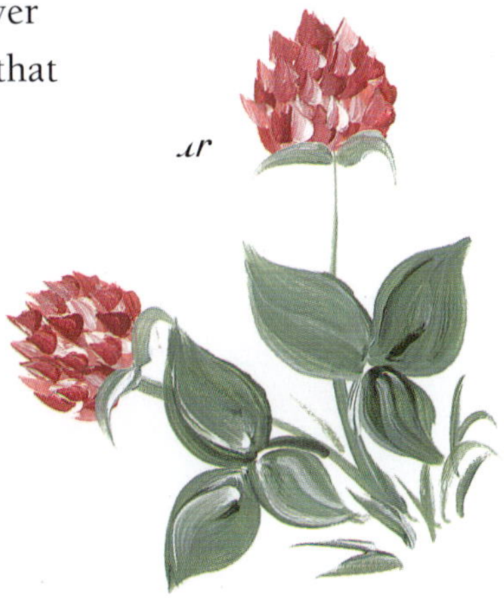

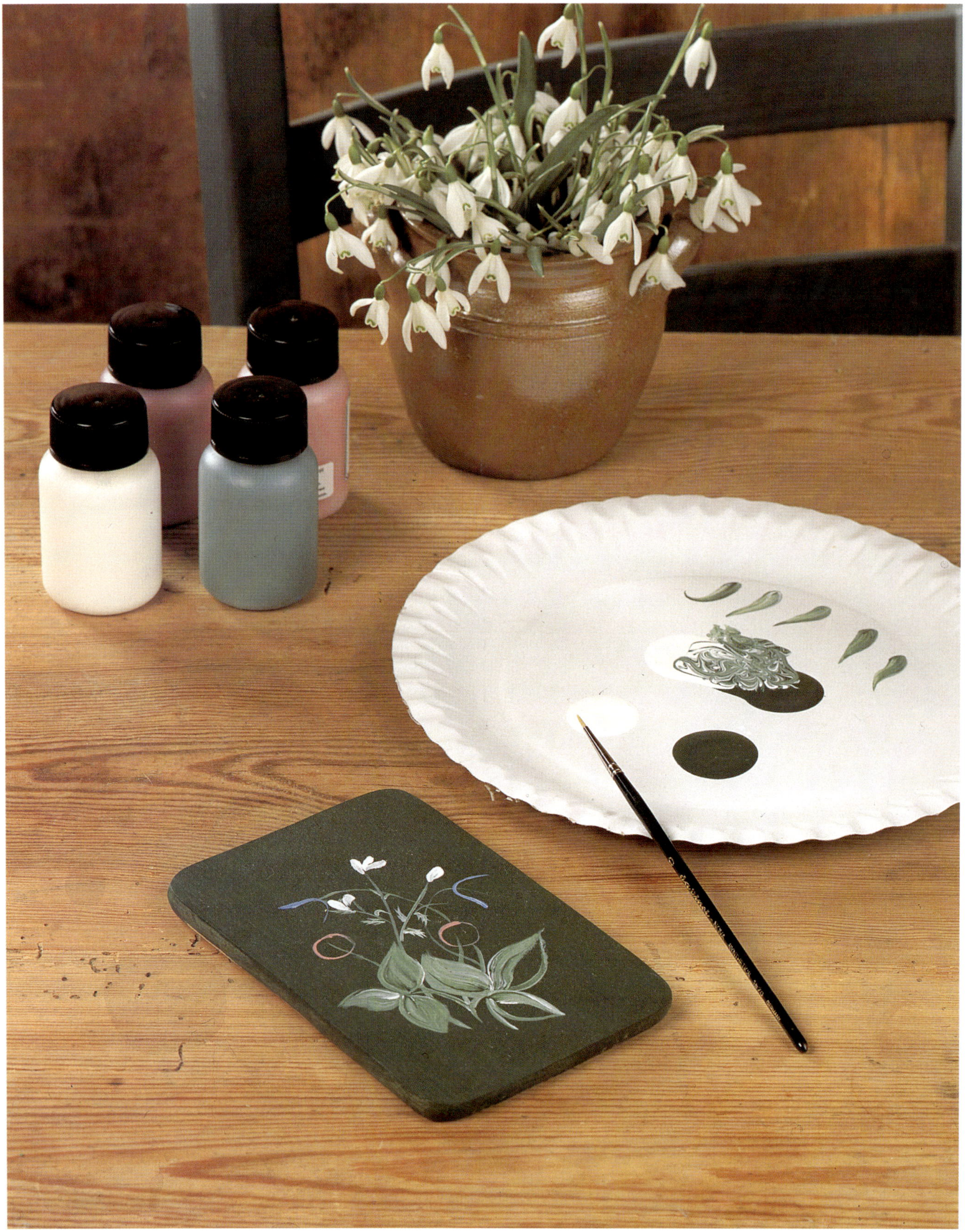

Some Tips Before You Start

Many of my designs are painted on a dark blue background. This color creates a natural contrast and produces a very desirable effect. It is also important to know that you can paint on a green base, even though the stems and leaves will be green. I'll show you how later in this book.

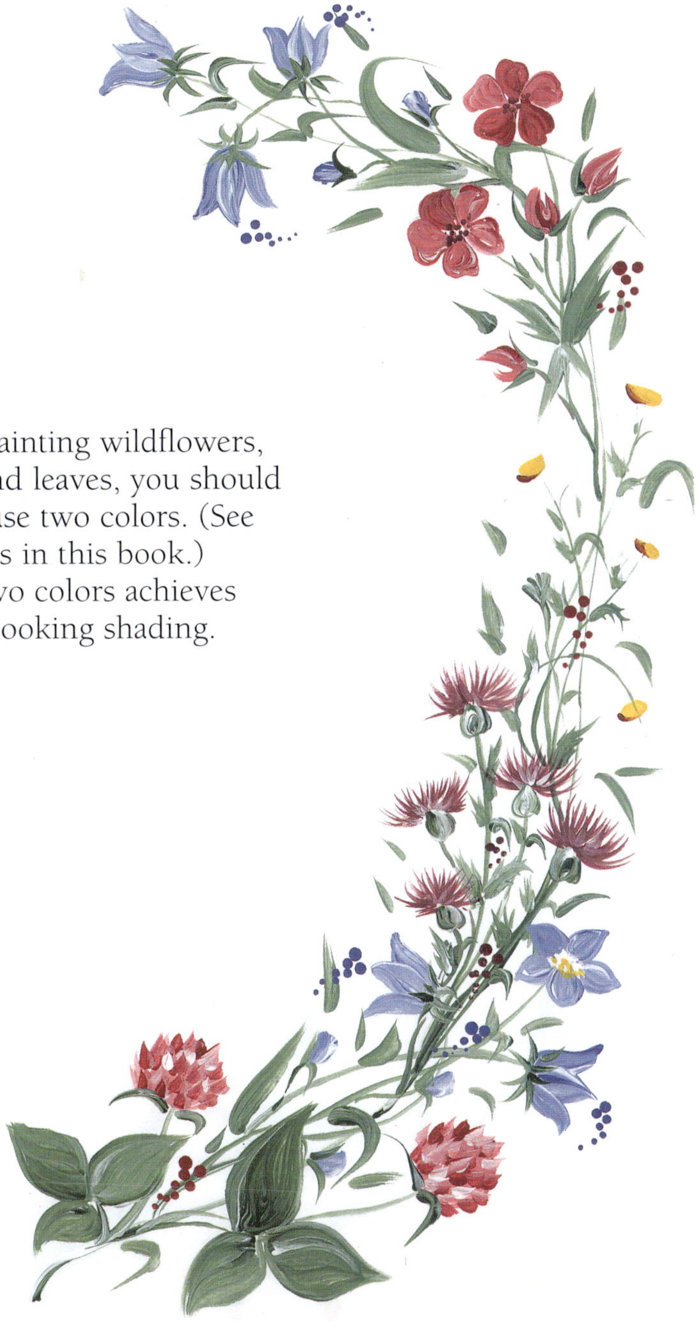

Materials to get started:

1. Paper plate or dish to pour paint onto. *(see photo on pg.4)*

2. Brush #0. I feel this is the best one to use for most flowers.

3. White paper to practice on. Do not practice on what you will paint on. Use colored paper for white flowers.

4. A thicker brush if you are using primer (make sure the bristles are not loose).

5. Paper towels and a glass of water to dip the brush in.

6. Colors you need: white, black, green, yellow, wine red, blue and purple.

When painting wildflowers, stems and leaves, you should always use two colors. (See examples in this book.) Using two colors achieves natural looking shading.

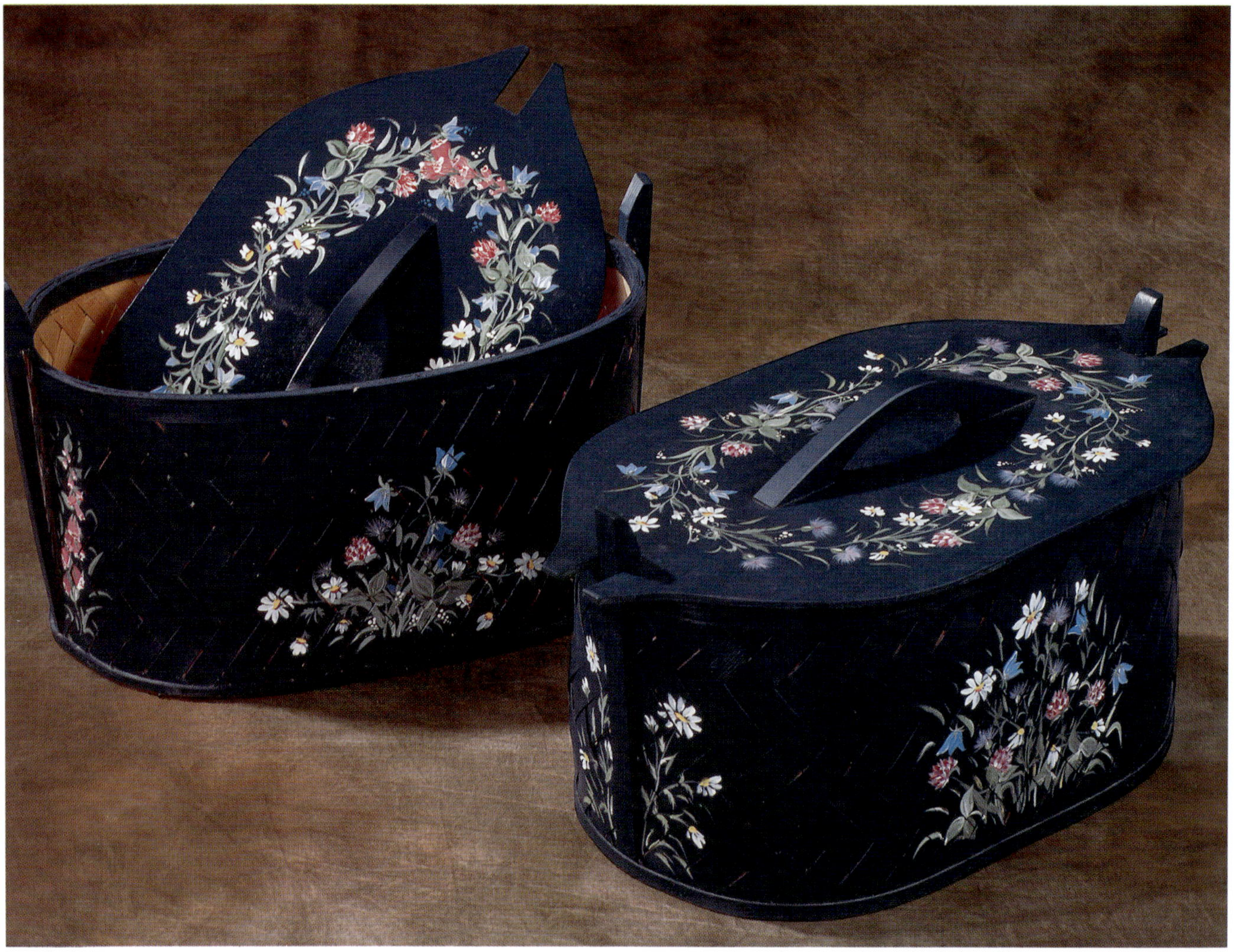

The Brush

Never let the brush stand in water with the bristles down as it will easily become bent and unusable. When you finish painting, rinse the brush well and put it in a glass jar or cup with the bristles up.

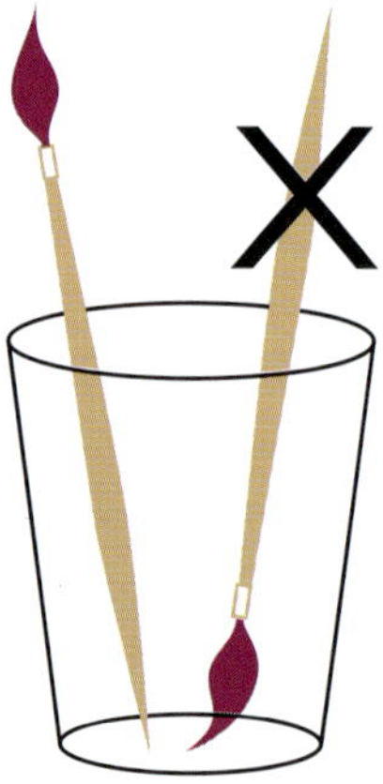

Shading

Always use two colors when you paint to achieve desirable shading effects.

Example: Pour a little green and a little white — mix the two colors together lightly, and you will get a nice shade to paint stems and leaves.

Background & Paint Colors

The piece on page 9 is painted with green on a green background. Here you can see how nicely stems and leaves show up, even though the base color is green. Just add a little white into the green so that you can mix a lighter shade of green. This also holds true for other colors.

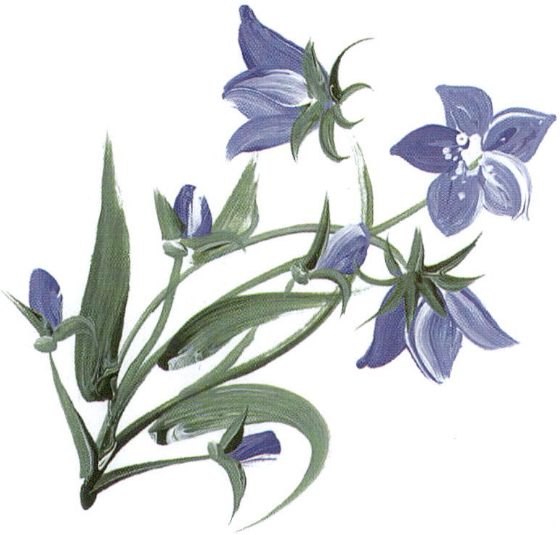

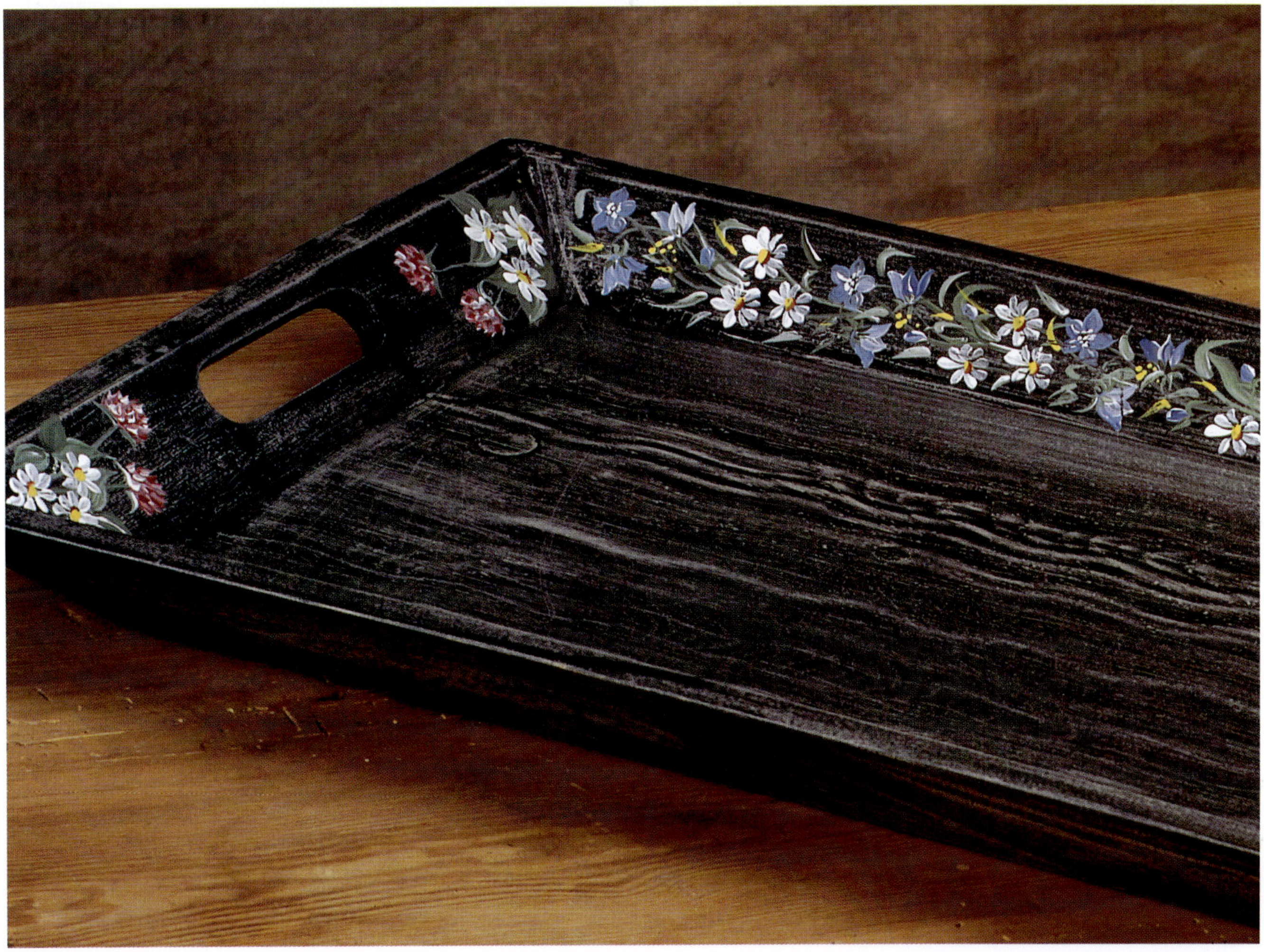

A Basic Color Lesson

Yellow + Blue = Green
Yellow + Red = Orange
White + a little Black = Grey
White + a little Red = Pink
Red + Green = Brown

It is important to know that white lightens and black darkens all colors.

For example: If you're painting a thistle, buy dark purple and lighten it with white. That way, you can obtain several shades and you can paint the thistles in various shades of purple.

Blend green and white for lighter shading.

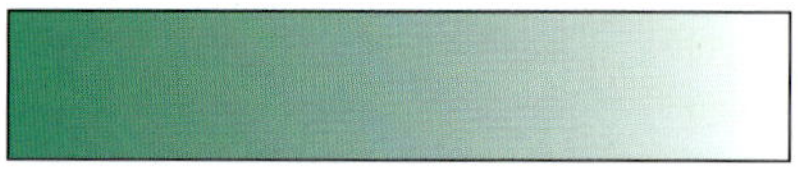

Blend blue and white for lighter shading.

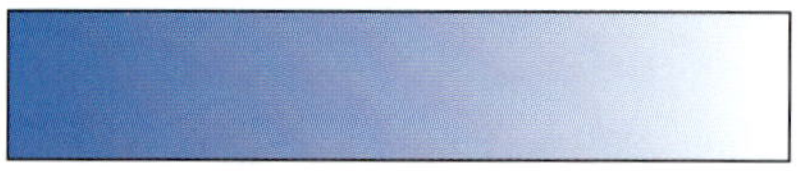

Blend wine red and white for lighter shading.

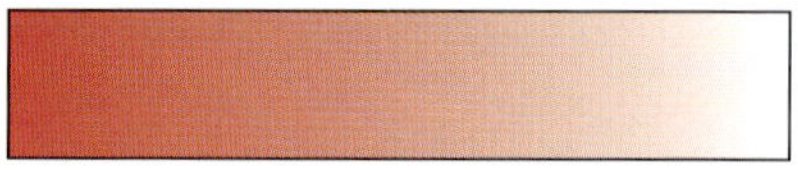

Blend purple and white for lighter shading.

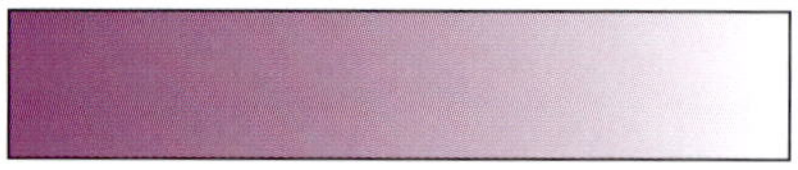

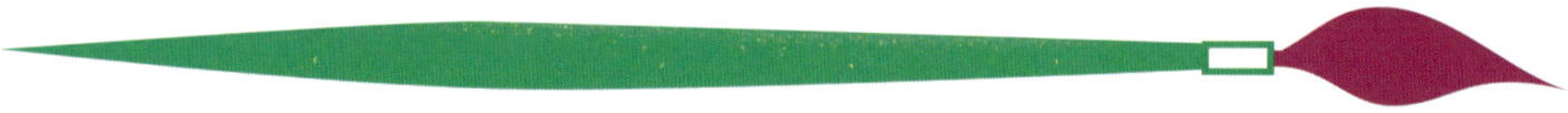

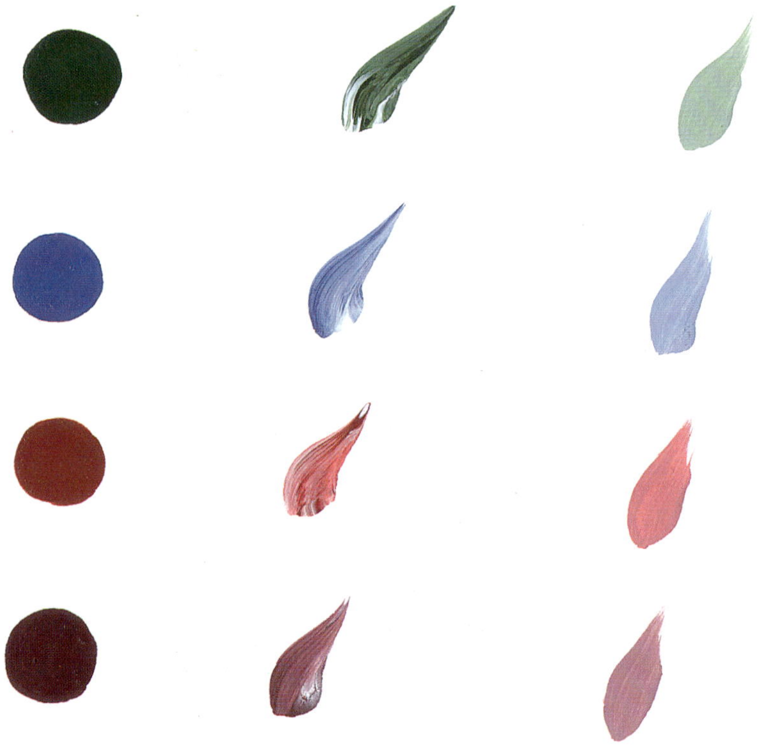

Green lightened with white

Blue lightened with white

Wine red lightened with white

Purple lightened with white

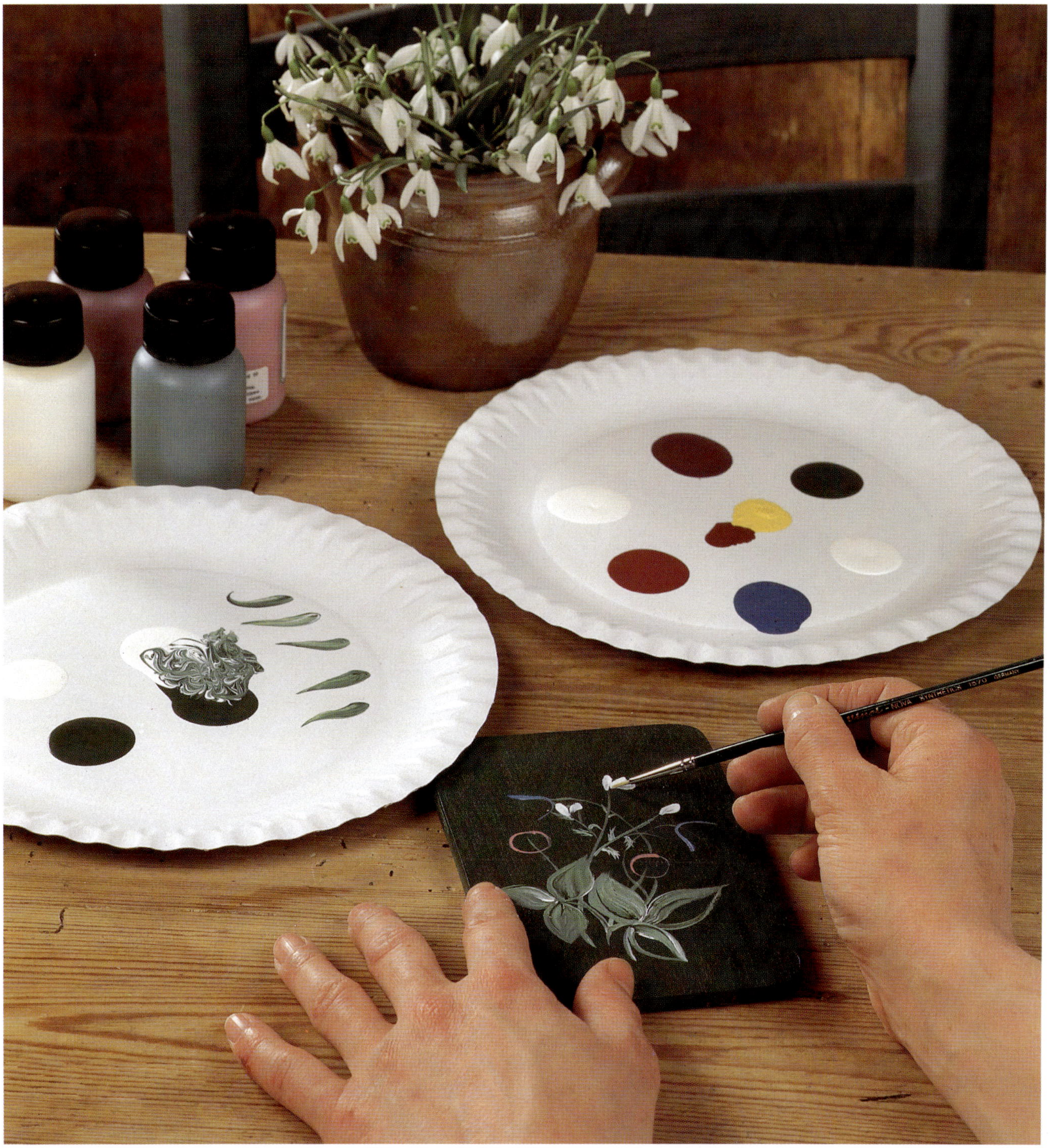

Pour out the paint you'll be using onto a paper plate so your colors are easily accessible. Tighten the lids on the containers to prevent the paints from hardening. Keep a glass of water handy to dip your brush in.

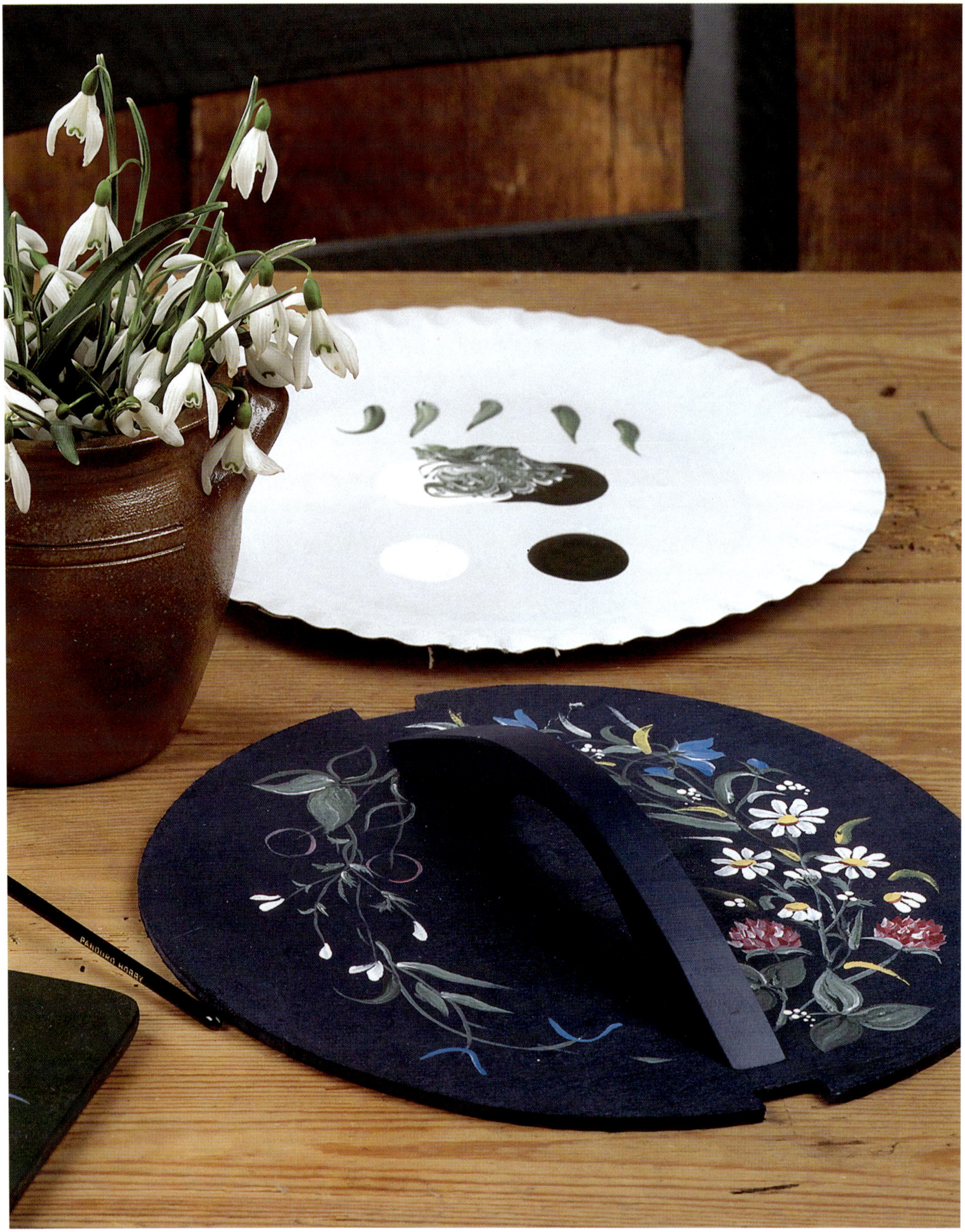
PANDURO HOBBY

Stem

Brush: #0
Colors: Green and white

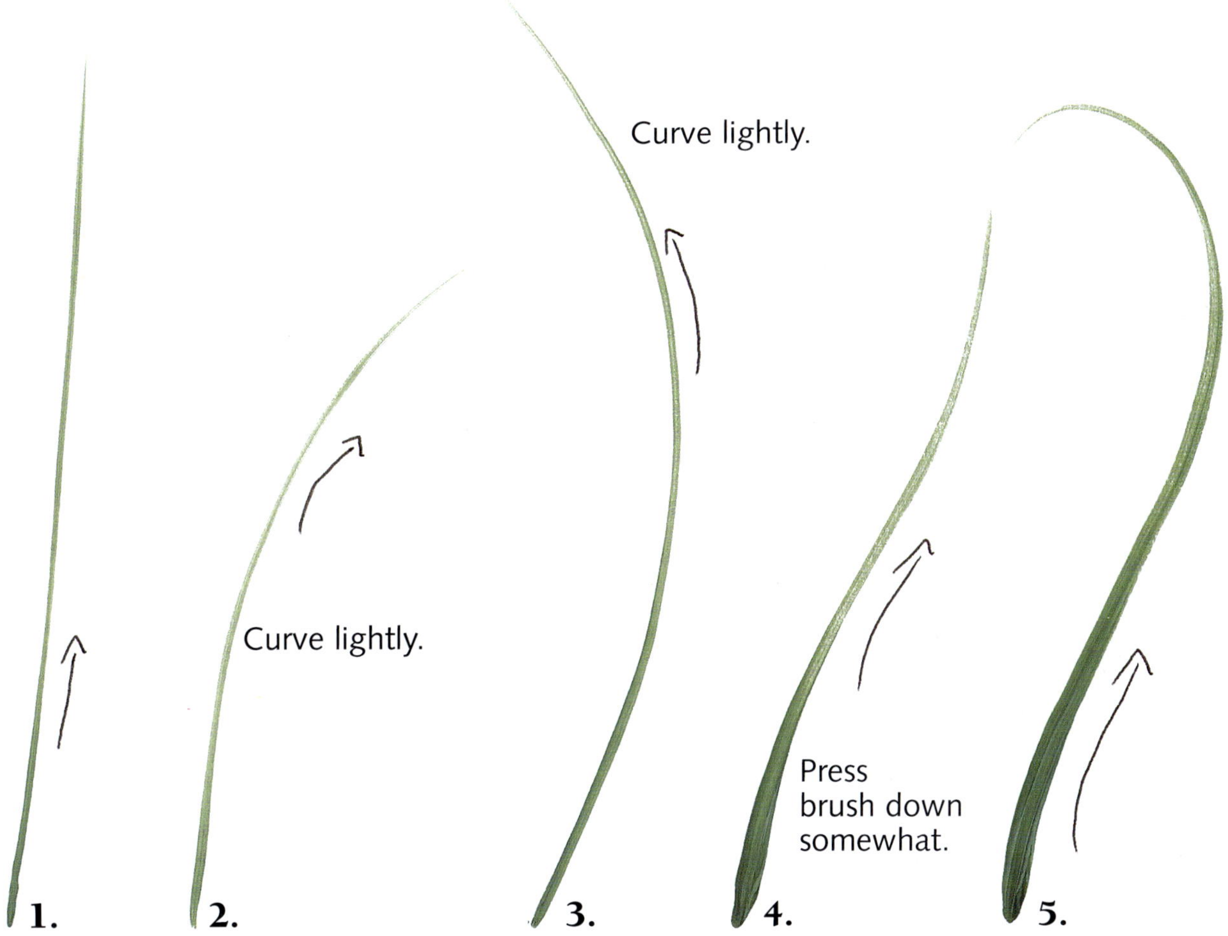

When you paint stems, you must fill your brush well with paint. From the start, be light handed. Pull brush, letting your hand follow, and you will get long, fine stems. If the paint is too thick, use a few drops of water to thin it, and you will find the brush glides nicely. When you press down on the brush, the stems will get thicker at the bottom.

Stems & Branches

Brush: #0
Colors: Green, brown and white

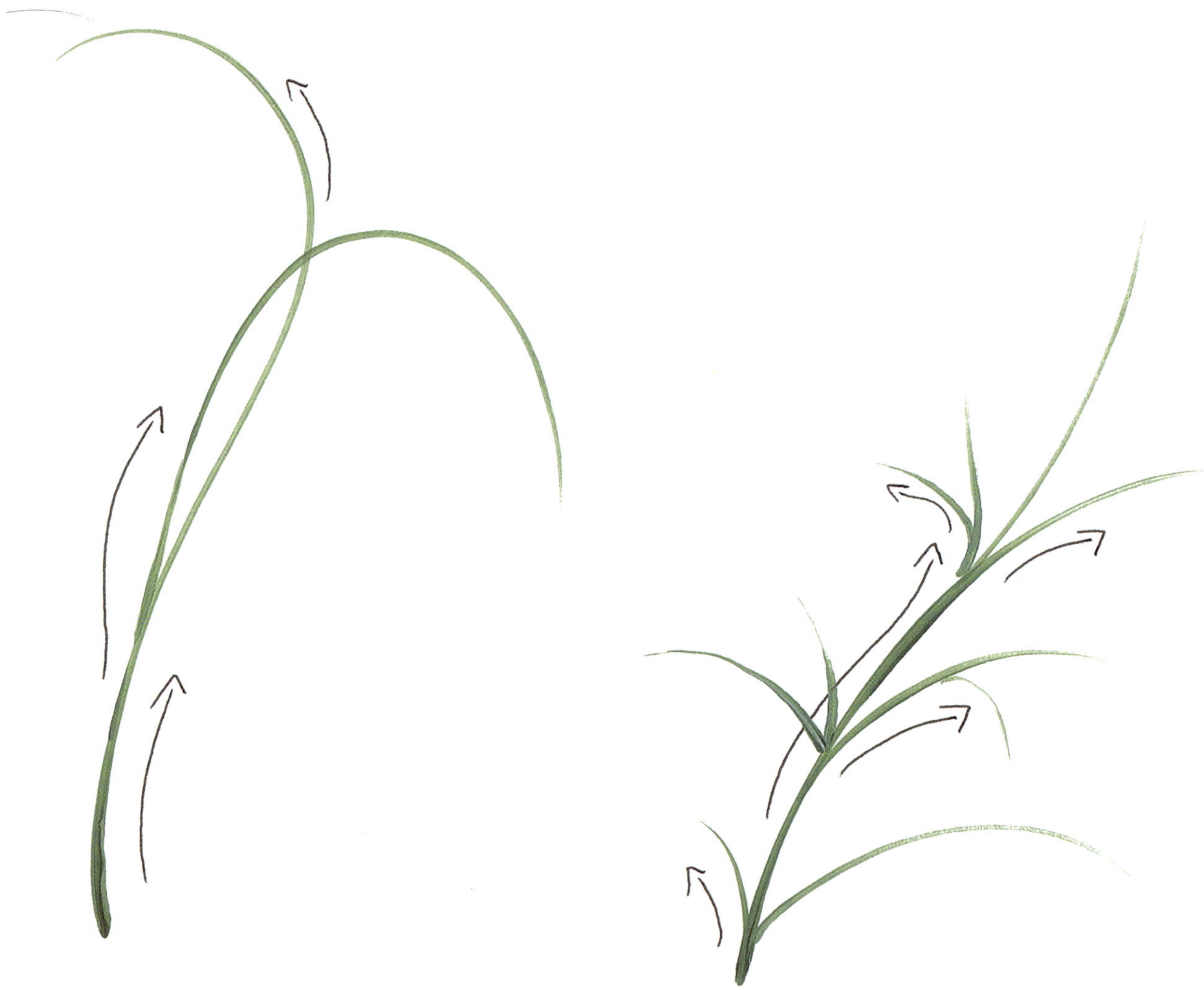

Practice painting stems and twigs thin. Be light handed and you will note as you practice that the stems and lines get lighter and finer. Always remember to have loose, fine paint and plenty of paint on the brush. Look at different plants to see whether the stem is green or brown.

Leaves

Brush: #0
Colors: Green and white

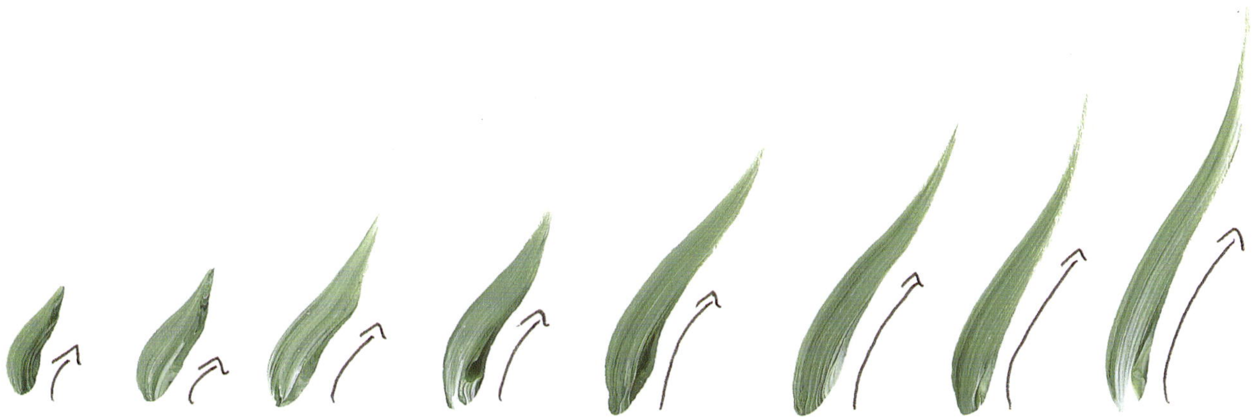

1. Press down and let up.

2. Start pulling the brush a little further, and the leaves get longer and finer.

3. Mix green and white for nice shading.

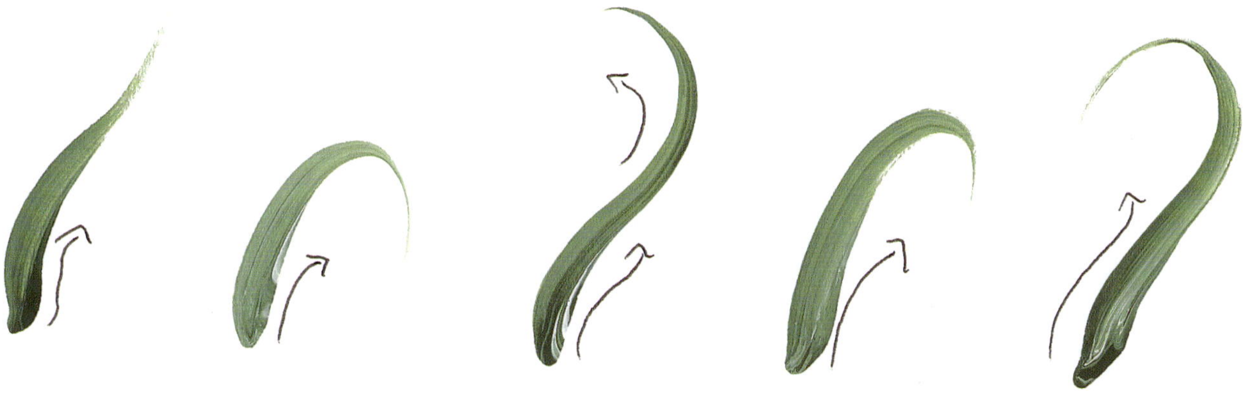

4. After you have practiced painting the leaves, then start adding graceful curves.

5. These leaves are the basis for painting leaves with lobes and spikes.

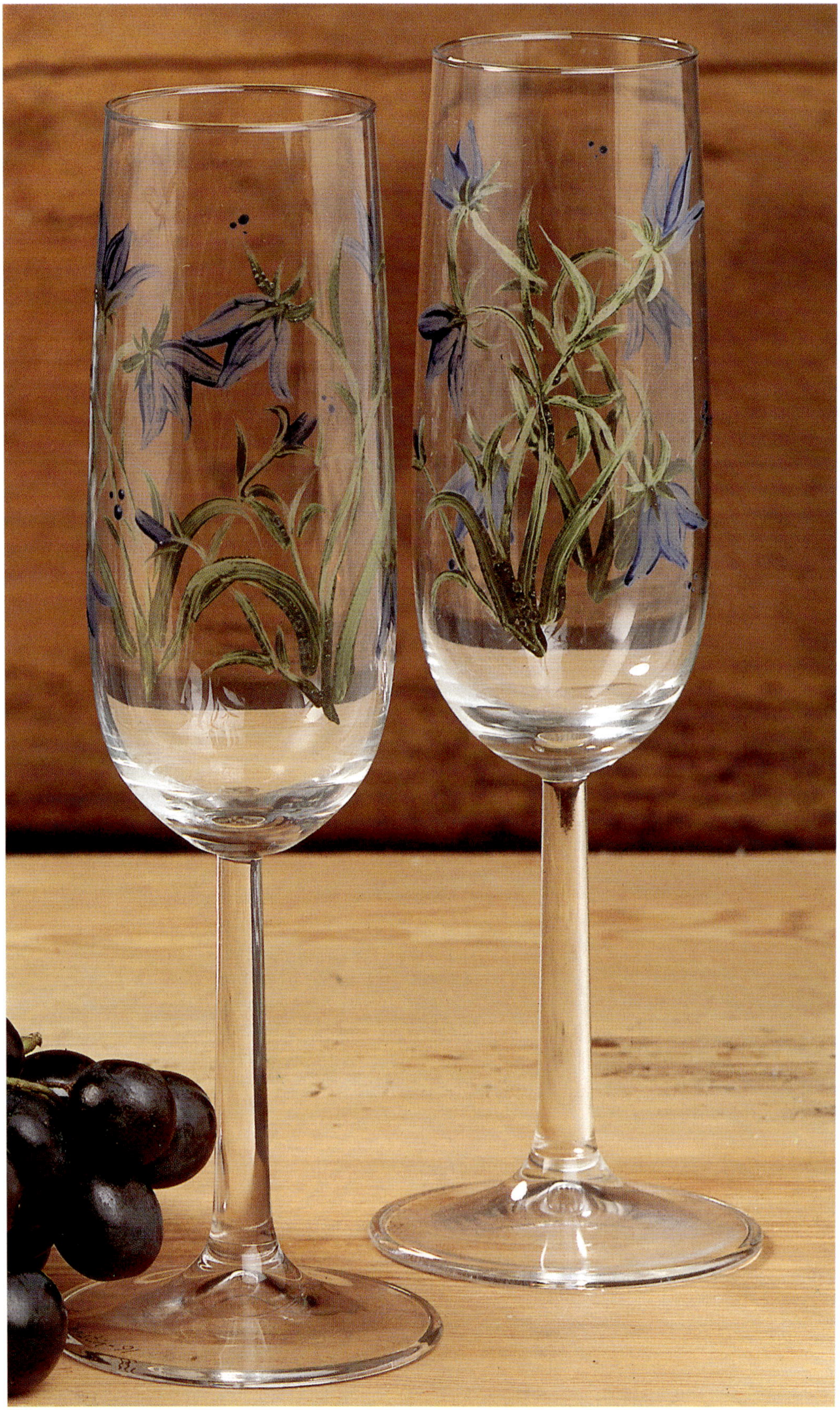

Bluebells

Stems and Leaves

Brush: #0
Colors: Green and white

When painting long, thin stems, fill the brush with paint. Be light handed — pull the brush upward and let your hand follow.

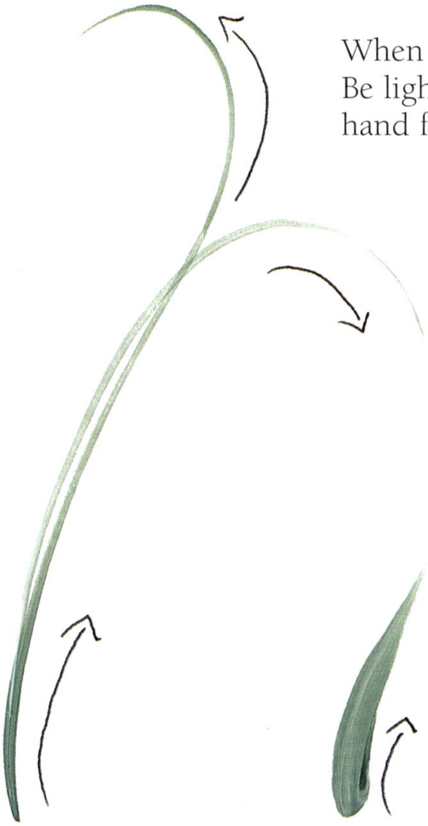

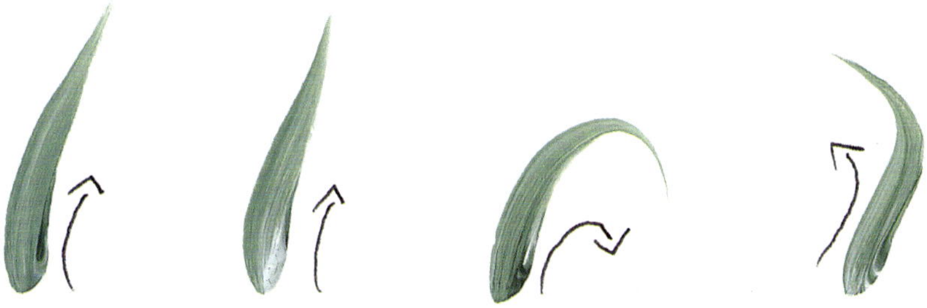

Stems

Leaves

Fill the brush with paint. Press down and pull the brush — let up. Practice this several times until you have mastered the technique. Then practice adding a curve to the leaves.

The Flower

Brush: #0
Colors: Ultramarine and white

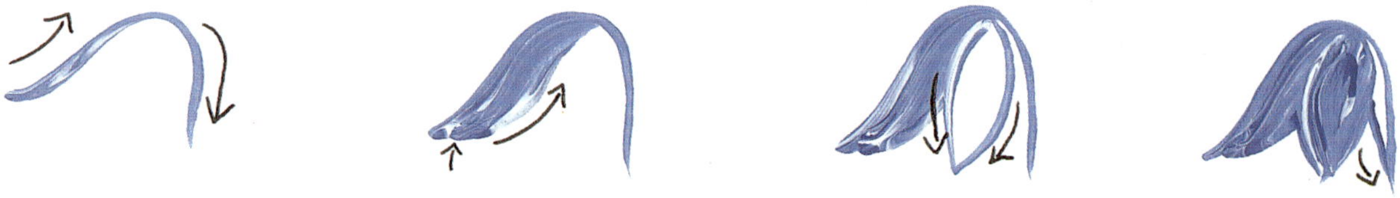

1. Light curve with one stroke.
2. Fill in a little where the arrow points.
3. Make a point that curves toward you.
4. Draw the last stroke and fill in.

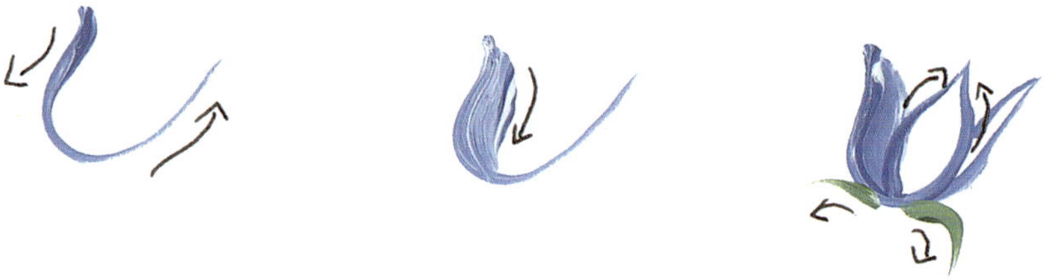

Turn the bluebell heads and follow the method described above.

Remember: Follow the direction of the arrows.

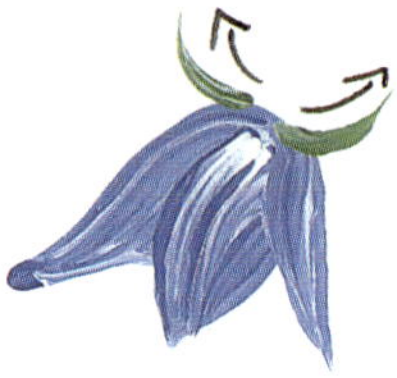

5. Make small green leaves in the direction of the arrows.

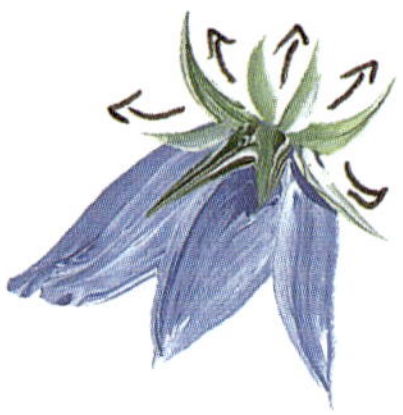

6. Add more green leaves.

The Bud

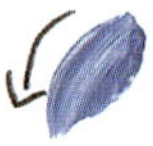

1. Press down and let up.

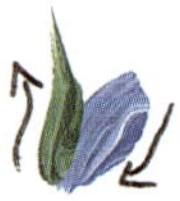

2. Make small green leaves on each side of the bud.

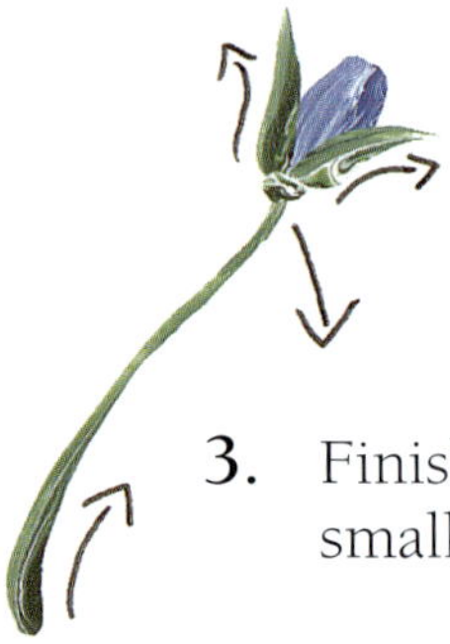

3. Finish with a small green bud.

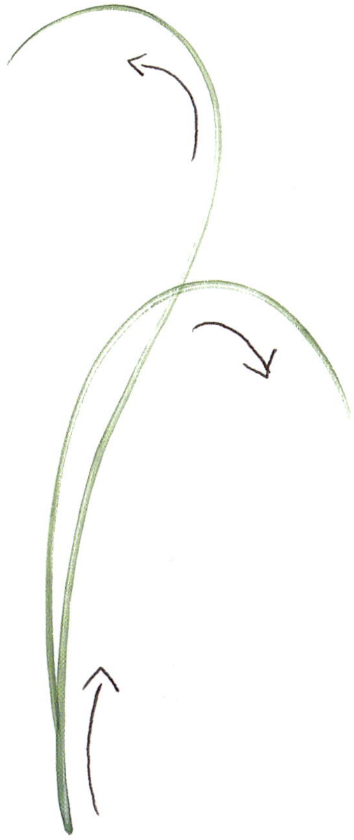

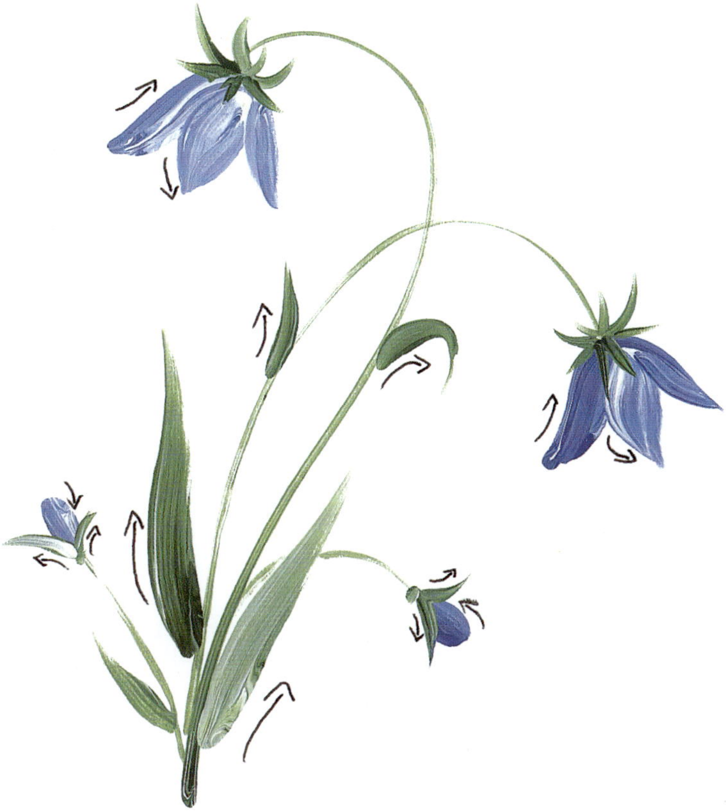

1. With a light hand and plenty of paint on the brush, draw graceful stems for the bluebells.

2. Paint leaves.

3. Paint bluebell heads following the directions on the previous page.

4. Finish with some buds.

Red Clover

Stems and Leaves

Brush: #0
Color: Arbor green and white (or whatever shade of green you have)

Try to curve the brush somewhat when filling in the leaves.

1. Draw two stems — one curved to the left, and the other to the right.

2. Remember: Be clever in shading, thus making the leaves look alive.

3. Outline the clover leaves in green. Fill leaves from inside and outward, note direction of arrows. It's important that you follow the same direction on all the leaves in order to make them look more natural.

4. If you want to add more white or green in the leaves, you must do it while they are still damp in order to make the paint mix well.

The Flower

Brush: #0
Colors: Pink, wine red and white

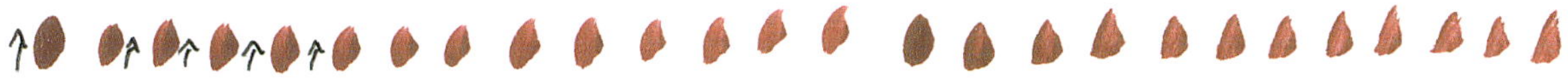

Practice on small petals by filling the brush with paint. Press brush down and let up. After a little practice you'll do fine. Follow direction of the arrows.

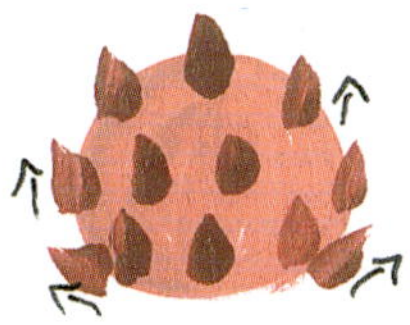

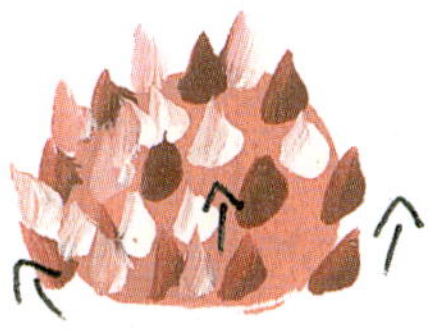

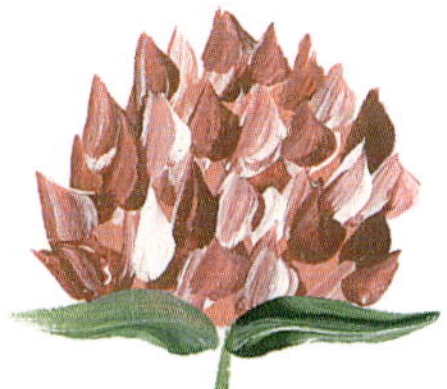

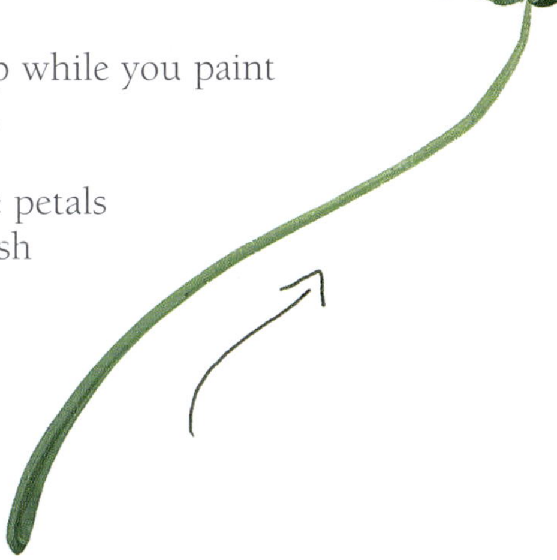

1. Make a pink ball. It must be damp while you paint the petals to achieve nice shading.

2. Dip your brush in wine red. Make petals evenly spaced by pressing the brush down and letting up.

3. Dry the brush somewhat, dip it in white and fill in the head of the clover.

4. Repeat this process with the flower until it gets nice and plump — or until you are satisfied. Note how alive the flower becomes as you paint.

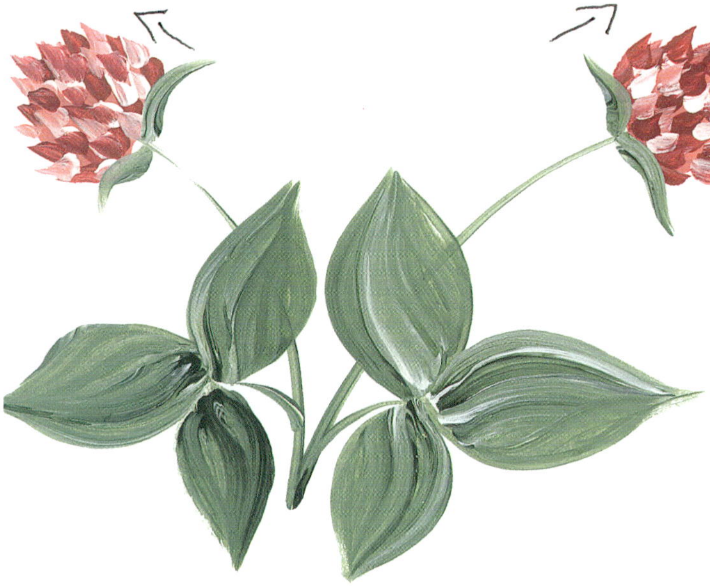

1. Paint the stems and leaves first.

2. Then, paint the clover heads.

Important:

Remember to turn your project so that the clover heads point the right way. Note arrows.

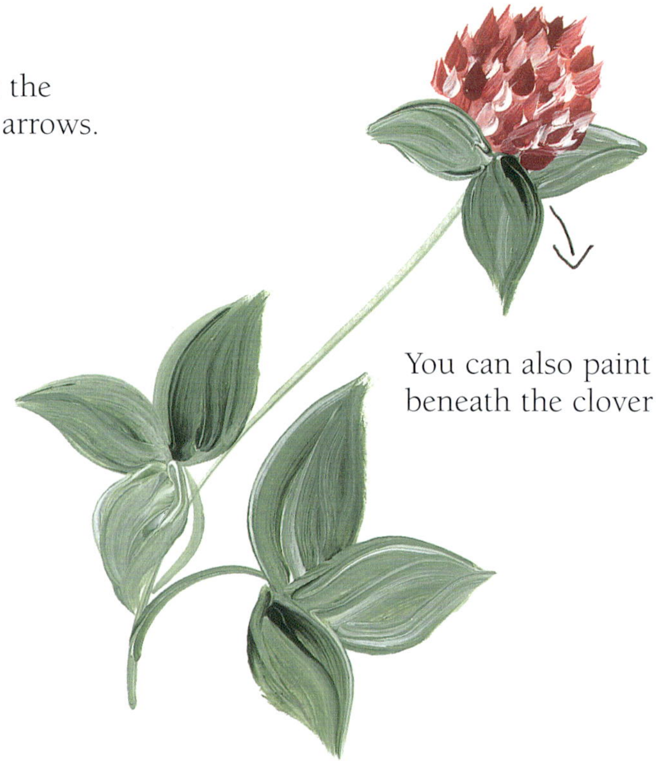

You can also paint leaves beneath the clover heads.

Thistle

Stems and Leaves

Brush: #0
Colors: Green and white

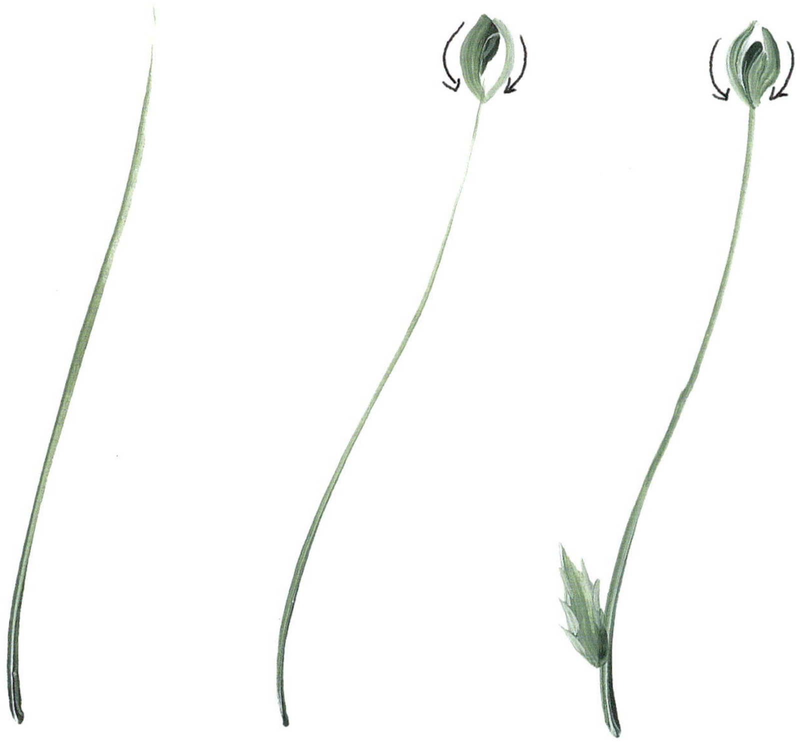

1. Make a long, thin stem.
2. When you paint the "head," fill the brush with paint, press down and let up (toward you).
3. Then, paint the spike leaf.

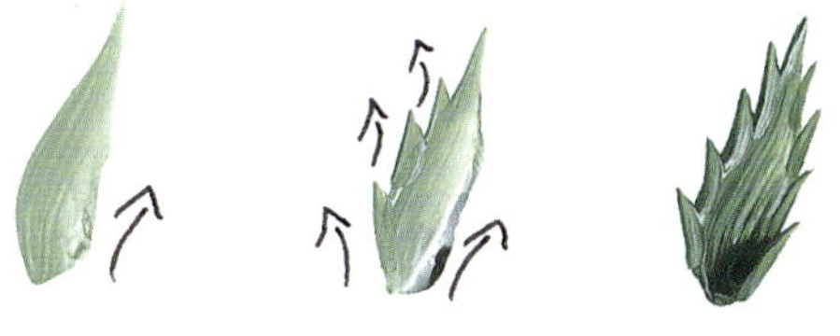

1. Press down and pull up — let up.
2. Drag out spikes with the tip of the brush. Remember the leaves must be fairly damp so they will appear natural and alive.

Thistle

The Flower

Brush: #0
Colors: Mauve and white

Stem and leaves are described on the previous page.

1.

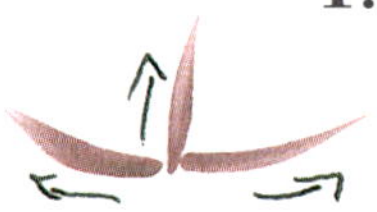

2.

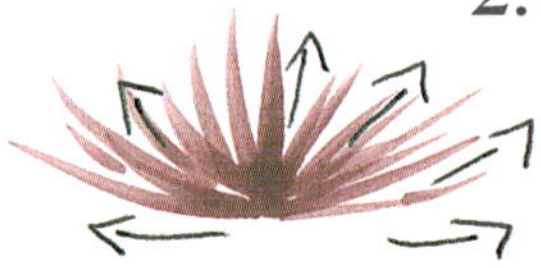

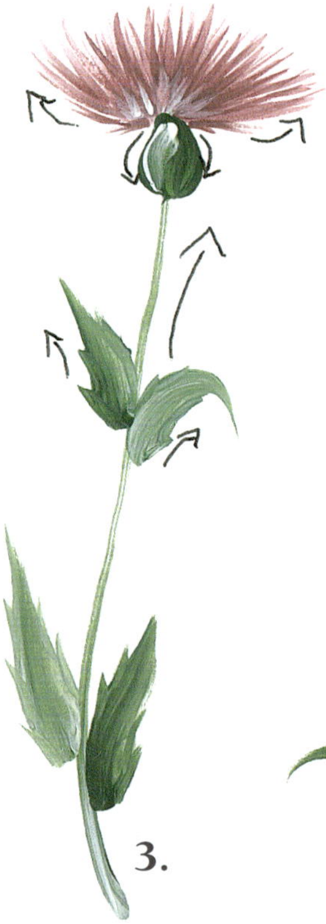

3.

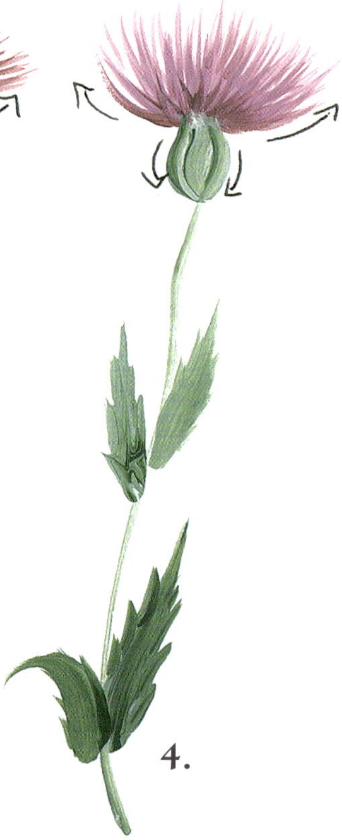

4.

1. Pull petals from inside to out, note arrows.

2. Keep a light hand and use only the tip of the brush. Fill the head of the thistle.

3. When making a thistle, first paint a thin stem, then the thistle head. Make a "ball" under the thistle head. Note arrows.

4. Make spike leaves. (See directions on previous page.) If you use more white in the mauve, the flowers will be lighter.

Blue Button

The Flower

Brush: #0
Colors: Ultramarine and mauve (maybe some white), wine red for stamens

Stem and leaves are painted with the same method as the bluebells.

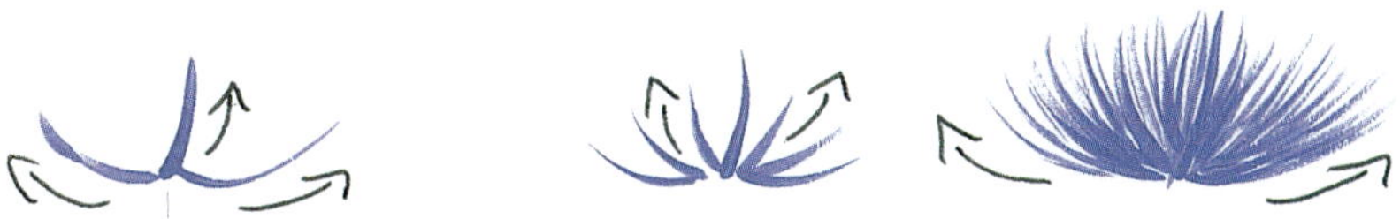

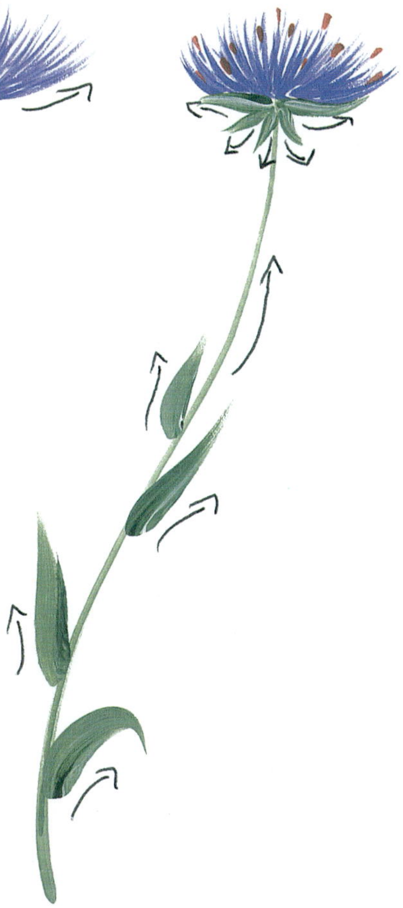

Method is the same as described under thistle.

Blue buttons have stamens that are wine red.

Look at other flowers and out in nature. There are many flowers you can paint using the same method, just by changing the color and altering the leaves somewhat.

Leaves

Press down and pull the brush — let up. (Same leaves as the bluebell.)

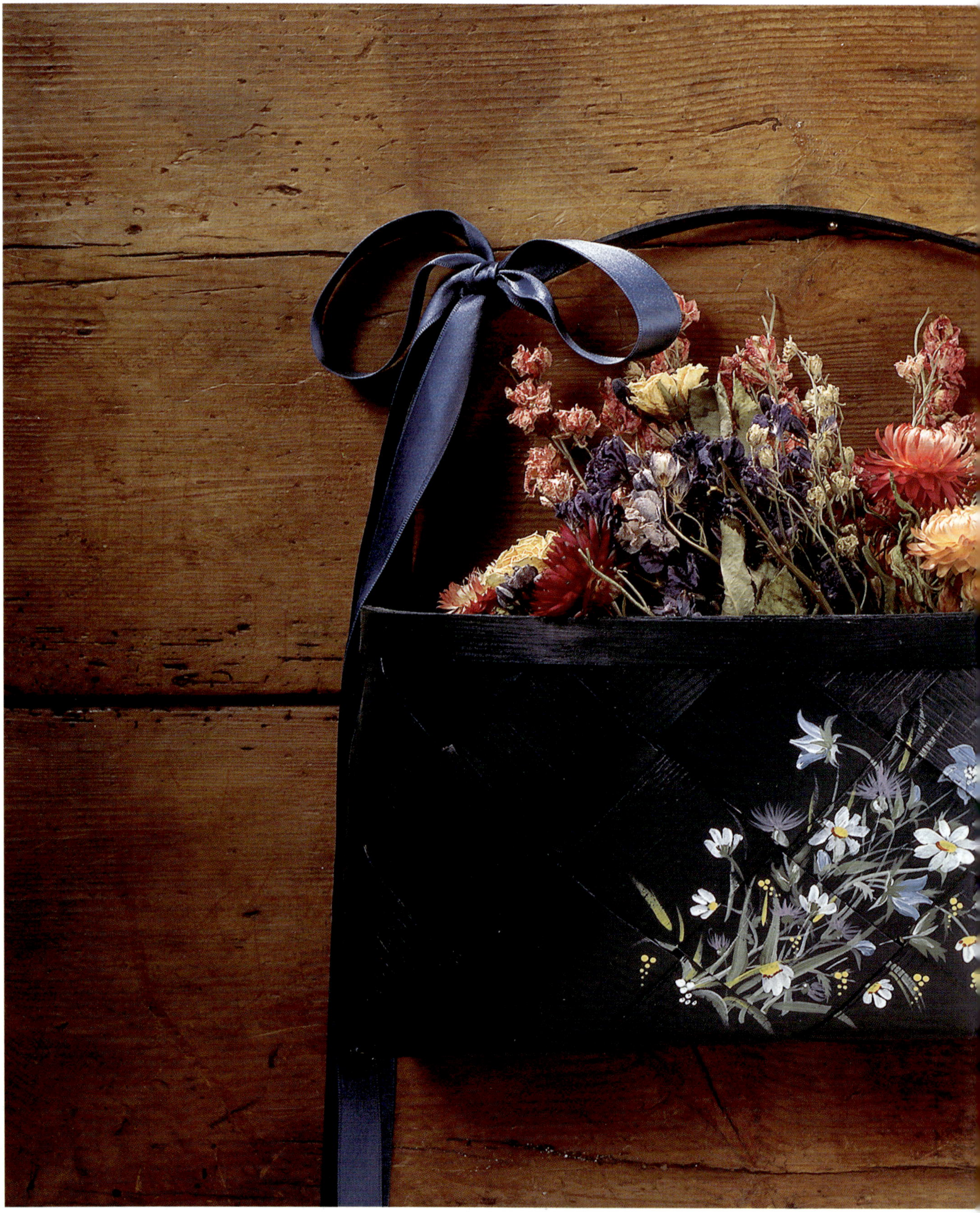

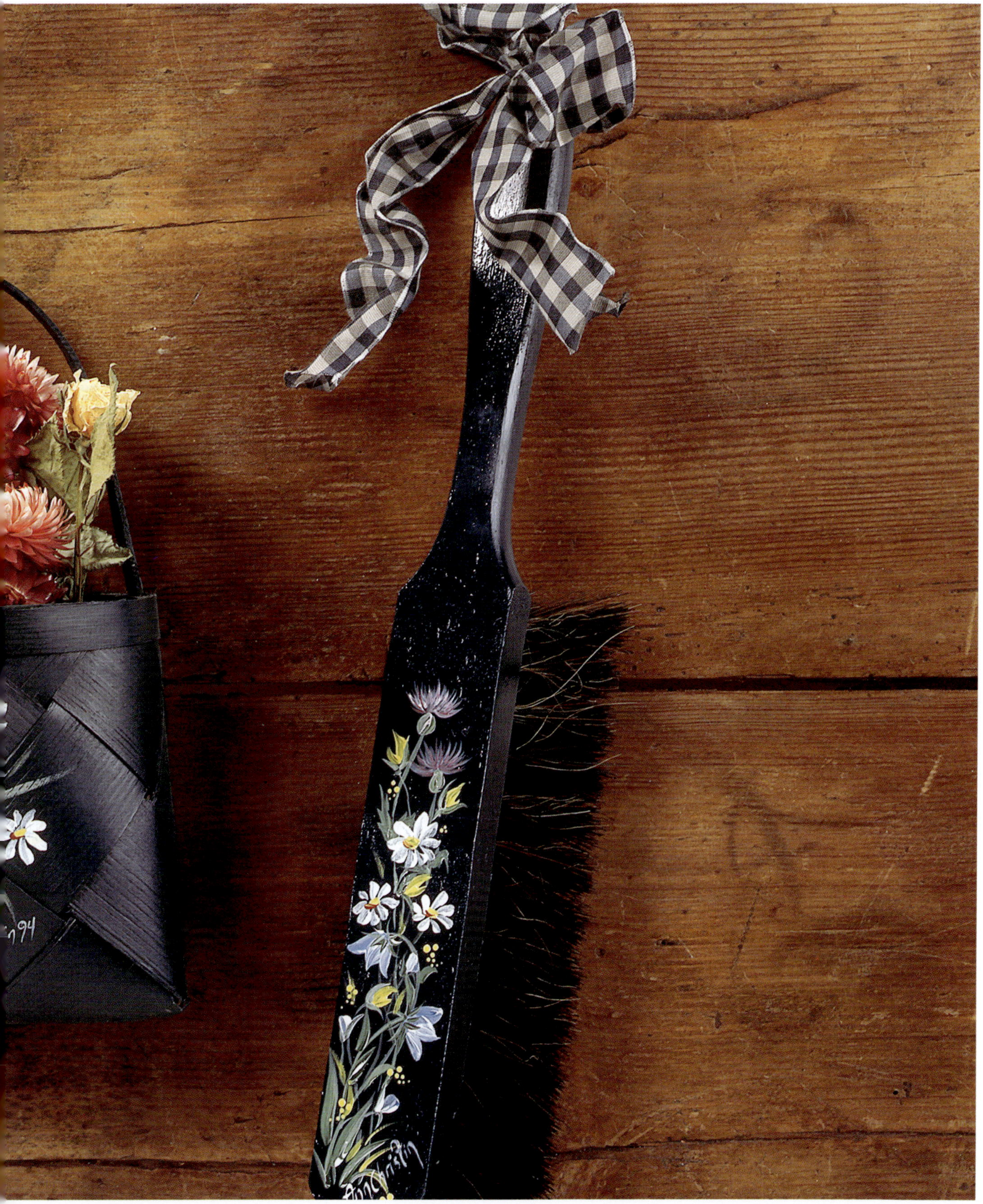

Foxglove

Stems and Leaves

Brush: #0
Colors: Green and white

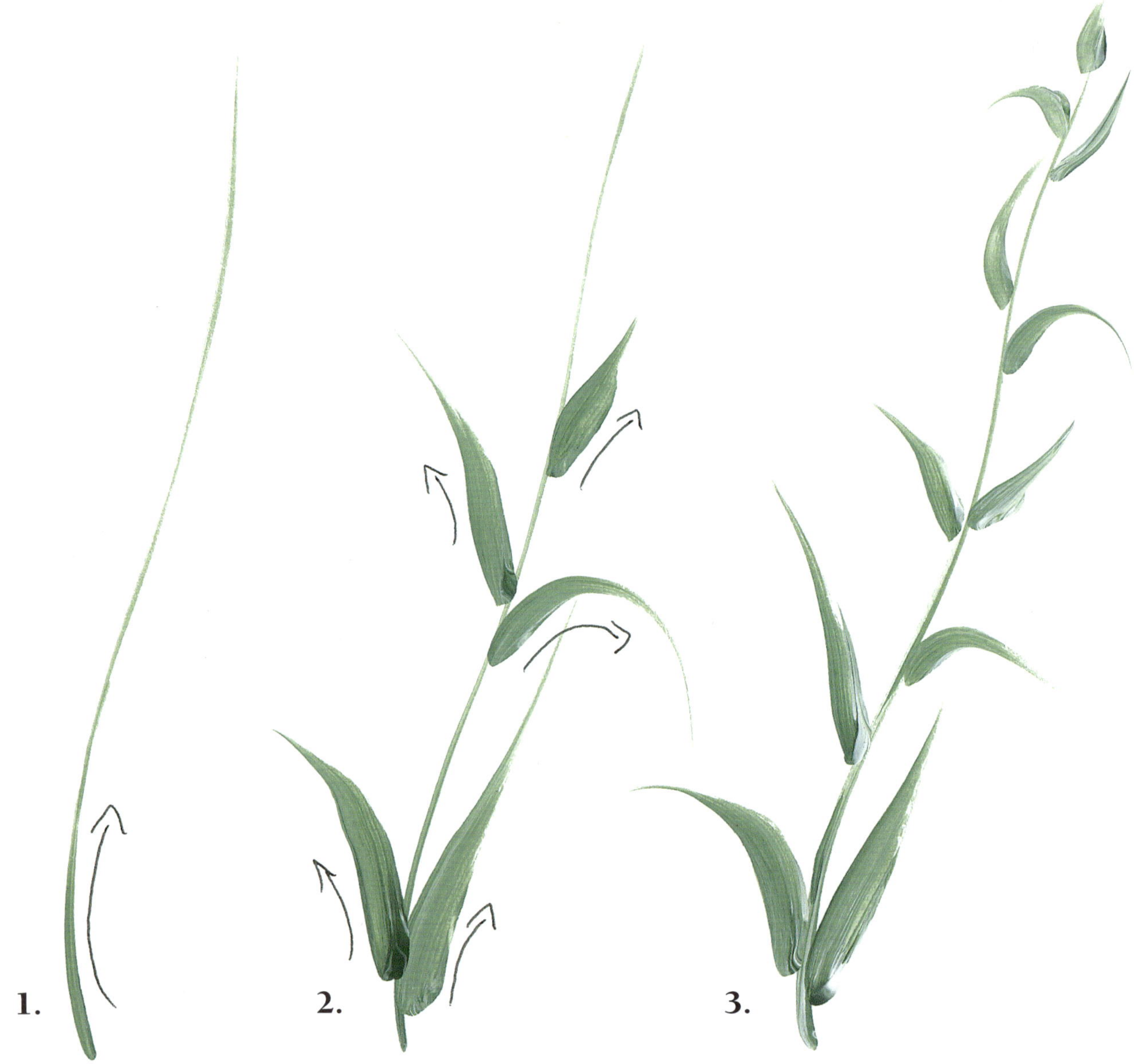

1. Make a nice long stem for the foxglove.

2. Paint the leaves evenly spaced, getting smaller and smaller.

3. Let the stem and leaves dry completely before painting the foxglove heads.

The Flower

Brush: #0
Colors: Wine red and white

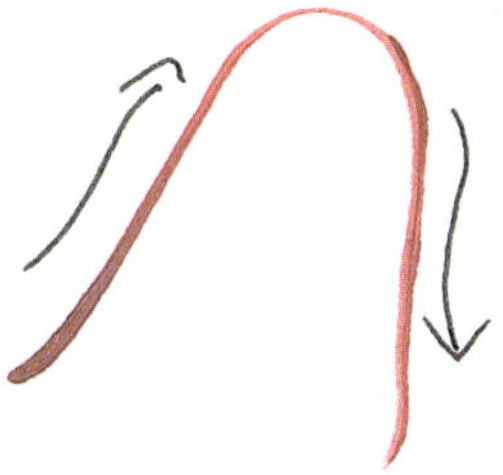

Make a bell.

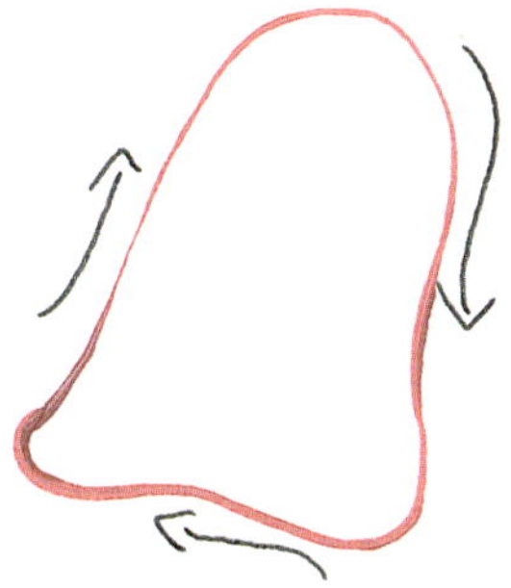

Follow direction of arrows.

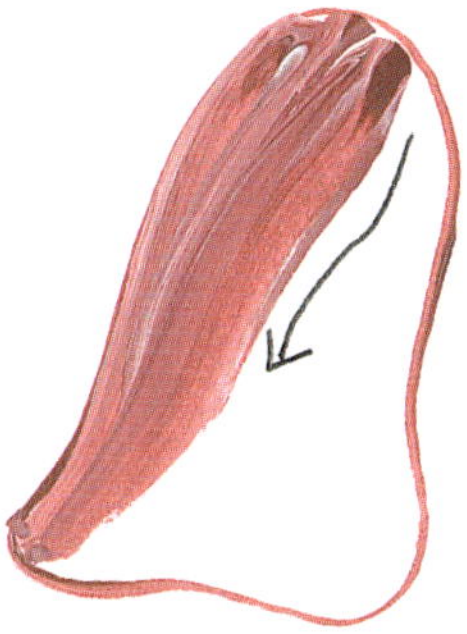

Follow direction of arrow.

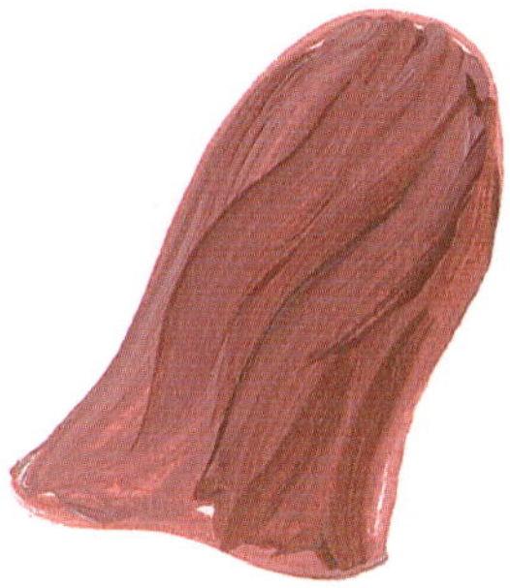

Fill completely.

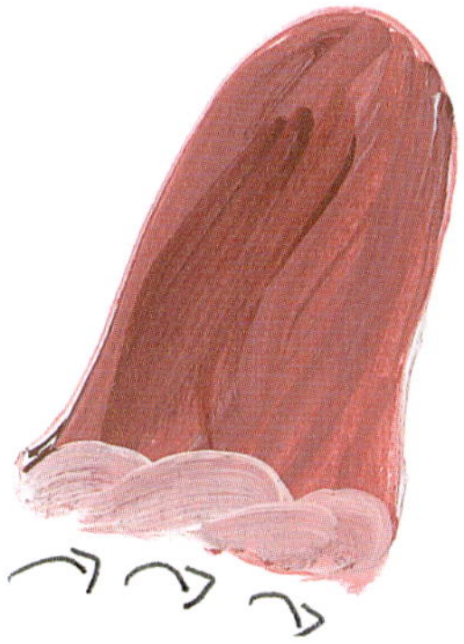

Dip in white and draw three curves.

Paint leaves.

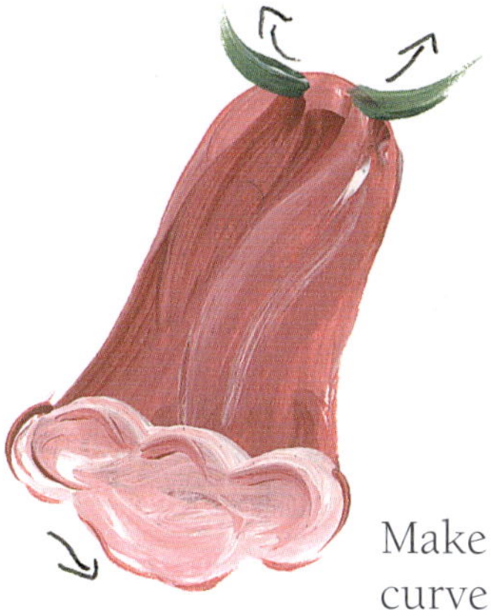

Make a curve.

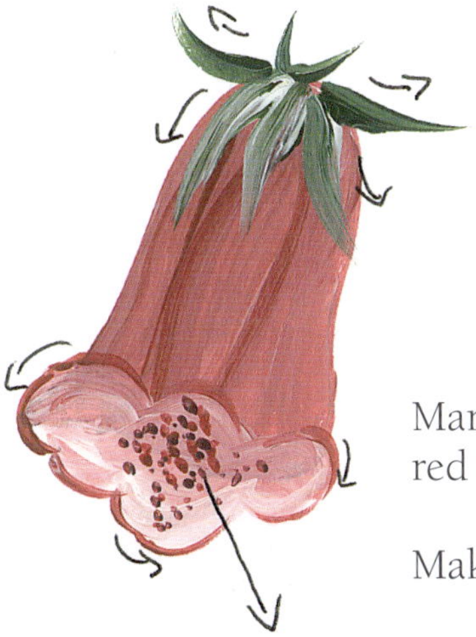

Mark "mouth" with a little wine red to make the flower come alive.

Make stamens with tip of the brush.

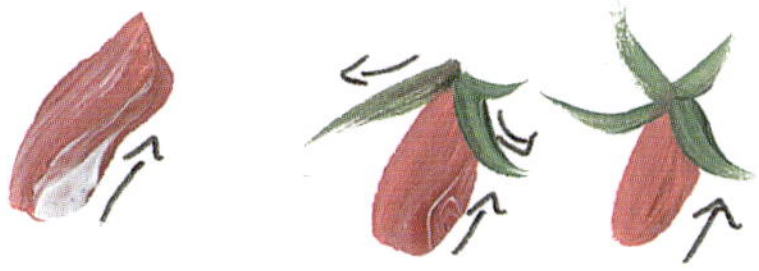

The Bud

Foxglove

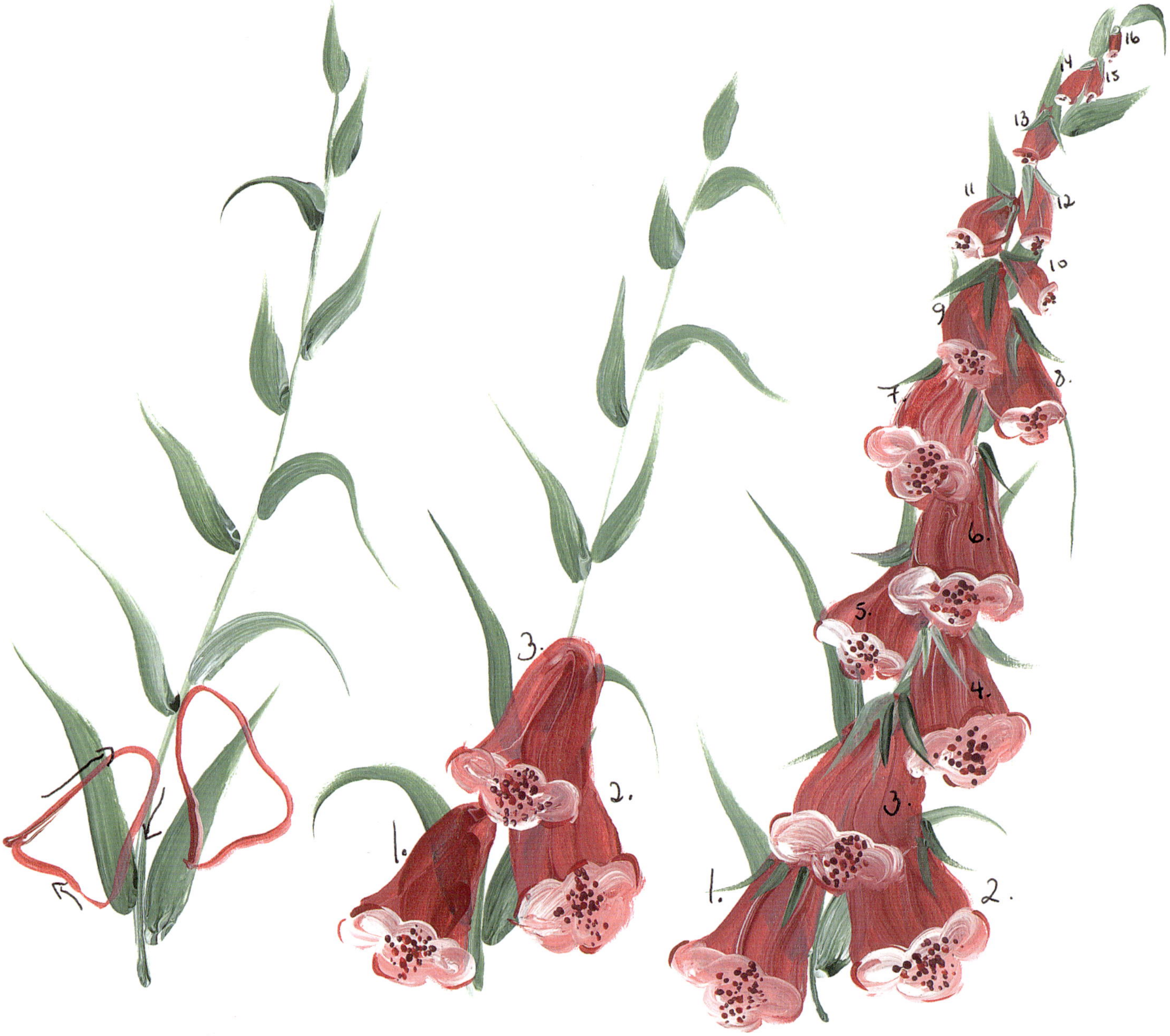

Note carefully how I paint the heads so that they partly cover each other.

1. Paint and fill the heads one by one.

2. Paint the stamens and small leaves last.

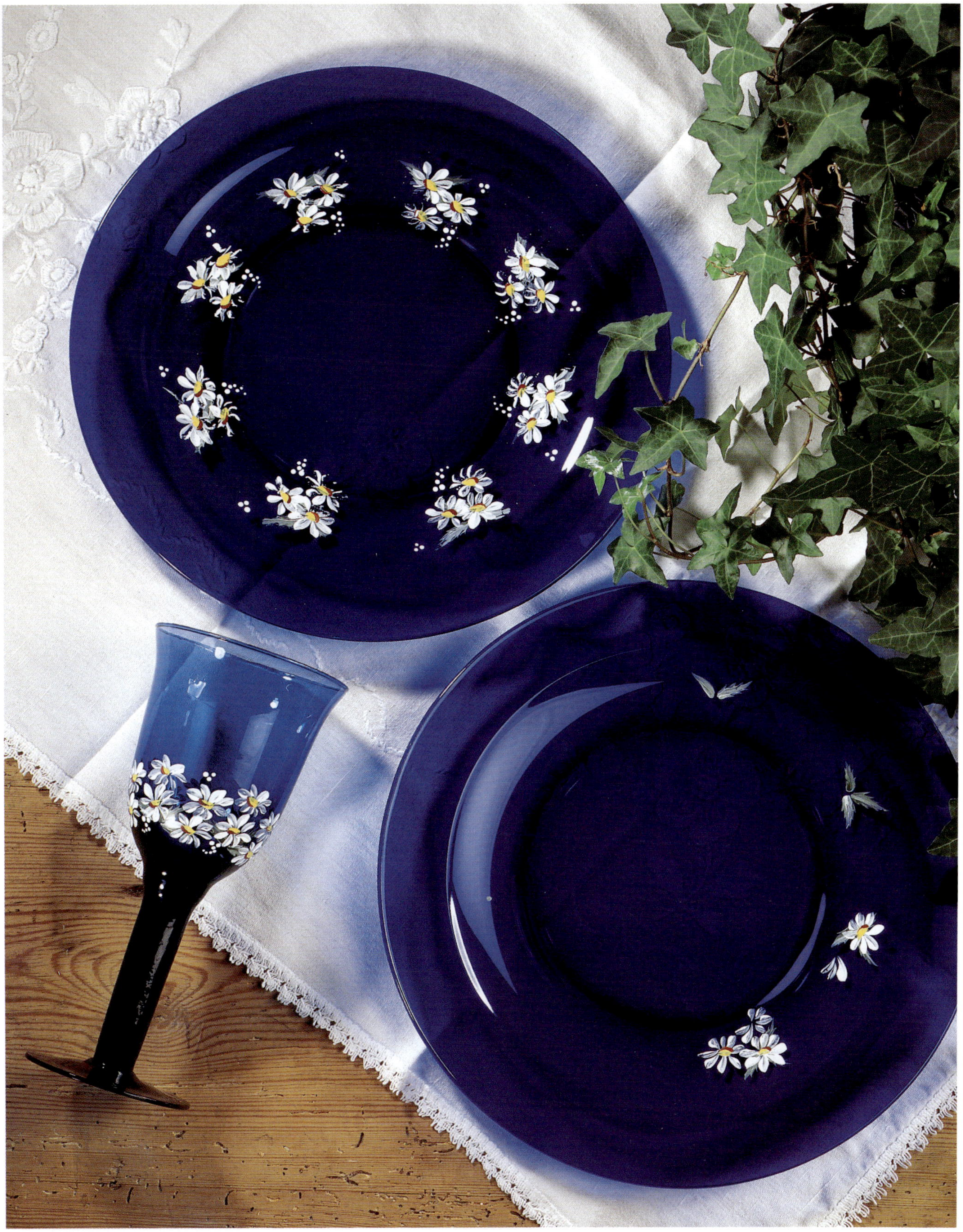

Daisy

Stems and Leaves

Brush: #0
Colors: Green and white

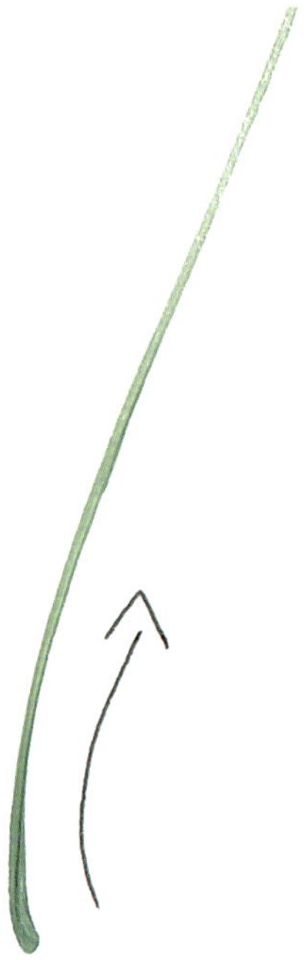

Paint long, narrow stems.

Remember:
Plenty of paint on the brush.

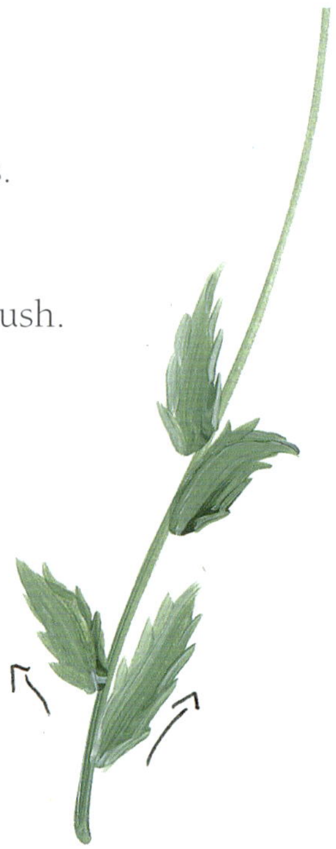

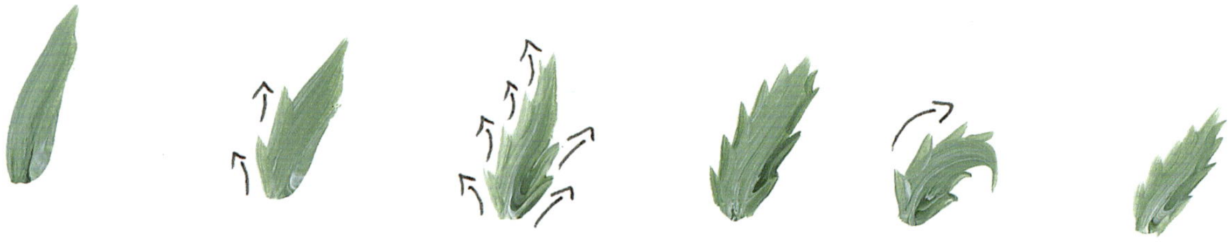

1. Press down and draw up a leaf.
2. Pull out spikes with tip of brush while leaves are still damp.
3. Try to curve the leaves somewhat.

Balderbra

Stems and Leaves

Brush: #0
Colors: Green and white

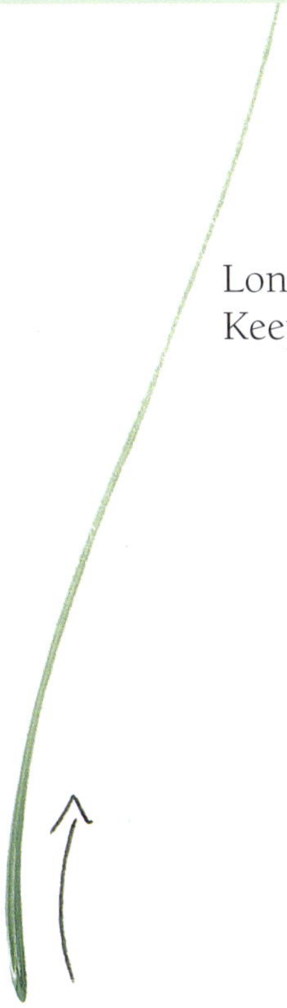

Long, narrow stems.
Keep a light hand.

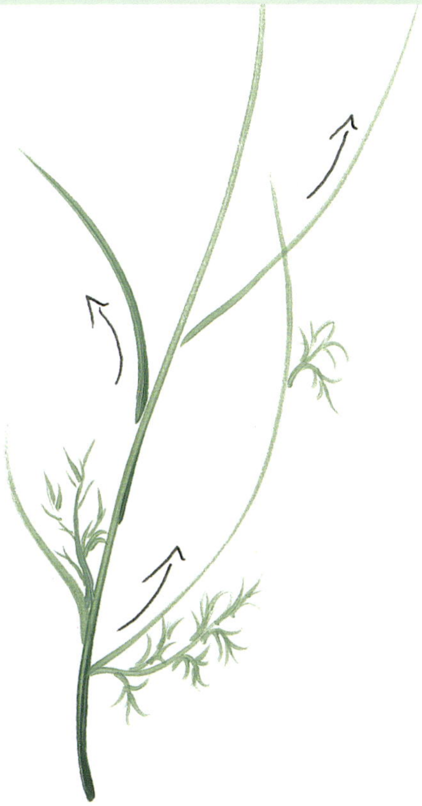

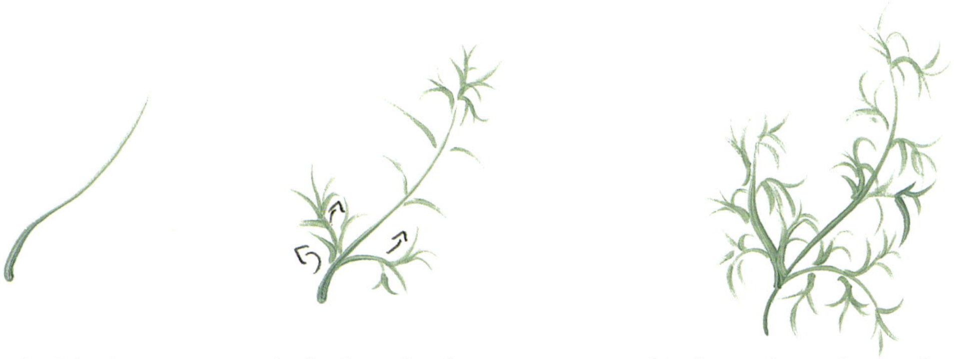

Leaves on "balderbra." Use a light hand when you paint the fine, thin "finger leaves."

Daisy & Balderbra

The Flower

Brush: #0
Colors: White, yellow and brown

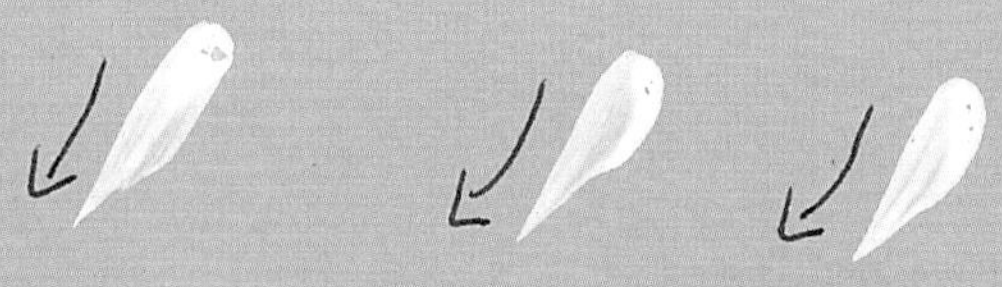

The Bud

Put a little green under the head.

1. Position the petals in a circle. Turn your work somewhat to make it easier to obtain a nice daisy head.
2. Put a little yellow in the middle.
3. Finish with a small brown stroke to put more life in the flower.

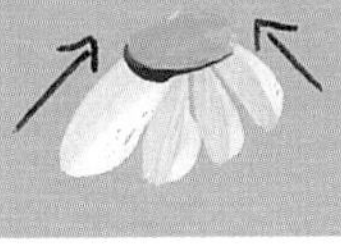

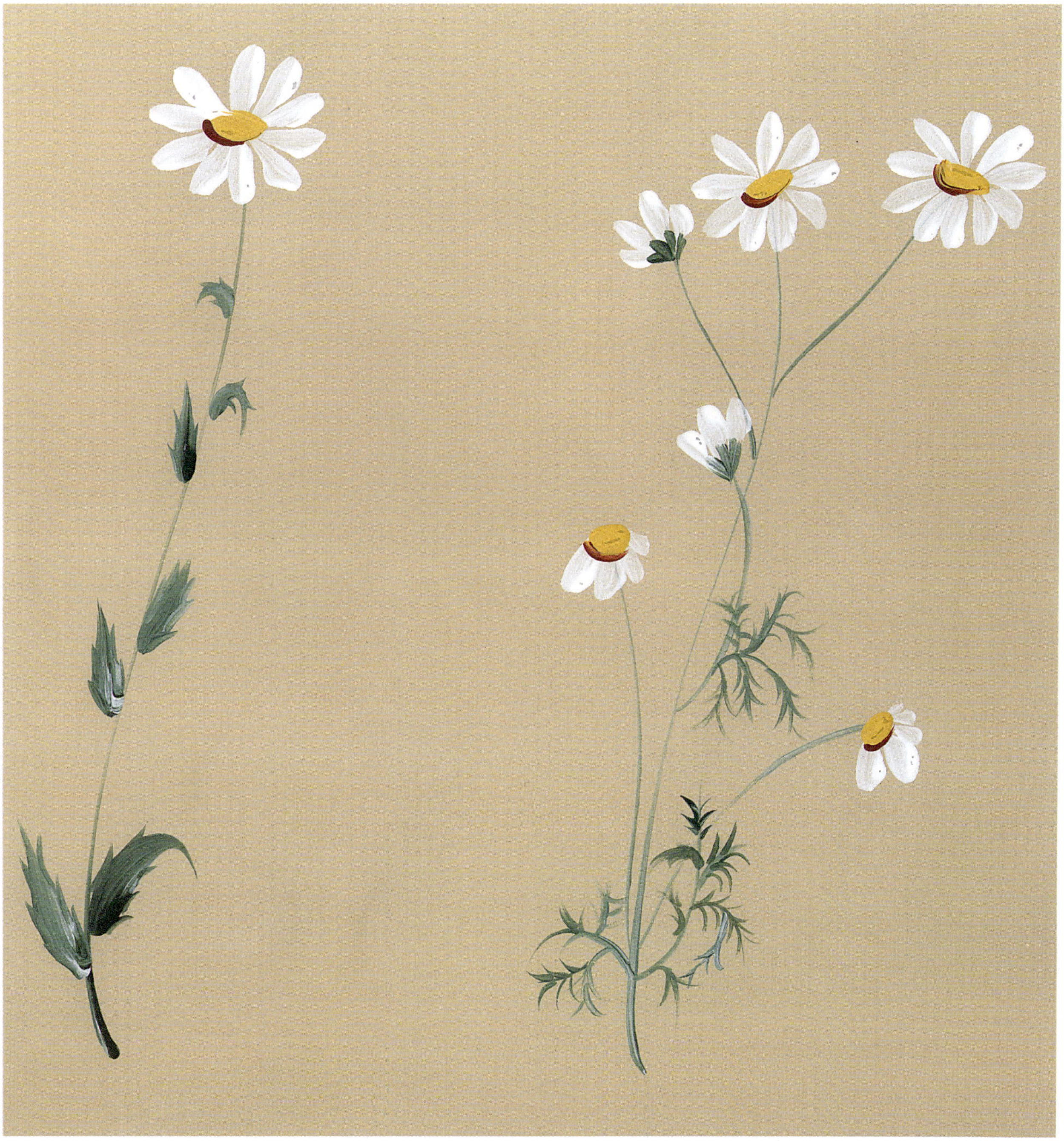

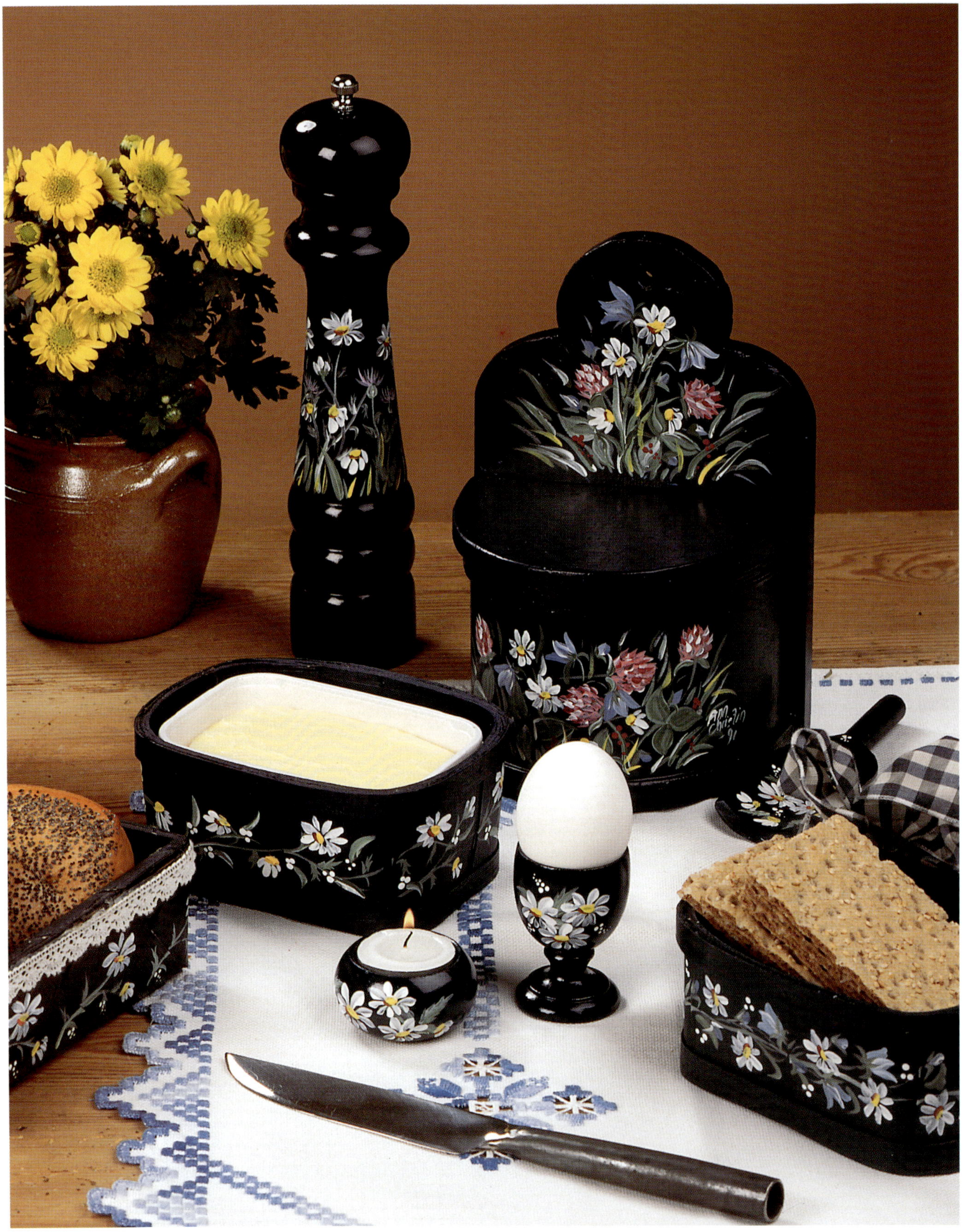

Meadow Buttercup

The Flower

Brush: #0
Colors: Yellow and a little brown

The stems and leaves are painted the same way as the bluebells.

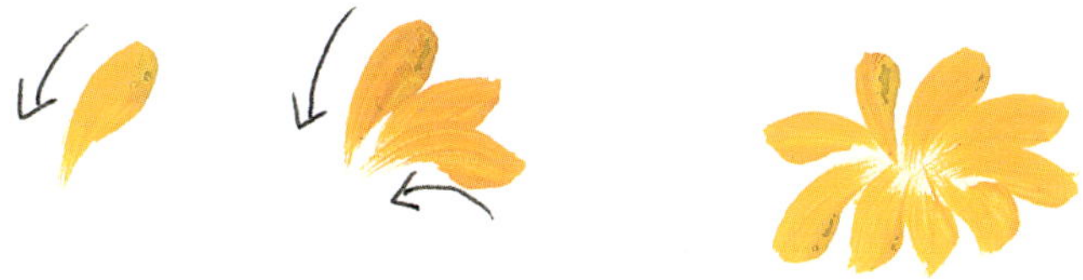

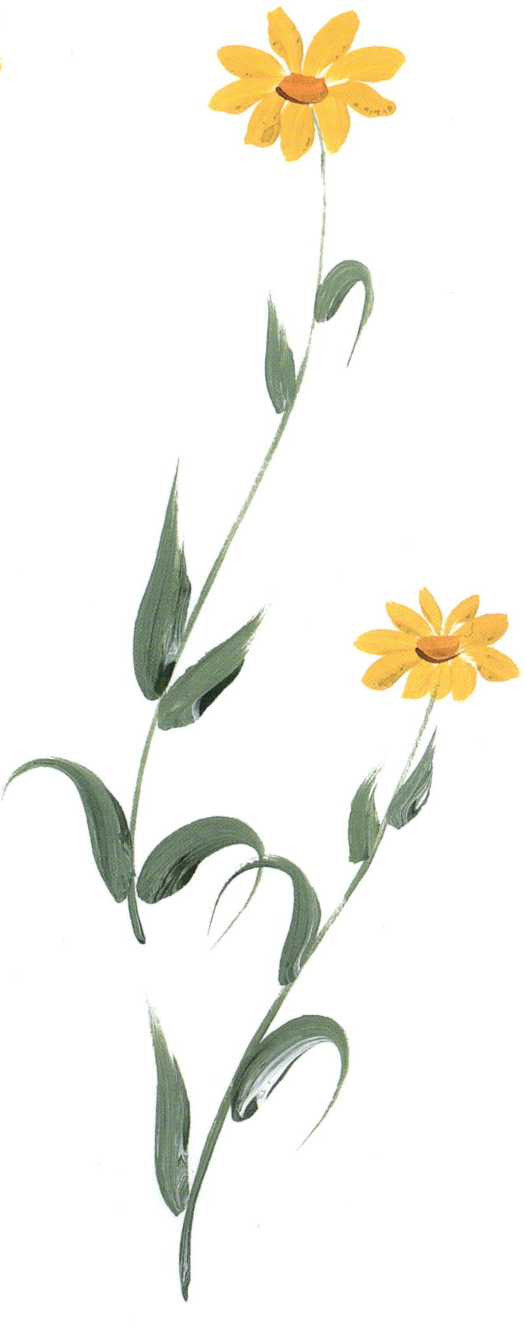

Paint the buttercup as you did the daisy.
Mix some brown in the yellow.

Paint leaves as on the bluebells.

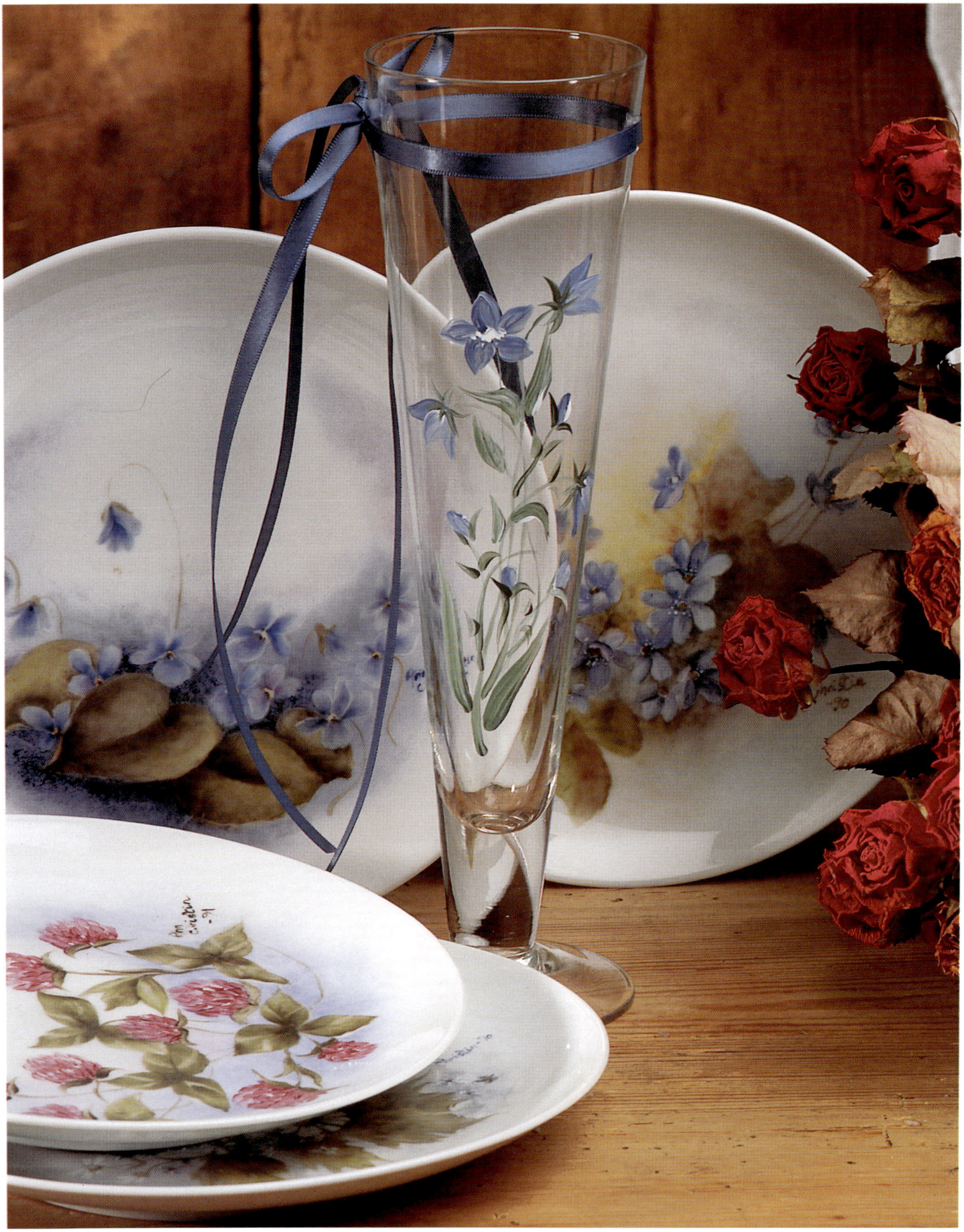

Forget-Me-Not

The Flower

Brush: #0
Colors: Ultramarine and white, yellow and black

The stems and leaves are painted the same way as the bluebells.

When you paint forget-me-nots, press the brush down and let up.
The point is toward the middle so that the flower itself is rounded with its petals.

1. The flower has five petals.
2. Fill the middle with white.
3. Then add some yellow.
4. Finish with a small black dot.

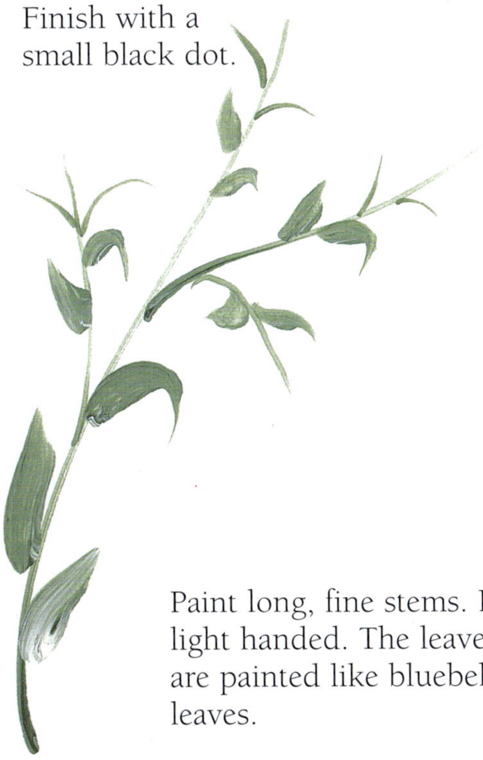

Paint long, fine stems. Be light handed. The leaves are painted like bluebell leaves.

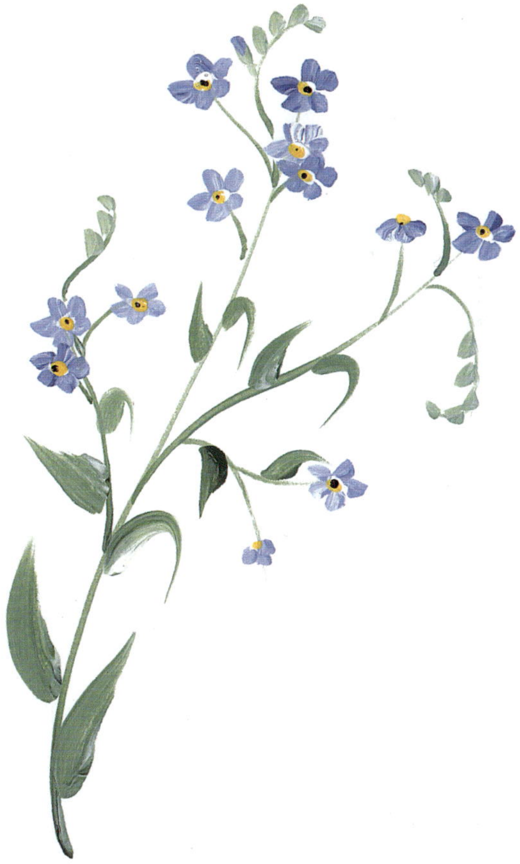

When looking at flowers in general, we see that most can be painted from a so-called "jack-in-the box," a name that I use with my pupils in class. This is easily understood, and the students see the possibilities for painting flowers themselves. This method of painting can be used for flowers with 5 or 6 petals, such as the crane's bill, white and blue anemone, buttercup, rose, fruit flower, pansy and violet. This is a simple technique that is very useful. By using this method, you can paint many flowers and see how they come alive under your brush.

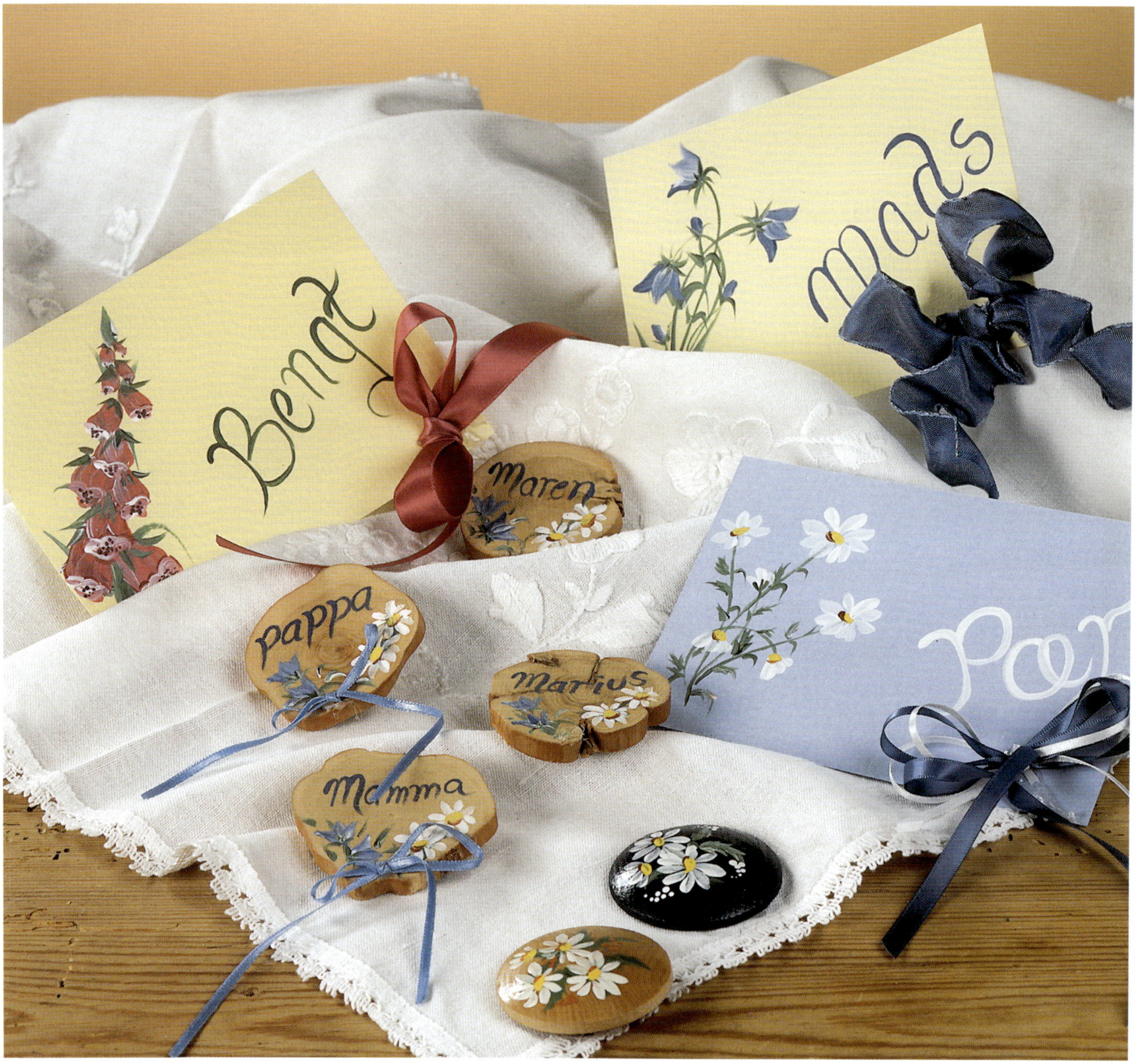

Jack-in-the-Box Flower

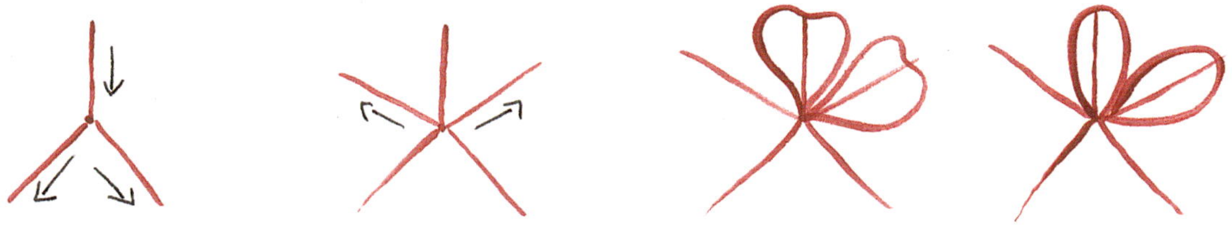

1. Start with a dot as the center of the flower.
2. Now paint the torso and a leg to each side.
3. Then paint an arm to each side.
4. We now have a way to paint flowers that are heart-shaped, such as the wood crane's bill, mountain pimpernel, rose, fruit flowers, etc.
5. Here we paint flowers with a rounder shape, such as sweet William, wood sorrel, etc.

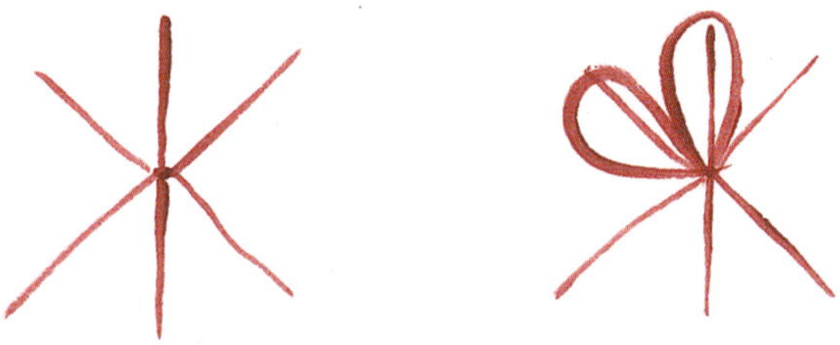

Here the jack-in-the-box has six arms, and we can paint white and blue anemones, etc.
Look at the flowers to see how many petals they have.

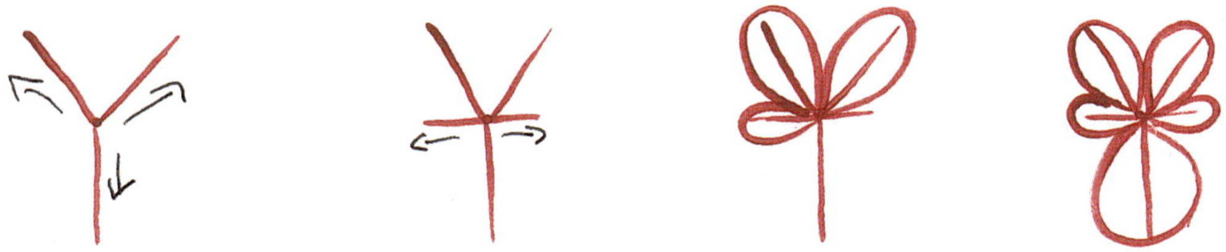

If we turn the jack-in-the-box somewhat, we can use it to paint violets and pansies.

Wood Crane's Bill

Stems and Leaves

Brush: #0
Colors: Green and white

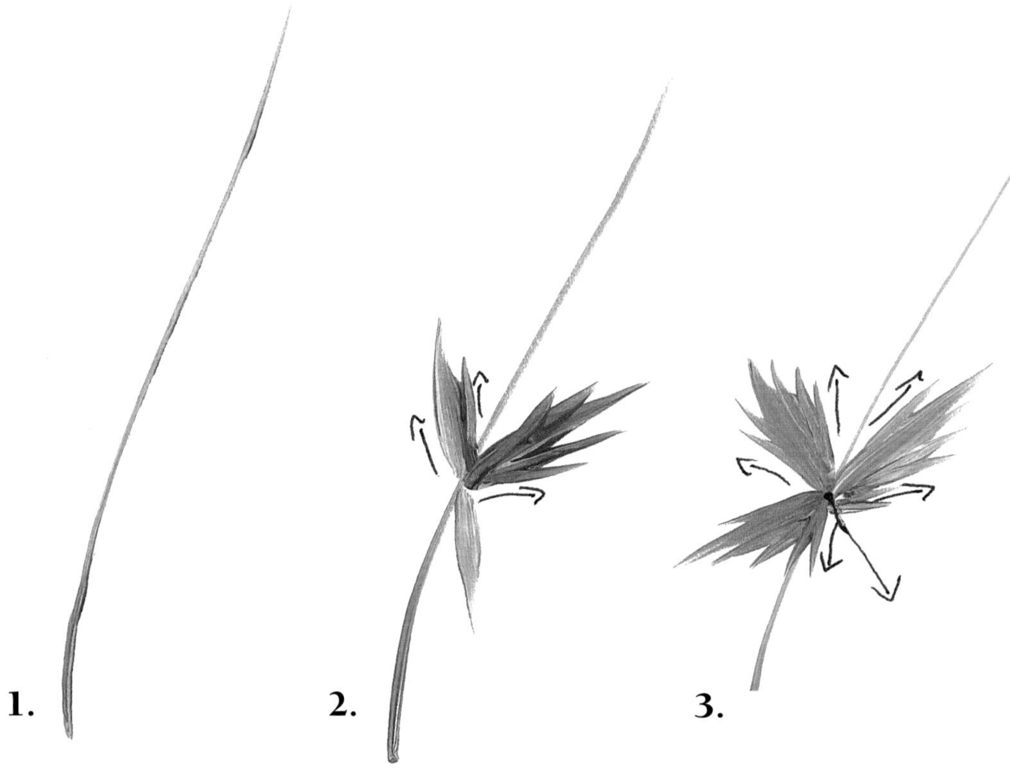

1. Paint a light, thin stem.

2. Use the same technique used to paint spike leaves on thistles and daisies. Pull out the spikes. An easy method for obtaining lobed leaves.

3. Remember to start from the middle.

The Flower

Brush: #0
Colors: Mauve and white

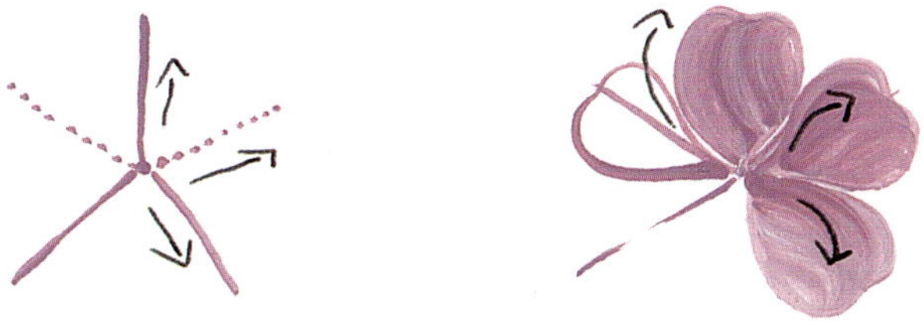

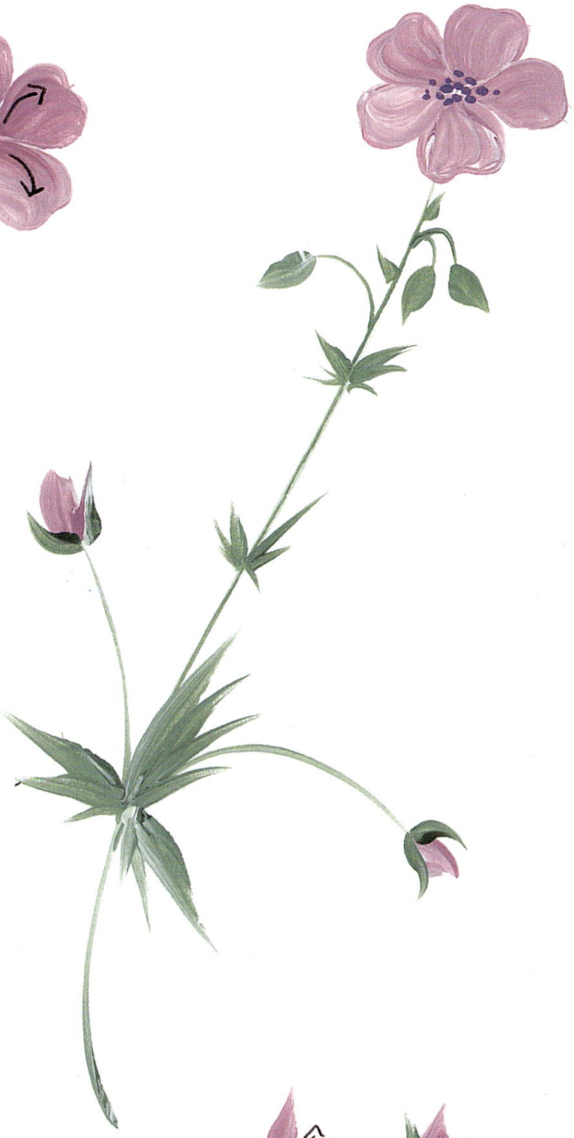

1. Make a jack-in-the-box with five arms.

2. Then outline the heart-shaped petals and fill them. Remember, you must fill in the same direction so the flowers will look natural and alive.

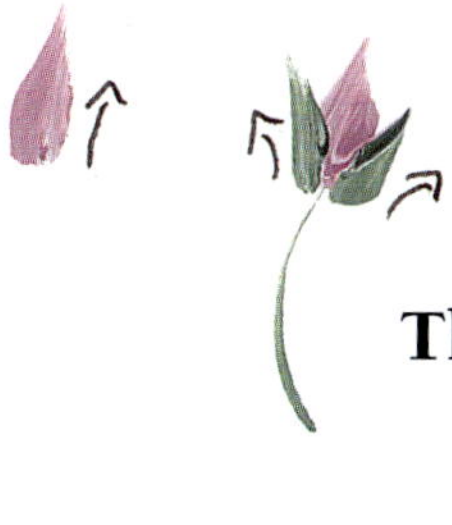

The Bud

Blood Crane's Bill

The Flower

Brush: #0
Colors: Wine red and white

Stem and leaves painted like the wood crane's bill.

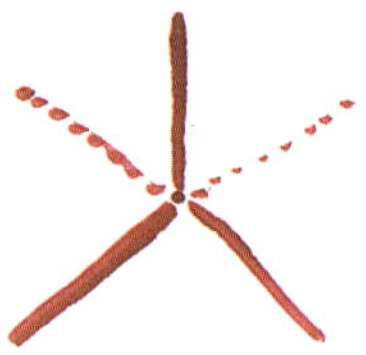

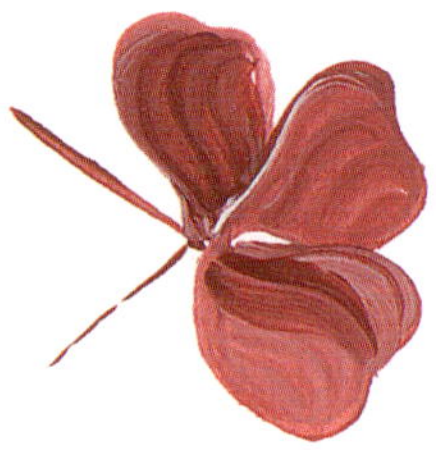

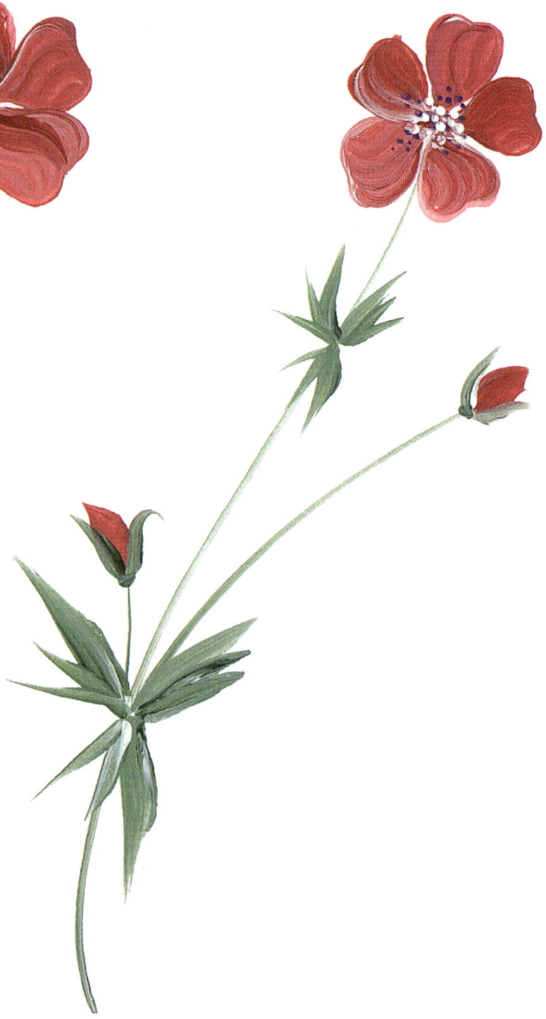

Here we also paint the jack-in-the-box with five arms, like the regular wood crane's bill flower. There are many different flowers that belong to the crane's bill family — only the colors are different. Just try it and you will find that you can paint most of these with some guide strokes.

Blue Anemone

Stems and Leaves

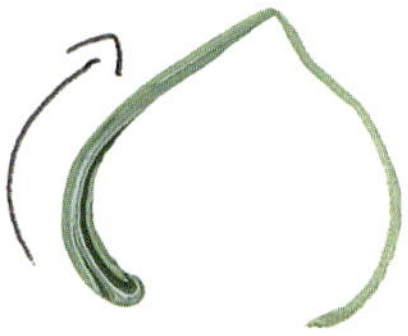

1. Form leaf. Note arrows.

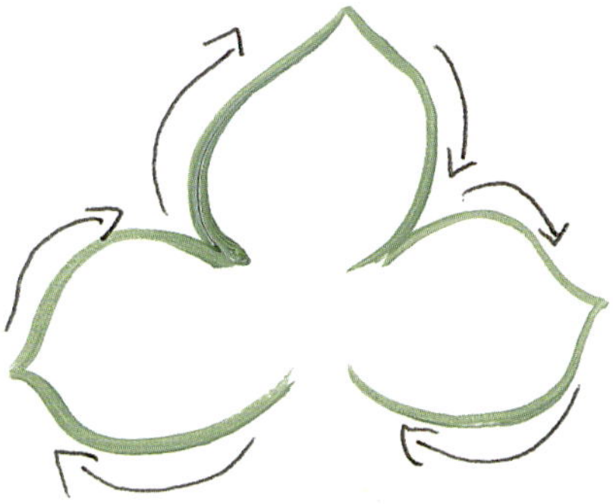

2. Make three leaves. Note arrows.

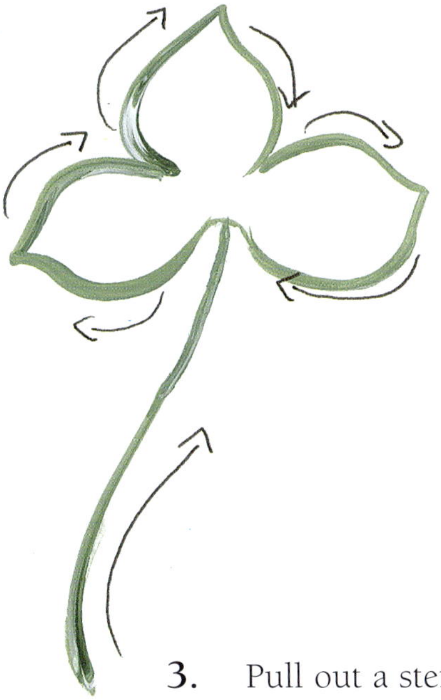

3. Pull out a stem.

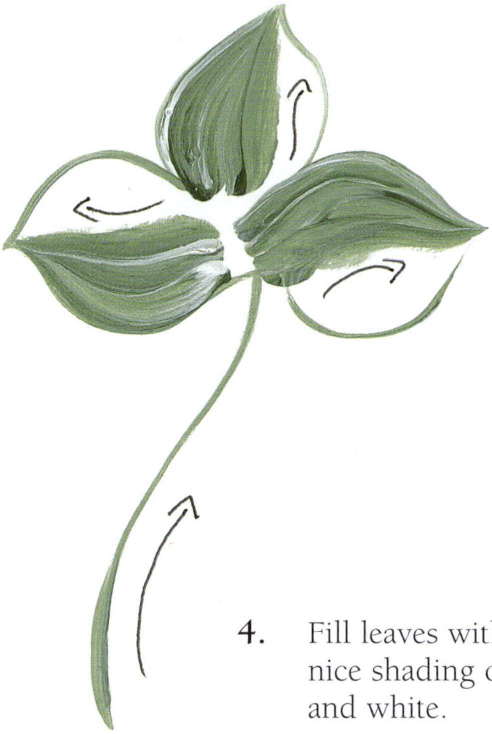

4. Fill leaves with a nice shading of green and white.

Blue Anemone

The Flower

Brush: #0
Colors: Ultramarine, a little navy and white

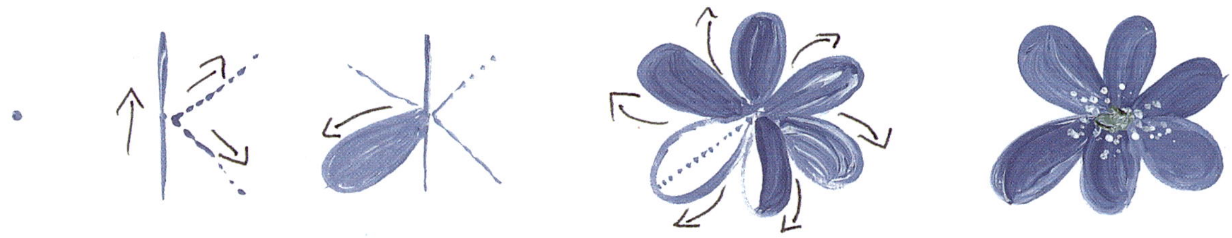

1. Make jack-in-the-box flowers as guide strokes. Paint six petals on the blue anemone. Fill each petal with a shade of ultramarine, a little navy and white from the center and out.
2. Put a little green in the center. Finally dip the brush in white and make stamens with the tip of the brush.

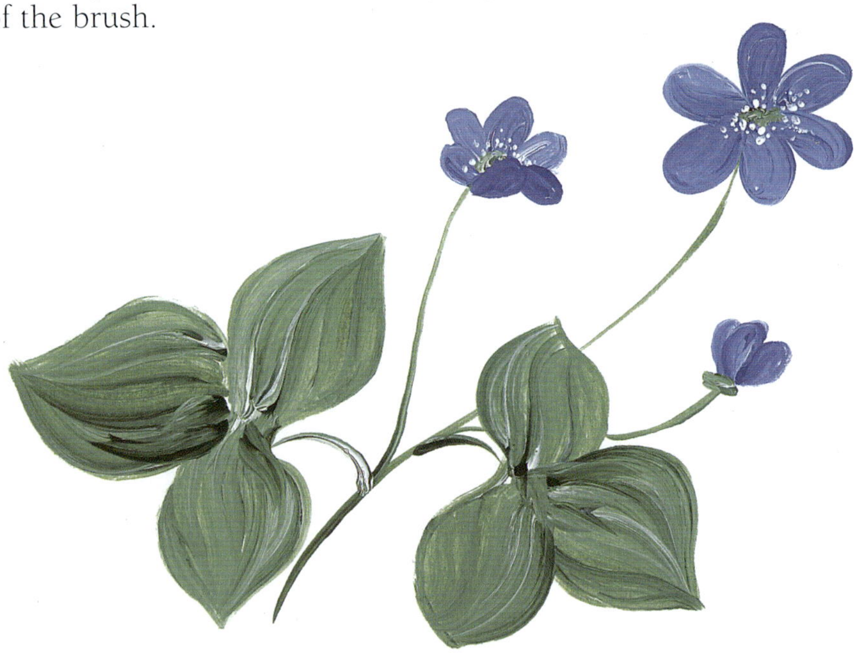

The Bud

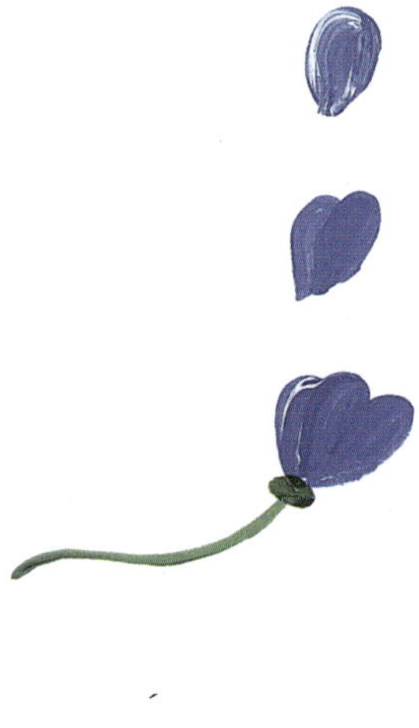

Place three petals partly over each other.

White Anemone

The Flower

Brush: #0
Colors: White, yellow, green and pink

Stem and leaves painted like the wood crane's bill.

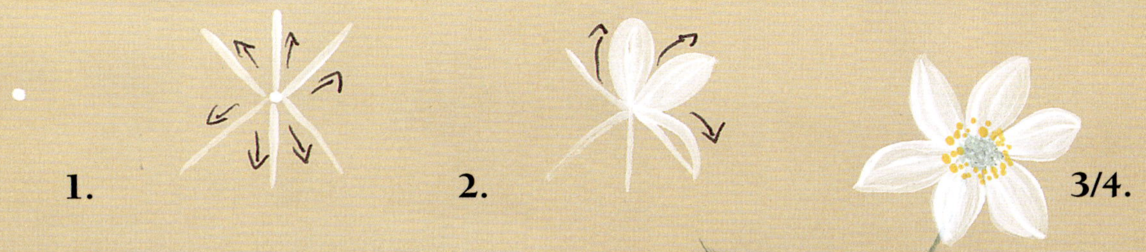

1. Paint a jack-in-the-box with six arms
2. Outline in white. Fill flower.
3. Green in the center.
4. Dot the stamen with yellow.

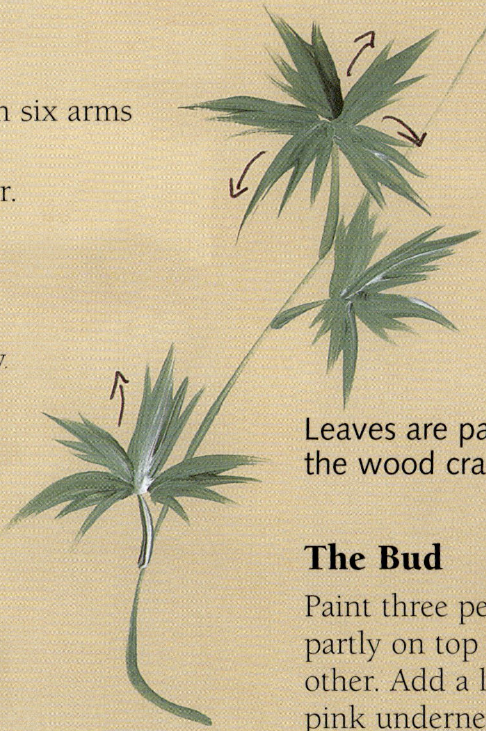

Leaves are painted as on the wood crane's bill.

The Bud

Paint three petals partly on top of each other. Add a little pink underneath.

Wood Violet

Stems and Leaves

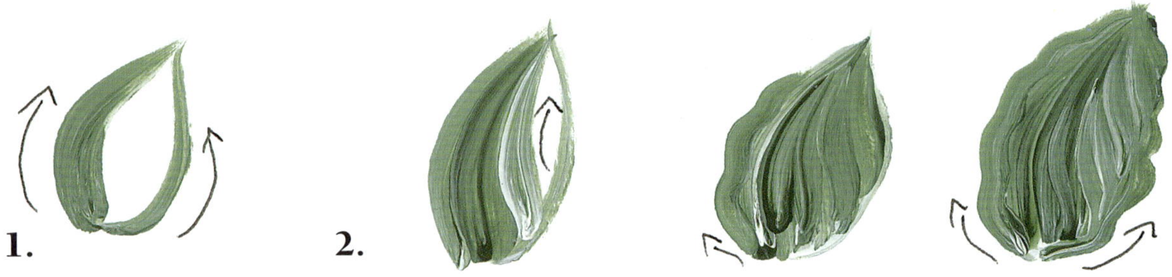

Shape and fill the leaf. Then place the brush at the bottom of the leaf and paint small curves around the leaf. Remember that the leaf must be damp.

The Flower

Brush: #0
Colors: Mauve (purple) and white

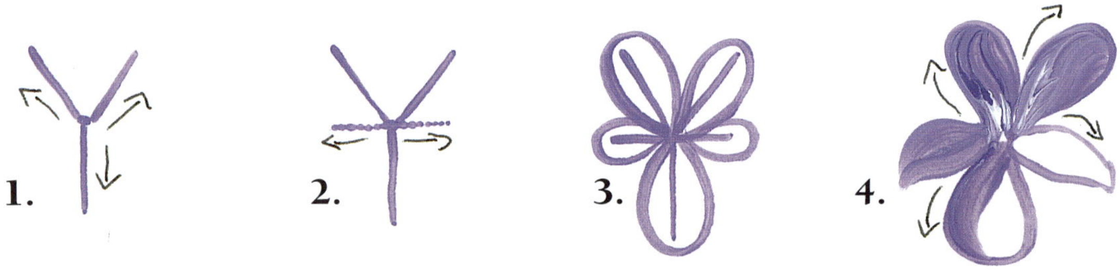

1/2. Make guide strokes.

3. Outline the petals with mauve.

4. Fill and shape the flower.

The Bud

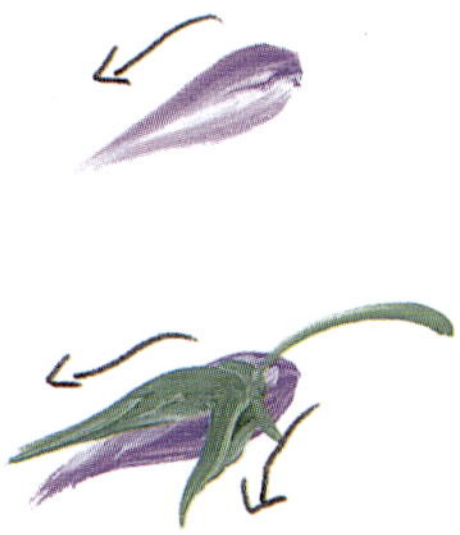

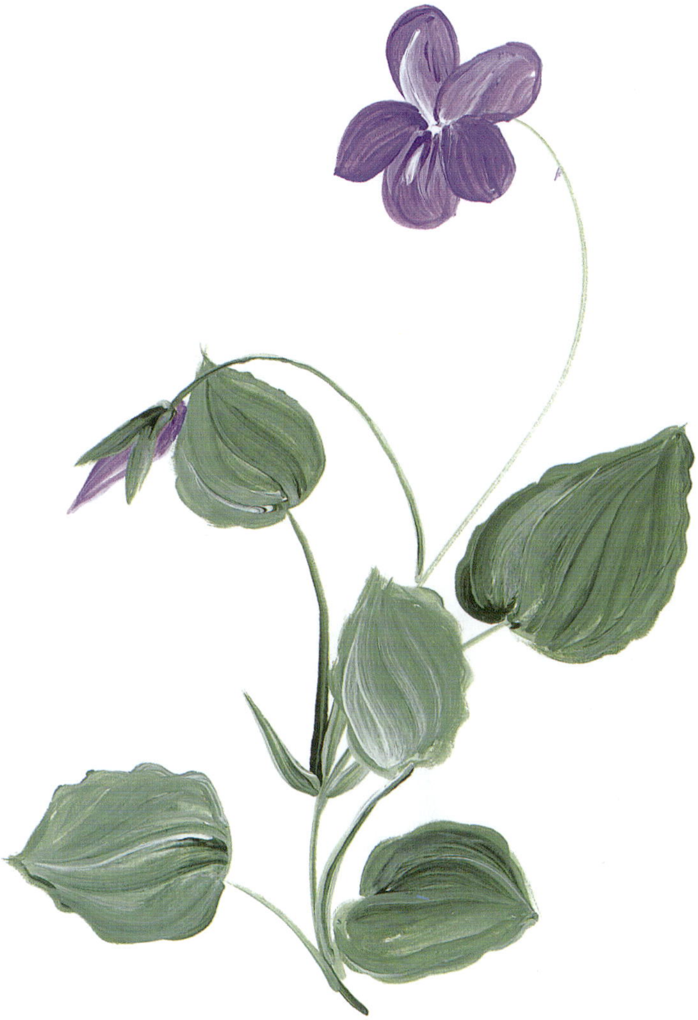

Violets have many colors and the petals are sometimes round and sometimes pointed. Use the "jack-in-the-box" for violets and pansies to start off, and you will see how easily you can change the shape of the flower. Be clever with shading.

Small Sorrel

The Flower

Brush: #0
Colors: Wine red and white

Stems and leaves are painted the same way as on the bluebells.

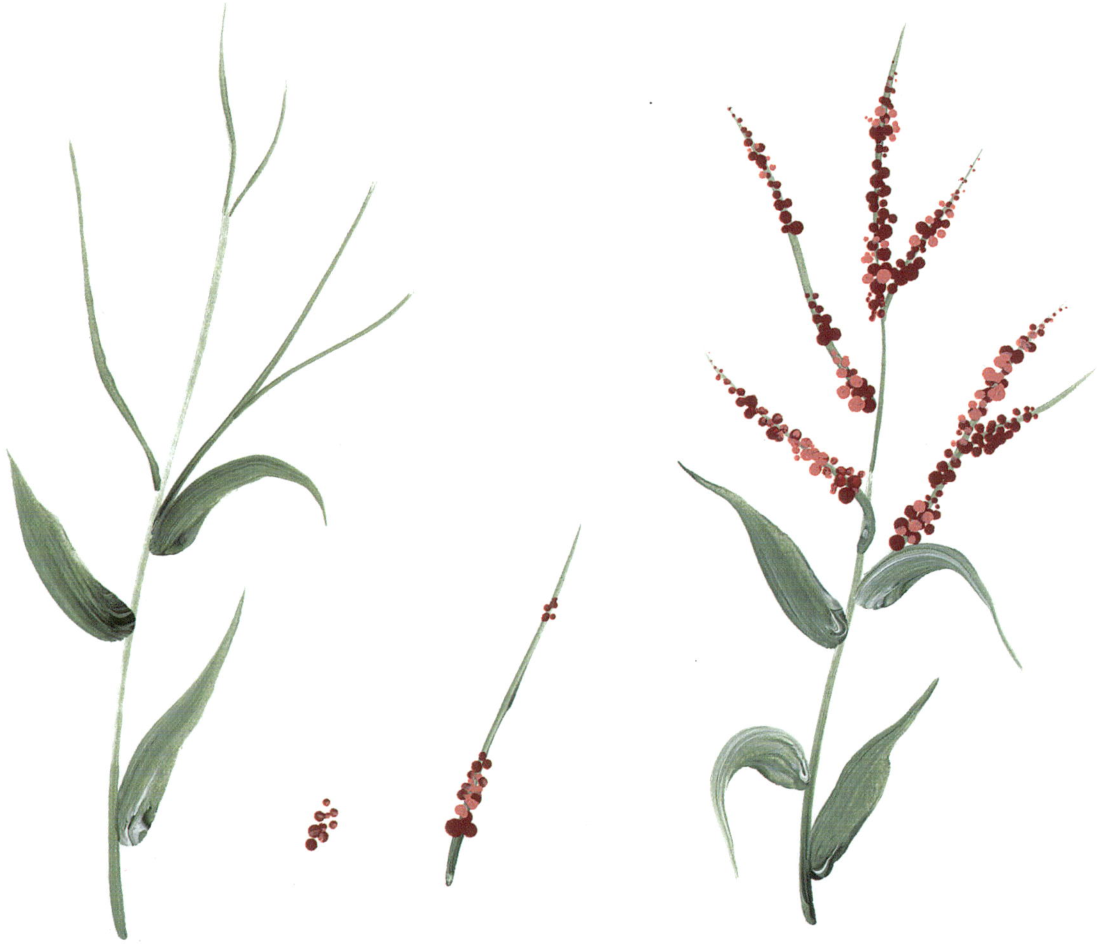

1. Paint long, fine stems.

2. Mix a little wine red with white to obtain pink.

3. Turn the brush and dip in paint. Make dots with wine red and pink, close together, and you will get a nice small sorrel flower — a simple but elegant flower.

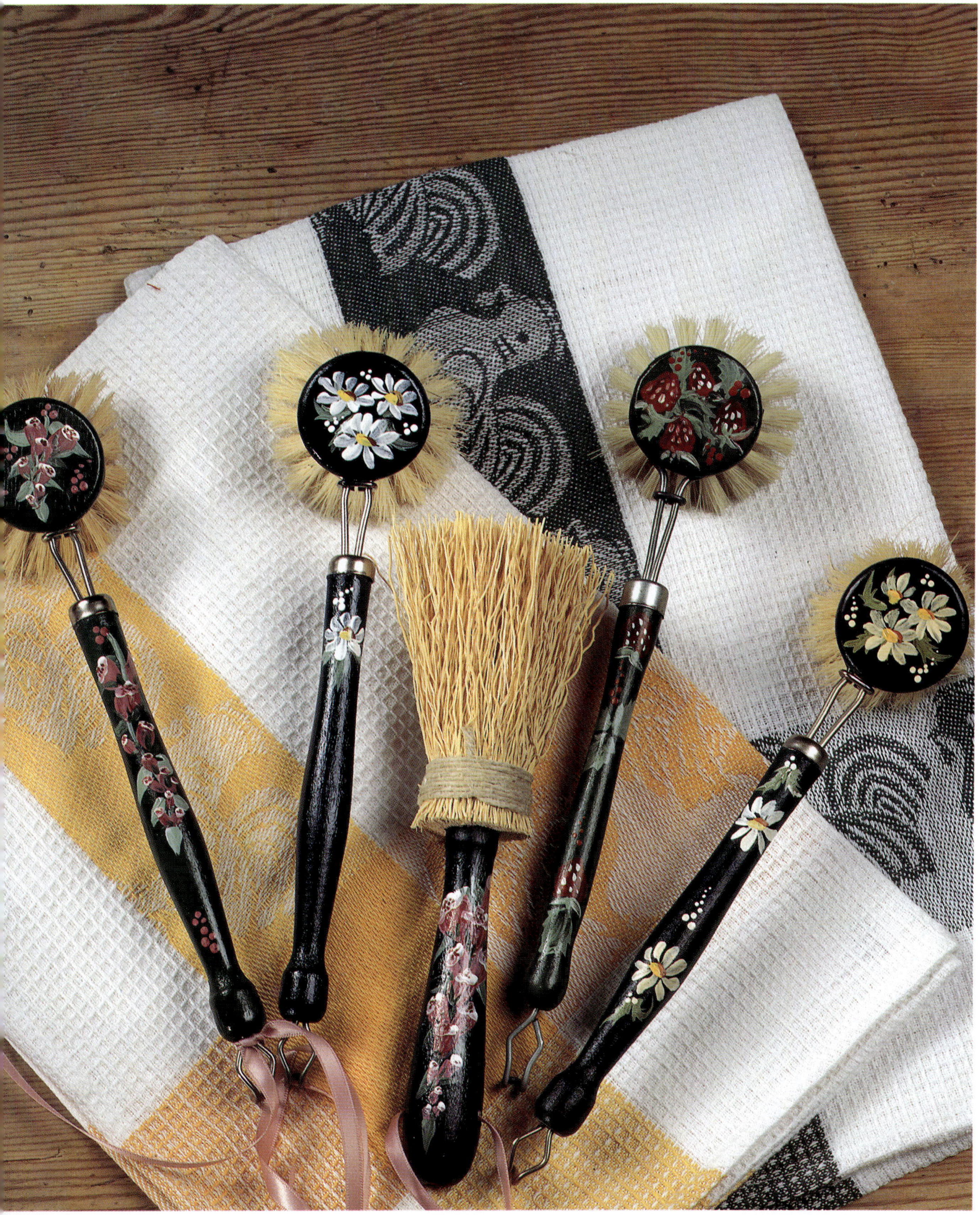

Stormarimjelle

The Flower

Brush: #0
Colors: Yellow and white

Stem and leaves are painted the same way as on the bluebells.

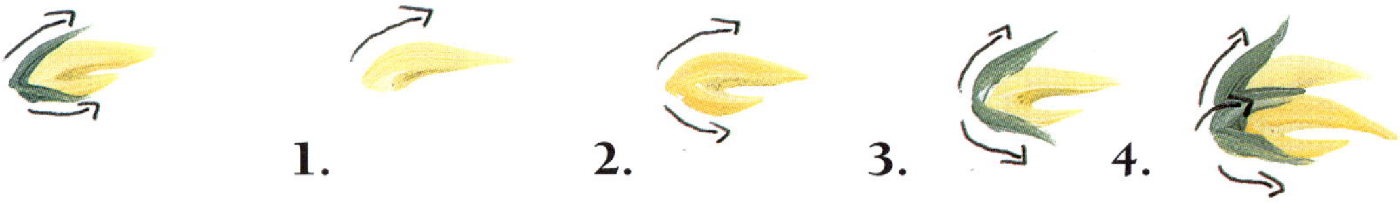

1. Press down — let up.

2. Press down — let up
   — somewhat shorter.

3. Paint a green leaf on each side.

4. This flower often has double flowers. Therefore, first paint one, then add the second flower somewhat on top of the first.

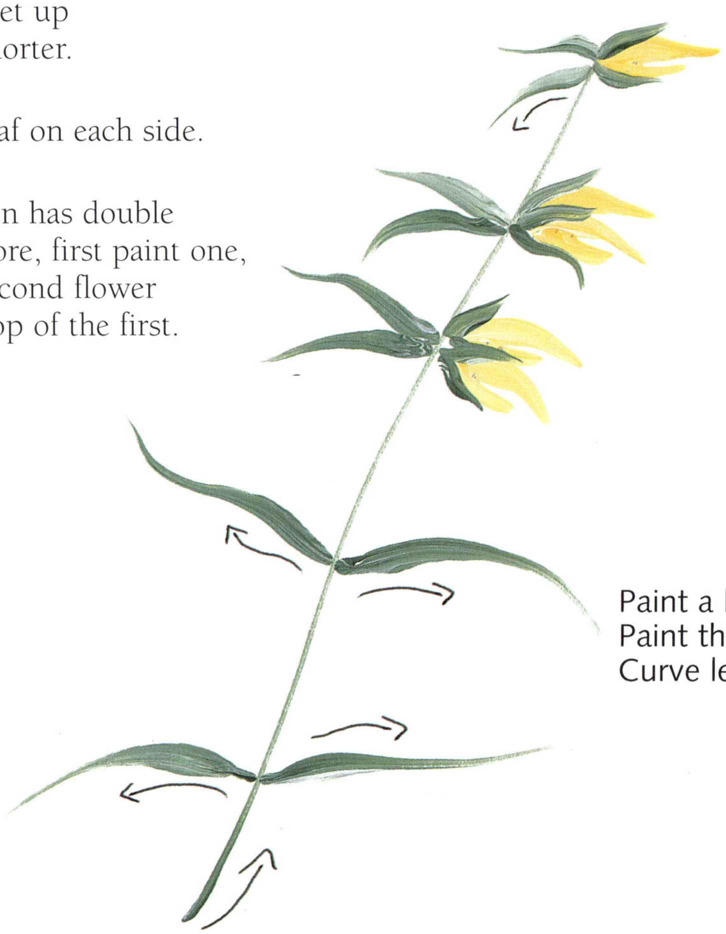

Paint a long, thin stem.
Paint thin, fine leaves.
Curve leaves a little.

Cornflower

The Flower

Brush: #0
Colors: Blue and white

Stem and leaves are painted the same way as on the bluebells.

1. **2.**

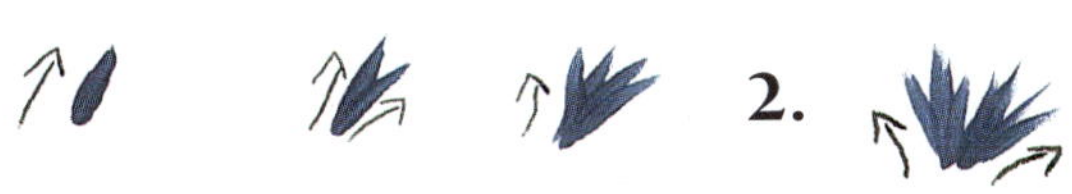

3.

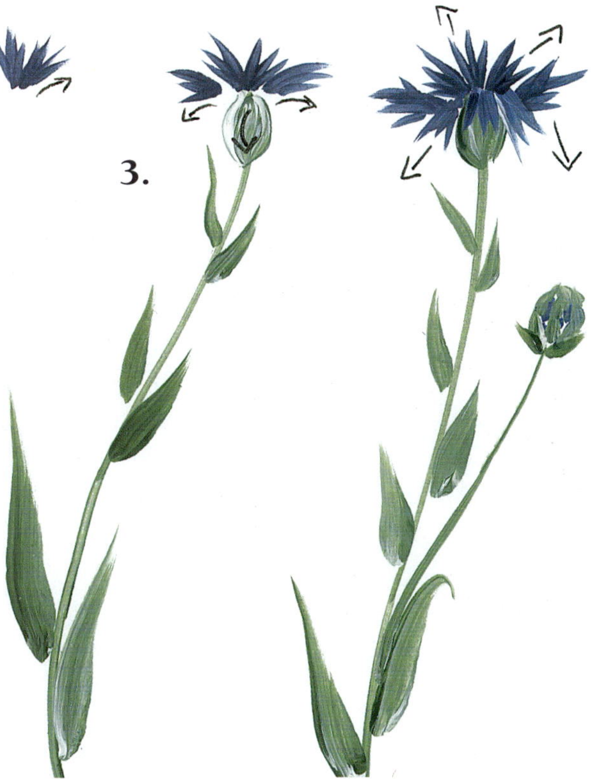

1. Use tip of brush to pull out spikes.

2. Put some small clusters together.

3. Make some small clusters on each side. Draw up a stem and make the green "head" so that you can paint some small clusters toward you. Note arrows. Leaves are the same as on the bluebells. Use shading and be light handed.

The Bud

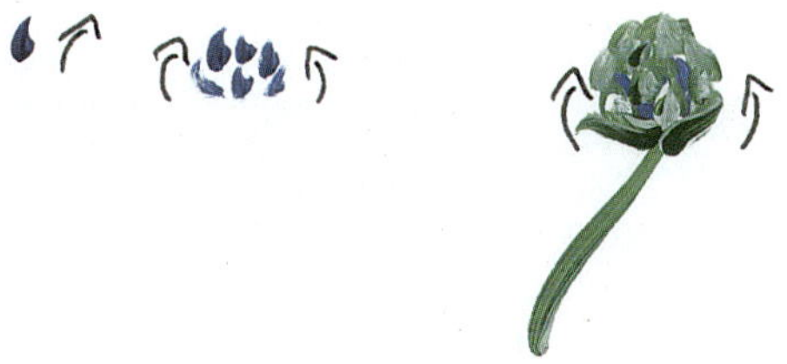

Press brush down and let up.
First make some dots with blue, then almost cover them with green.

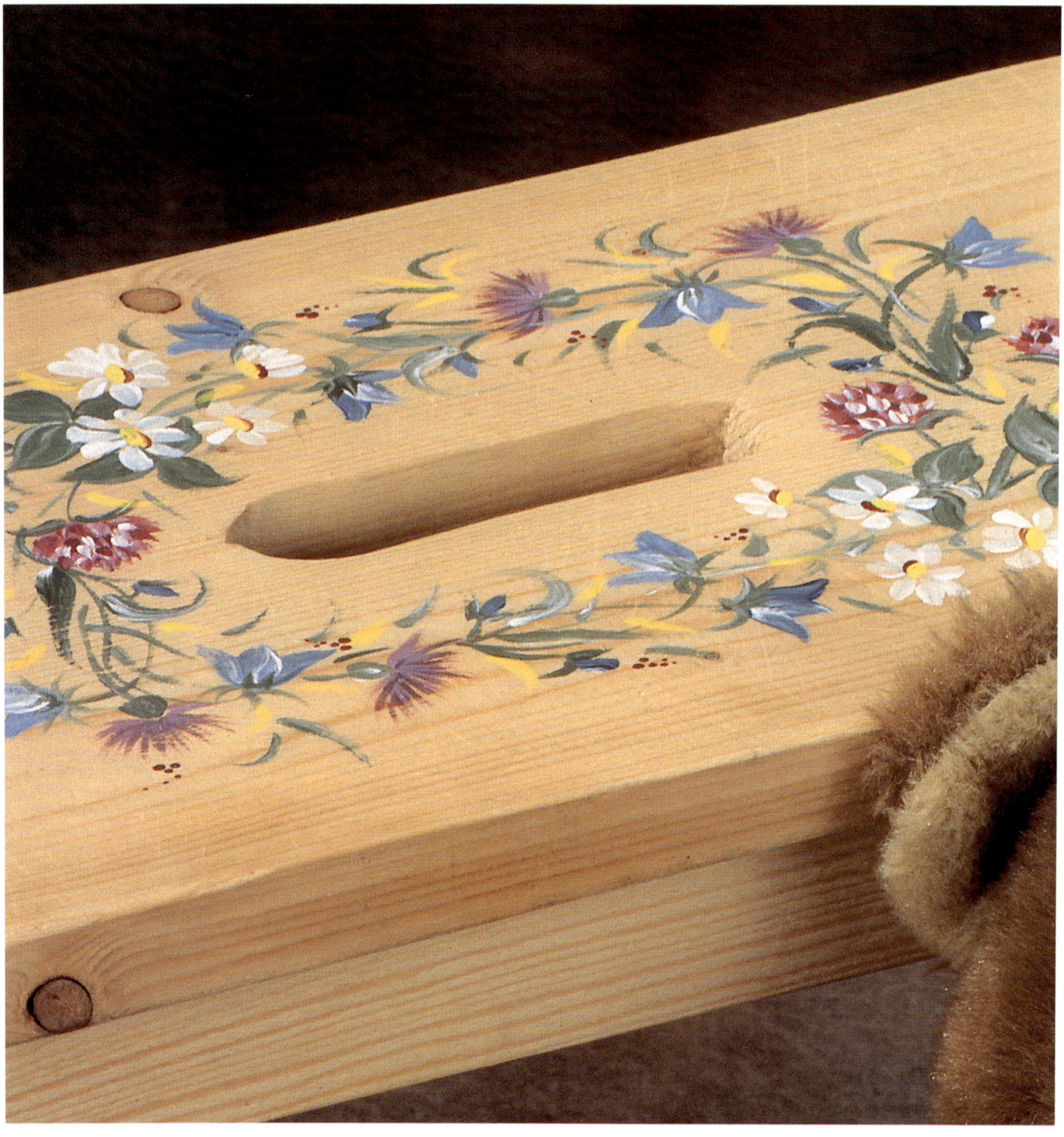

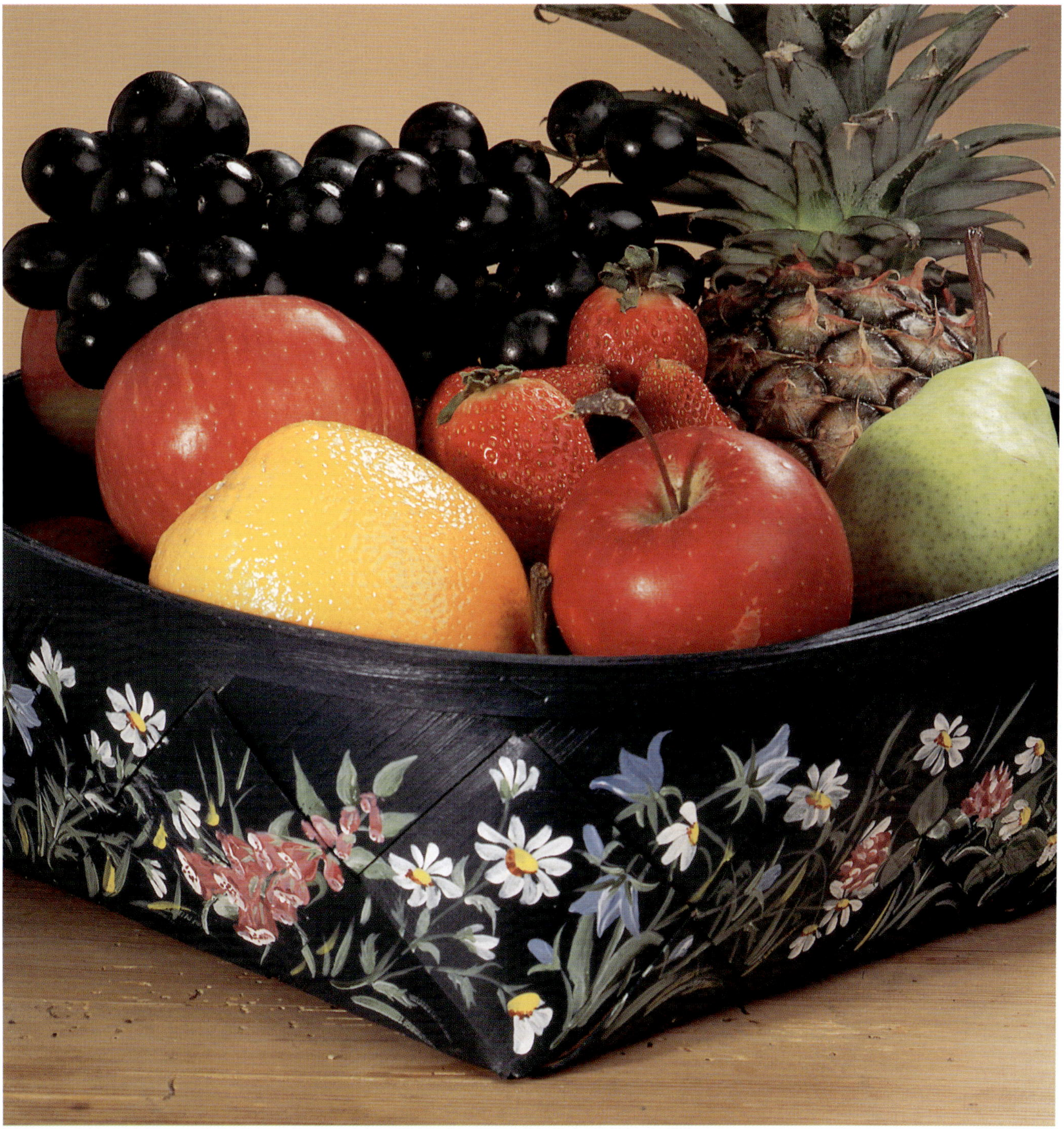

Dandelion

Stems and Leaves

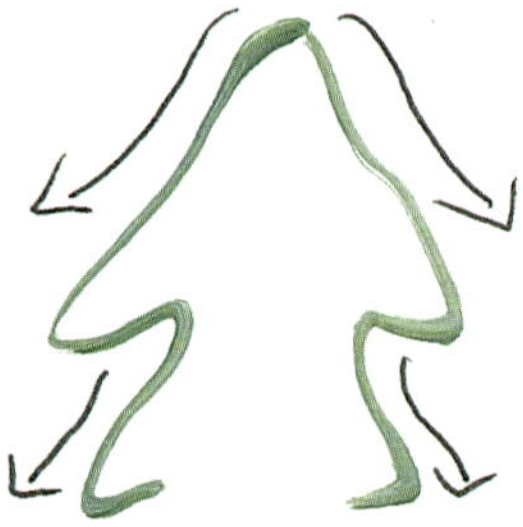

1. Shape the leaf.

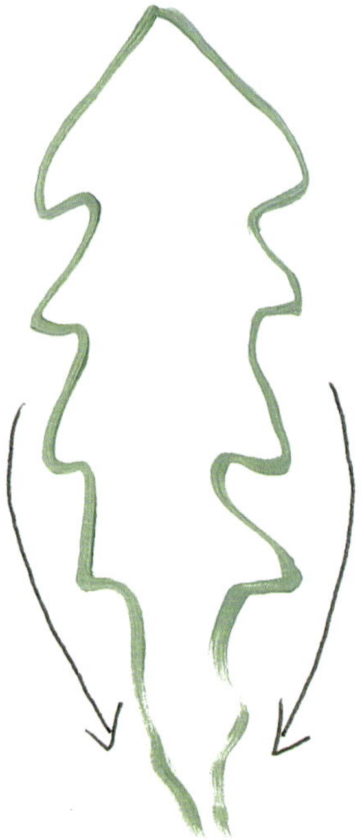

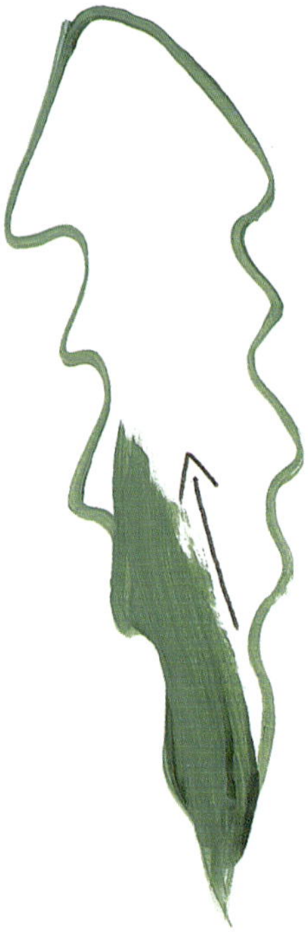

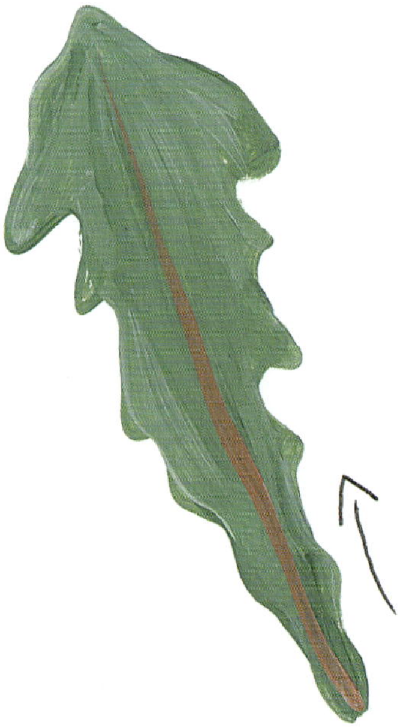

2. Dandelion leaves are dominating. They are more solid on the outer edges and thin down toward the root.

3. When filling the leaf, fill your brush with paint. Put a little white in the green and pull brush upward. Try filling leaf as evenly as possible, it works great if you keep it damp the entire time.

4. Finish by drawing up a brown vein in the leaf.

The Flower

Brush: #0
Colors: Yellow and brown

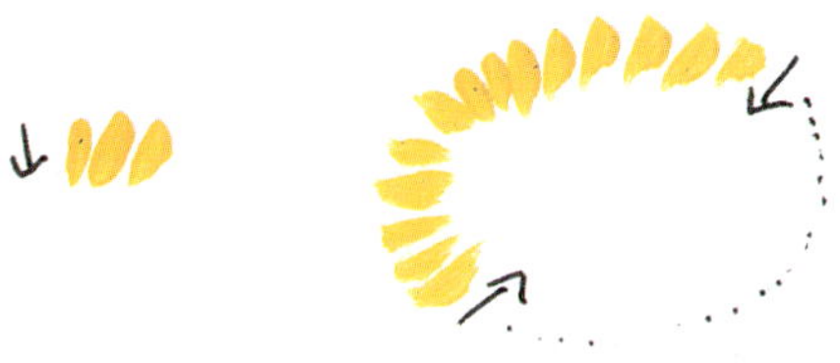

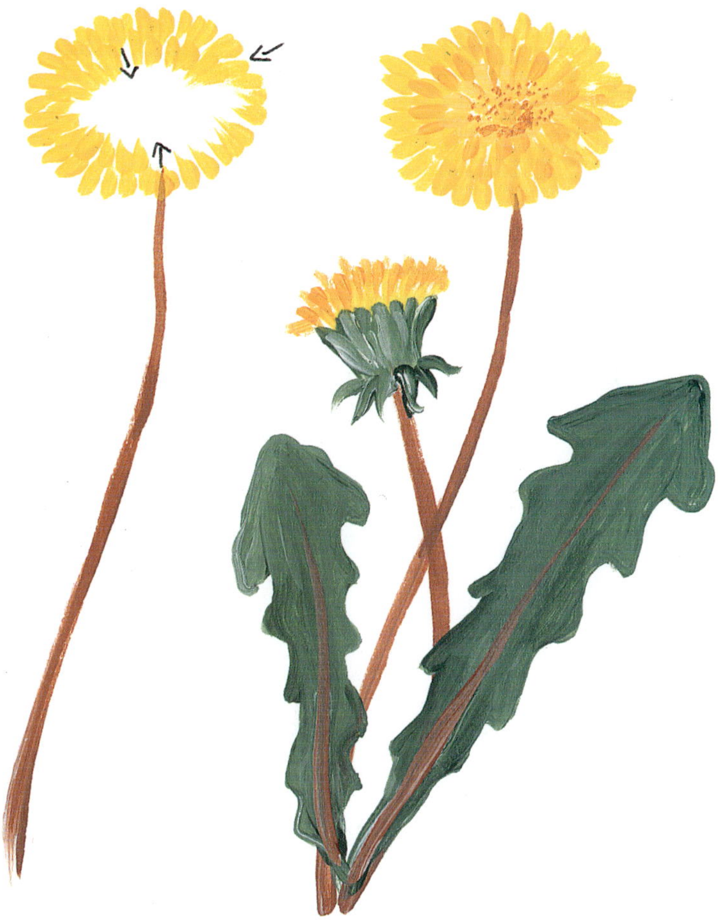

Press brush down and let up. Make a circle that forms the head of the dandelion. Fill head of flower completely. If you add a little brown in the yellow, it will make the flower stand out more.

Stems on dandelions can be somewhat brownish.

The Bud

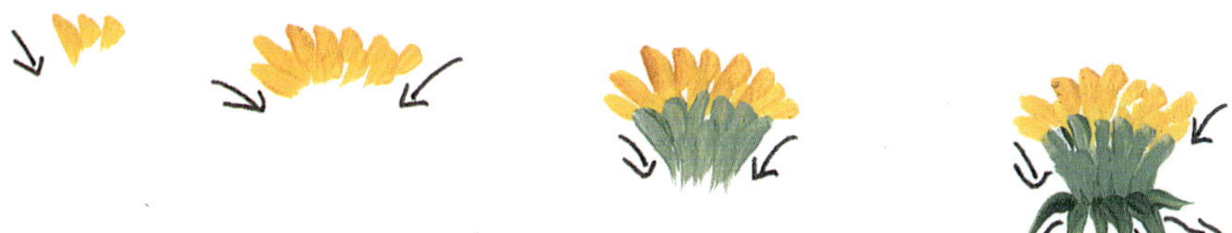

1. **2.** **3.** **4.**

Press down, let up. Shape the bud. Then dip brush in green. Press down and let up. Finally, make the "cuff". Note arrows. Press down, let up.

Tansy

Stems and Leaves

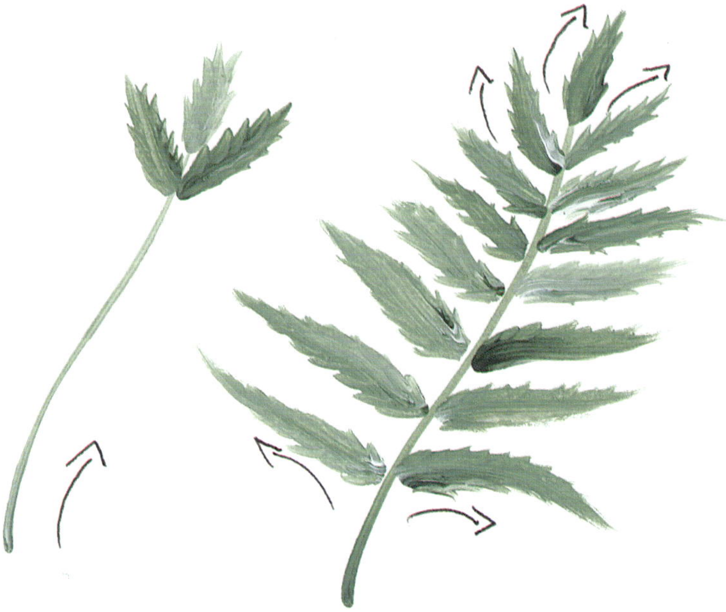

1. Paint a fine stem with spike leaves. (See thistle.)

2. Pull leaves evenly to each side. Use white and green together.

The Flower

Brush: #0
Colors: Yellow (possibly some brown and white)

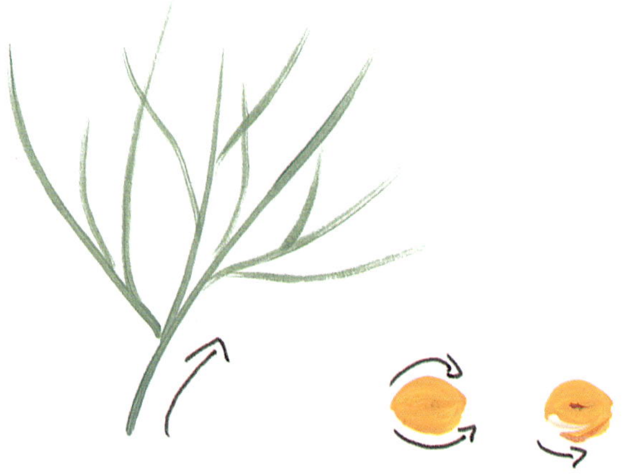

3. Make thin stems for the flower heads.

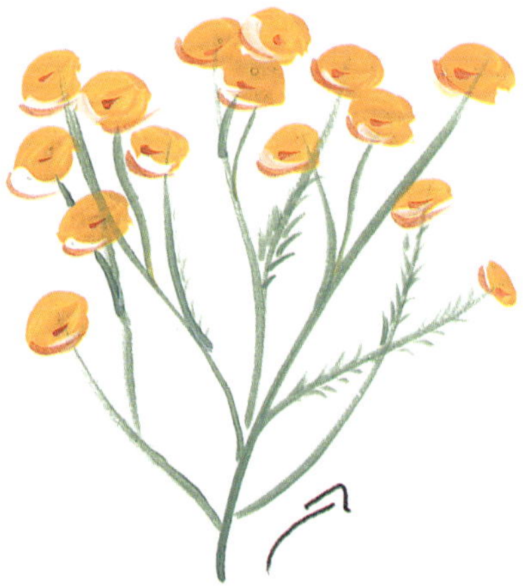

4. Paint round flowers. Dip brush in white — press down and let up. Dip brush in a little orange (add a little brown to yellow), press down and let up.

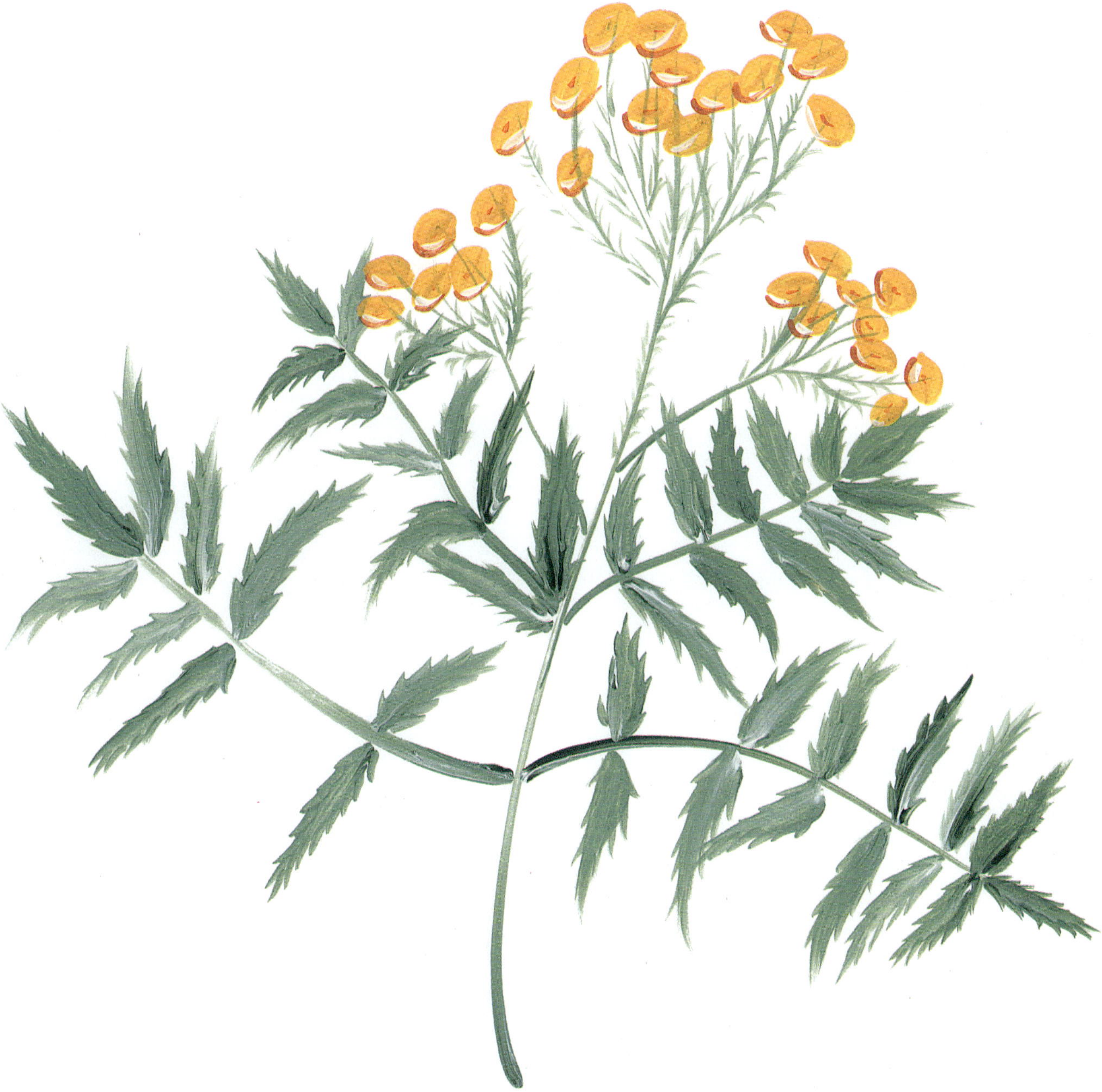

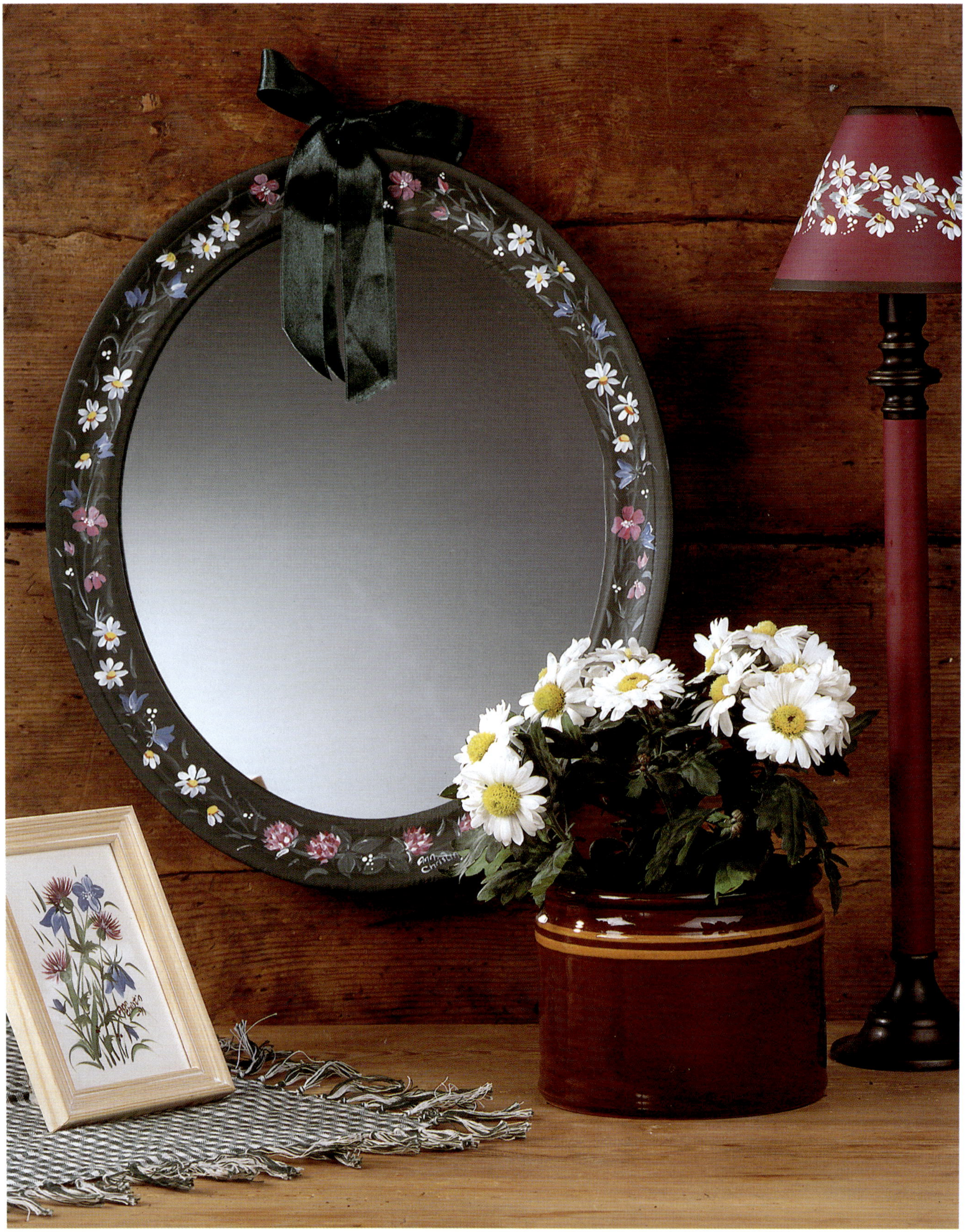

We will now put together some of the flowers we have learned to paint, into one composition.

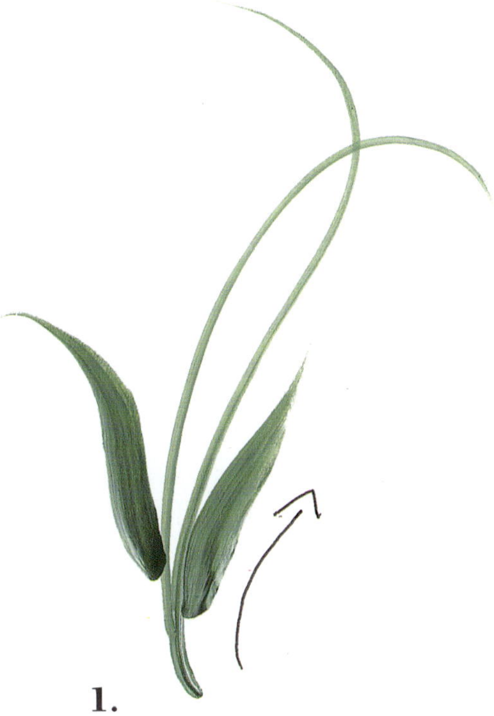

1.

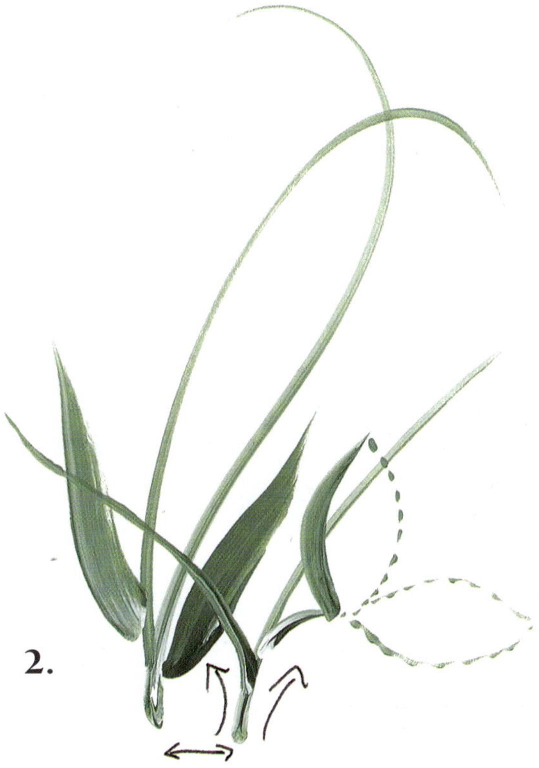

2.

1 cm.

1. When putting together several flowers, you can start with the bluebell stem. Draw it up. Make sure to leave room on each side for filling in with several flowers.

2. Start approximately one centimeter from the stem and draw up a stem for red clover. You must draw this stem across the bluebell stem and leaves so they will fit together naturally. Finish painting the red clover leaves.

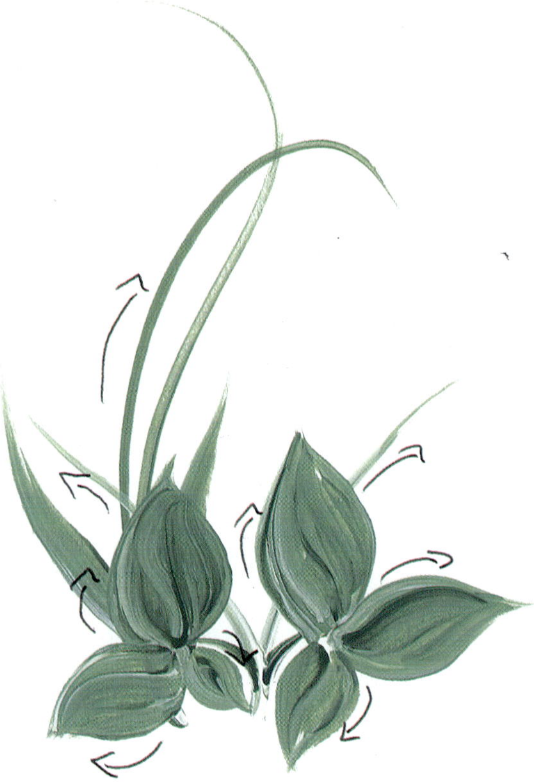

3.

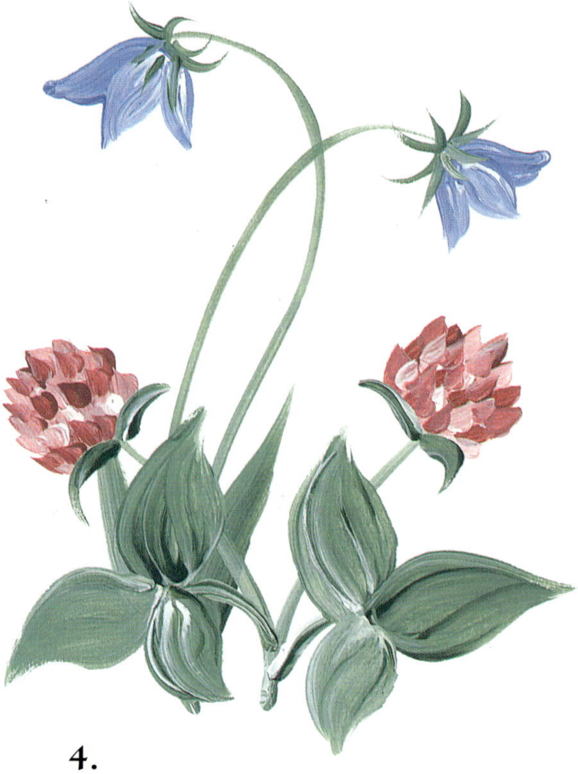

4.

3. Here you see that the leaves have been filled. Remember to mix white and green together for natural shading. Never try to shade where paint has already dried.

4. Now paint the flower heads for bluebells and red clover. Finish painting the red clover leaves.

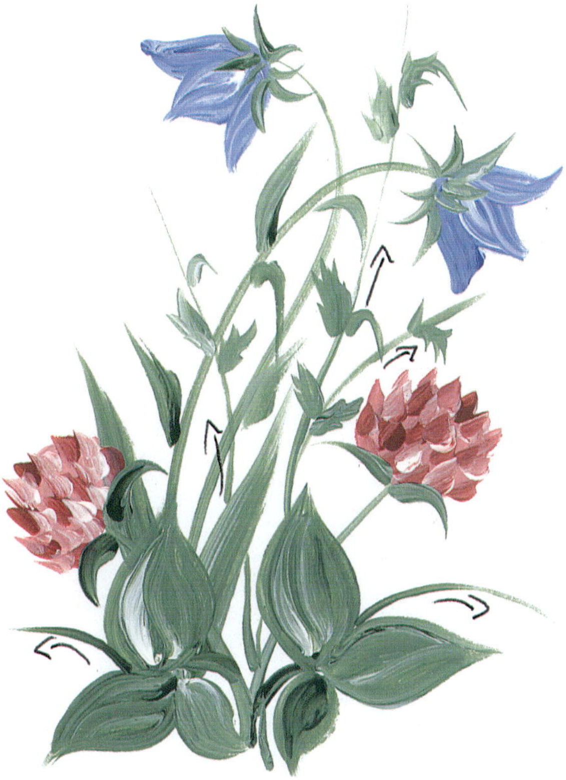

5.

6.

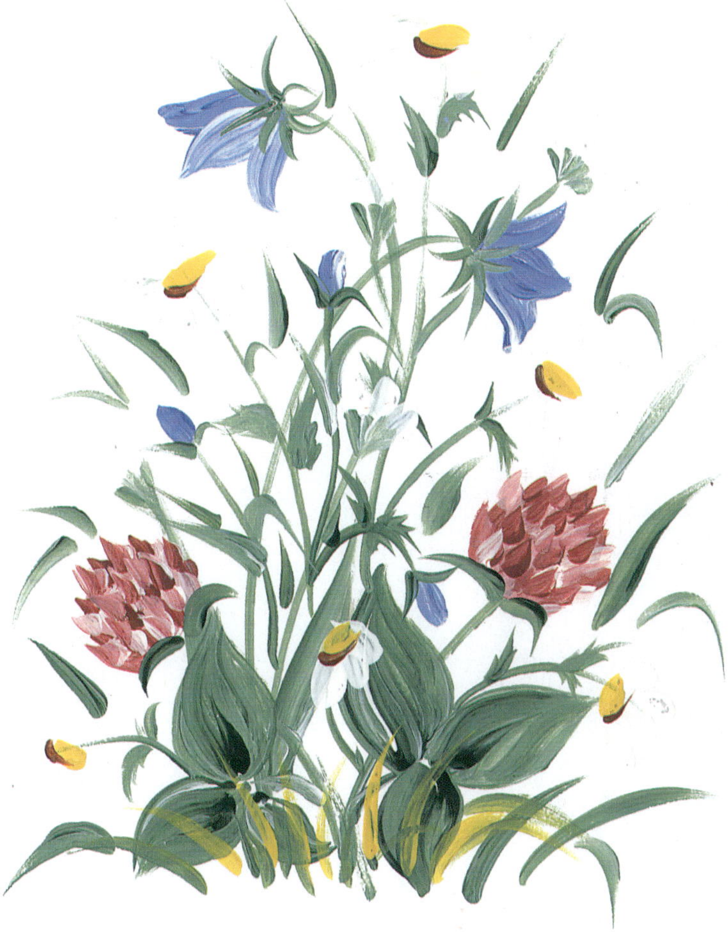

5. Paint a few more leaves on the bluebell stems. Now you will "cheat" a little. Start between the clover leaves and draw up thin stems for the daisies. Add more leaves.

6. Paint daisies. Let your imagination soar. Make some buds and leaves for a well-rounded design. Finally make some grass straws (thin leaves). Presto, you have a simple design!

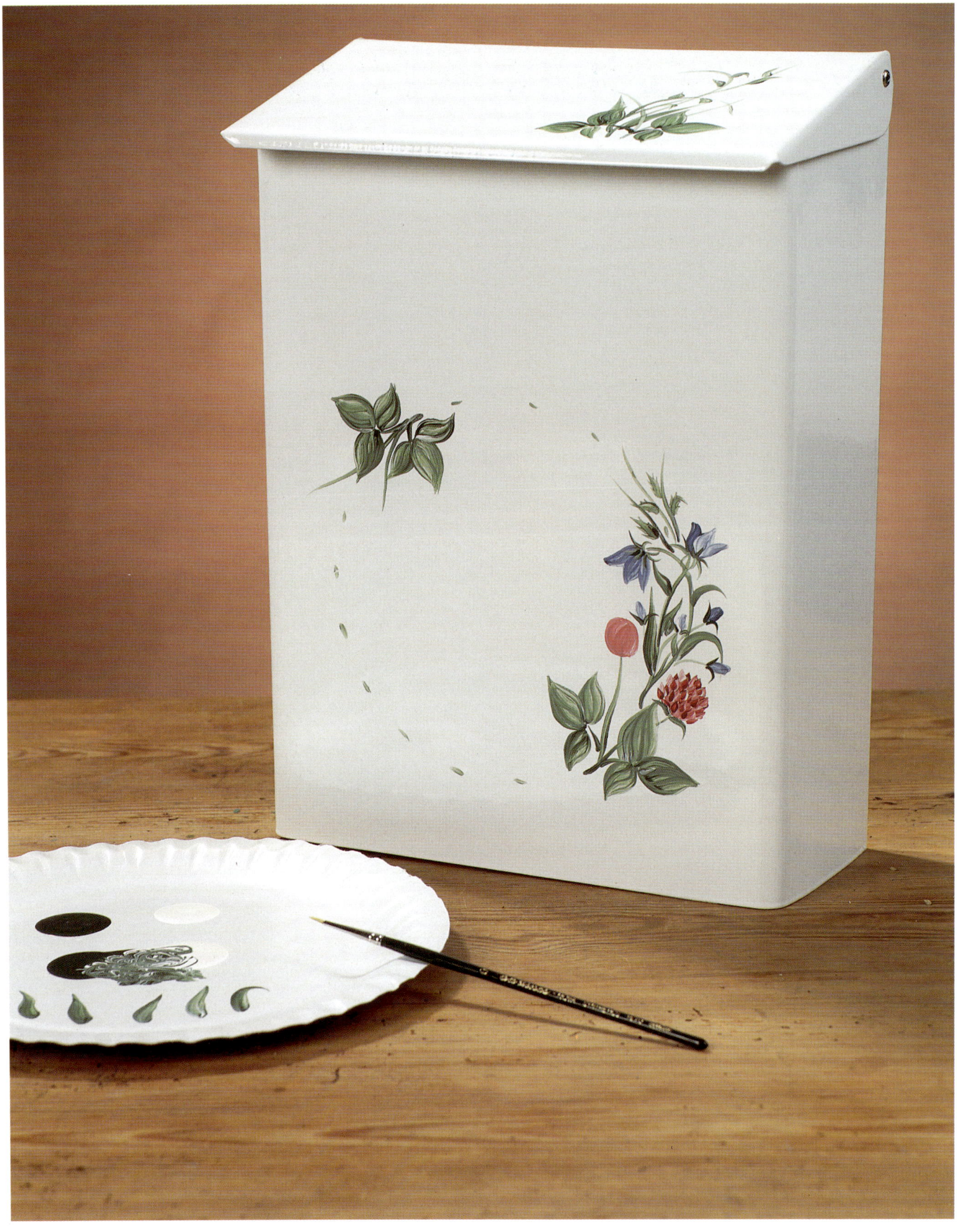

How to Paint a Wreath

Use a cup or something similar, turn it upside down on the background that you will be painting on. Hold the cup steady while you dot around it with green. The size of the wreath depends on the size of the cup/plate. The green dots form the center of the wreath.

The illustration shows the beinning stages of a wreath. Green was used so that it will blend in with the leaves and stems, and your guide lines will not be visible.

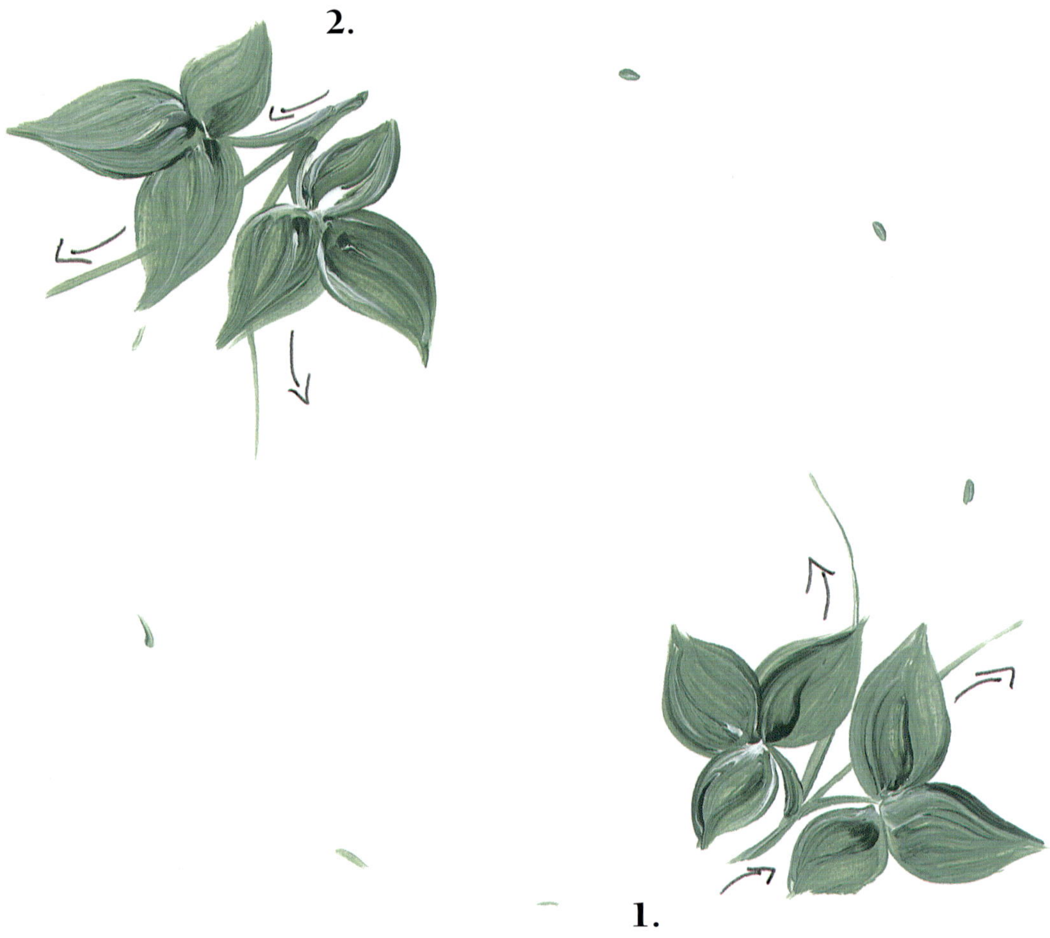

1. Start with clover. Put your brush on one of the dots and draw a stem to each side. Finish painting the leaves.

2. Turn the project. Place your brush on another dot and paint a stem to each side. Fill the leaves. We now have the starting points.

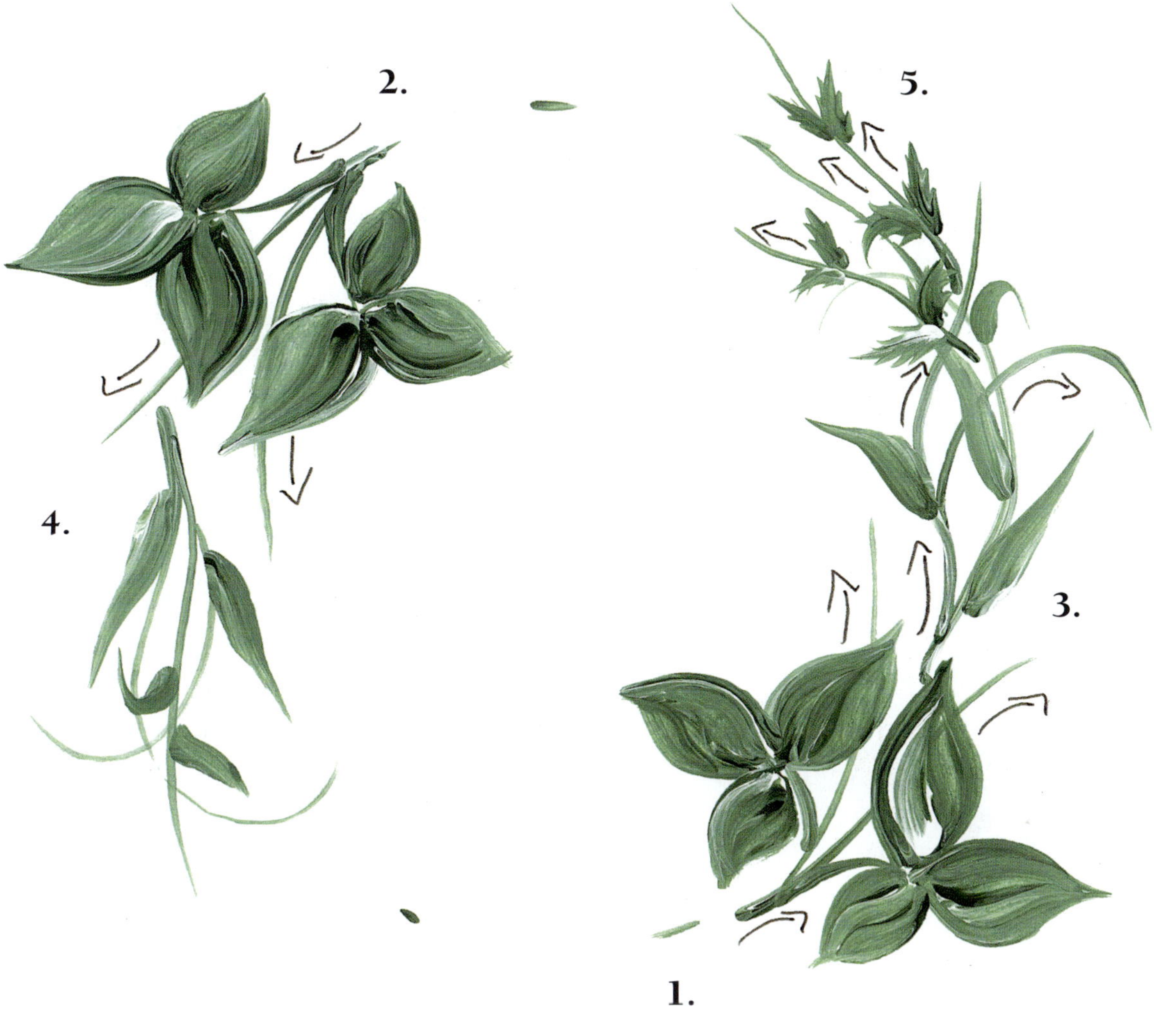

1. Paint clover stems and leaves. Do not paint the flowers.
2. Turn and paint more clover stems and leaves.
3. Turn and paint a bluebell stem and leaves.
4. Turn and paint a another bluebell stem and leaves.
5. Turn and paint three stems for thistle with leaves.

This is how the wreath looks without flowers. Work on the stems and leaves first. (Note numbering and follow accordingly.) If you have a large project, you can include several other types of flowers.

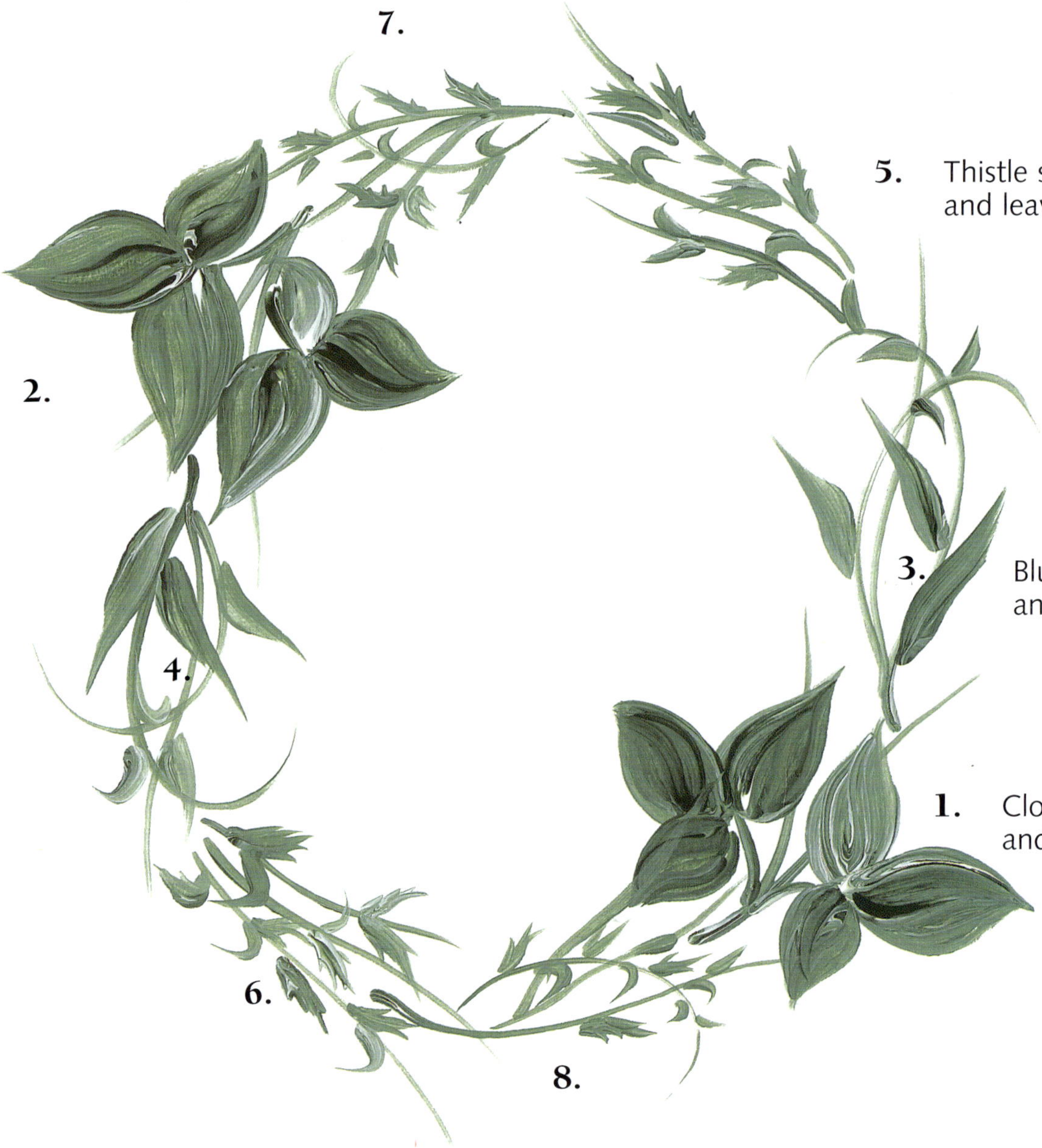

1. Clover stems and leaves. Turn.
2. Clover stems and leaves. Turn.
3. Bluebell stems and leaves. Turn.
4. Bluebell stems and leaves. Turn.
5. Thistle stems and leaves. Turn.
6. Thistle stems and leaves. Turn.
7. Daisy stems and leaves. Turn.
8. Daisy stems and leaves. Turn.

We now have a wreath with stems and leaves and are ready to paint the flower heads.

1. Start with the clover heads.
2. Paint the bluebell heads.

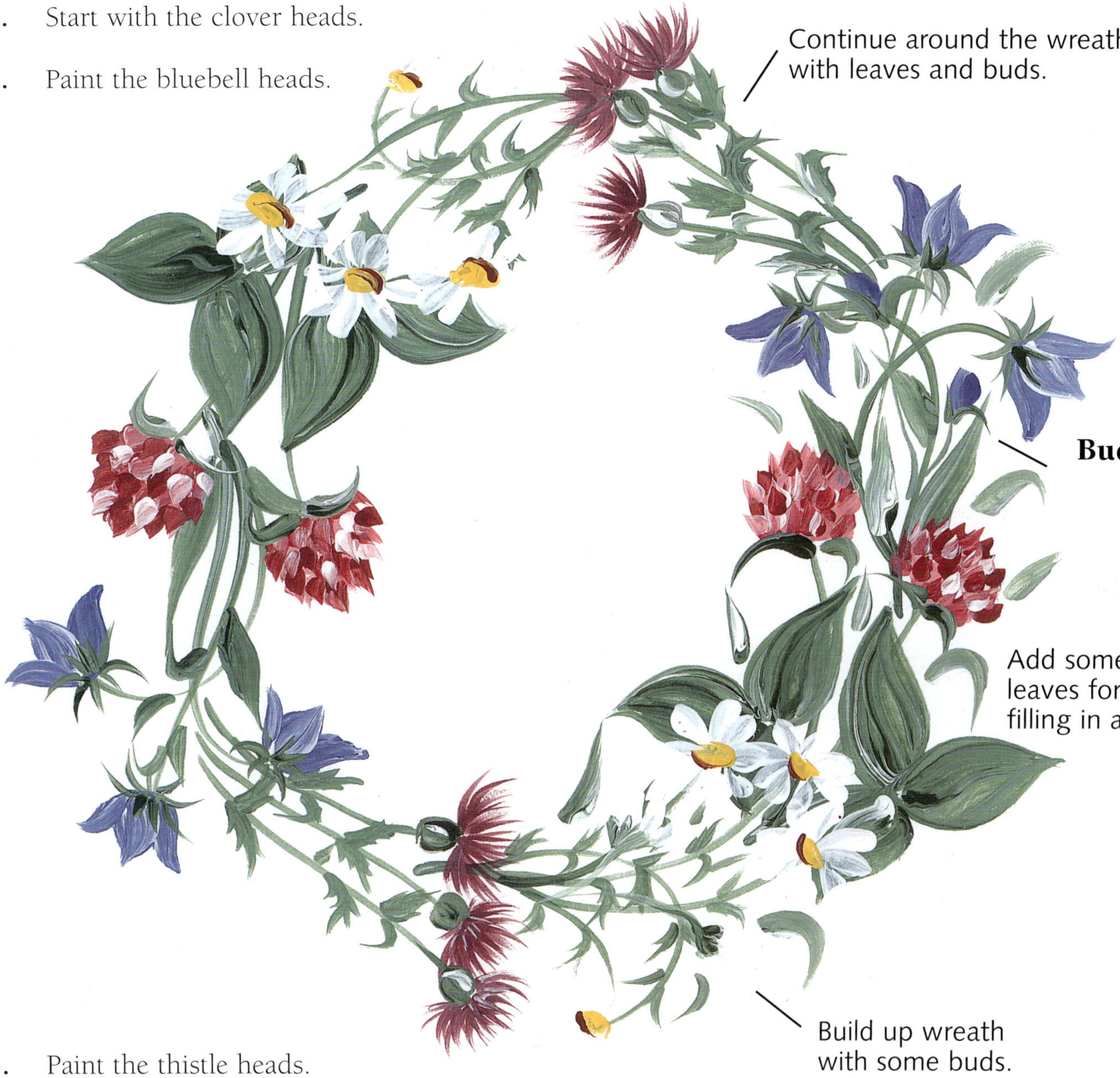

3. Paint the thistle heads.
4. Paint the daisy heads.

Finally, we fill in with some buds and leaves. Do you see how nice and simple this is?

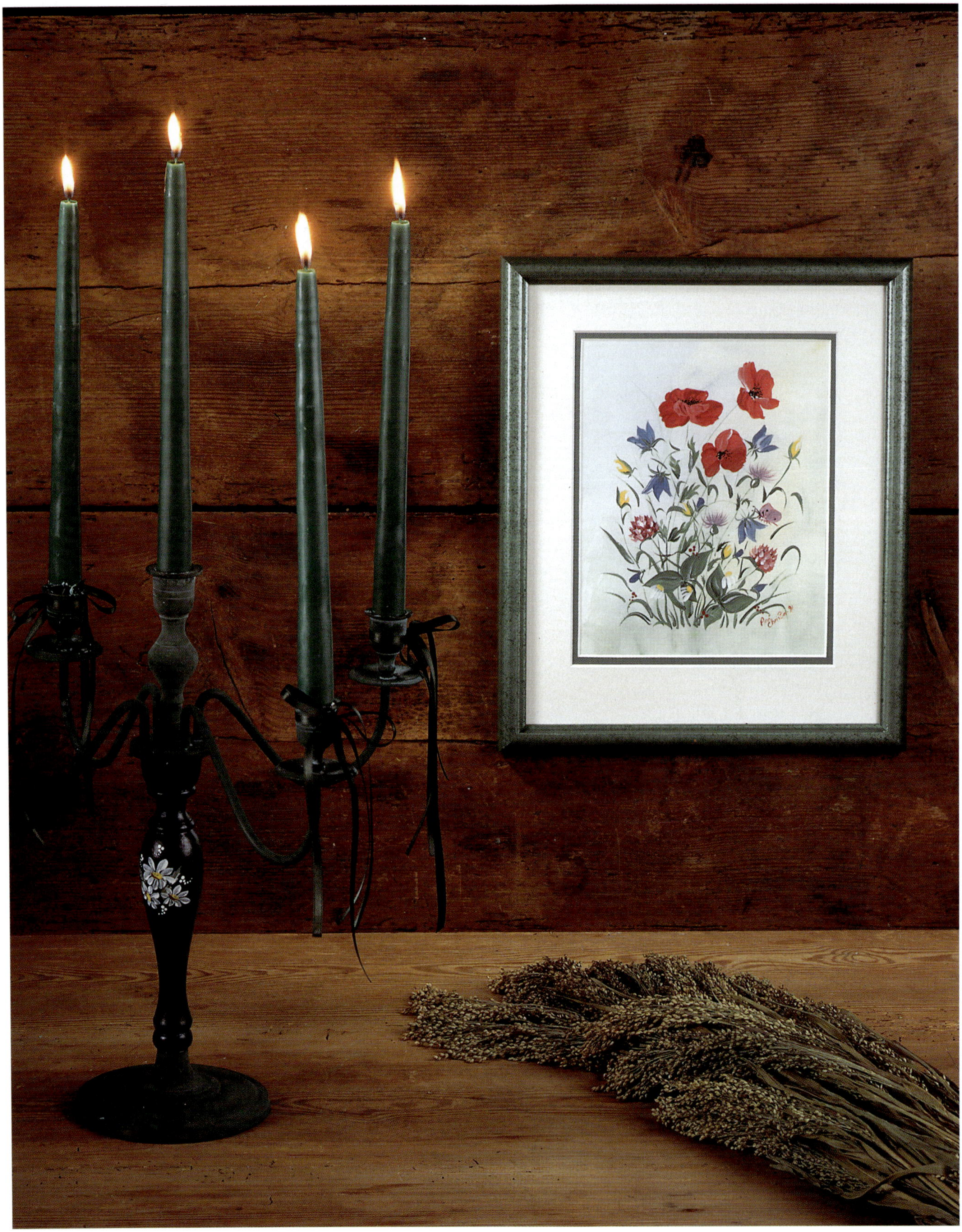

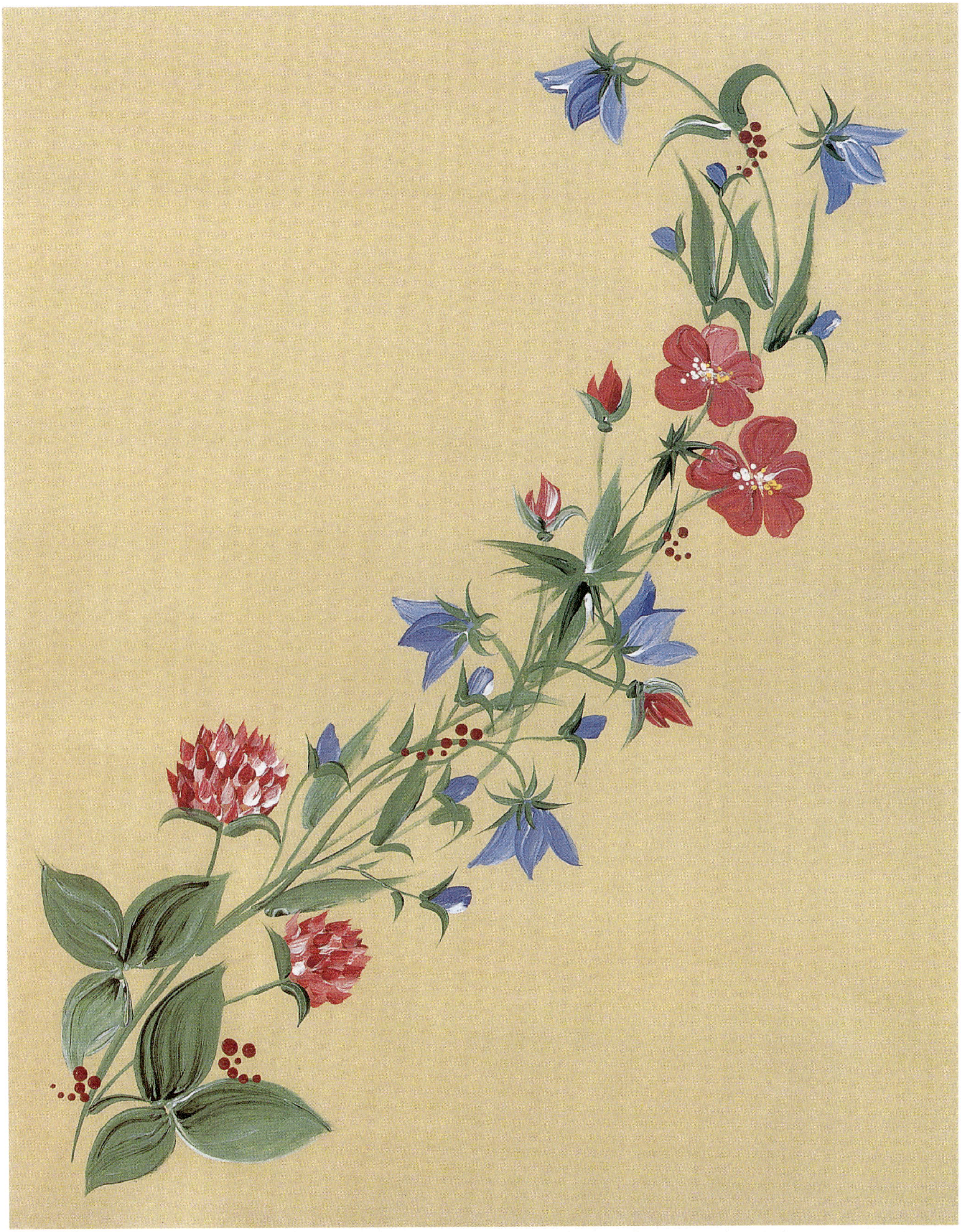

Bell Heather & Ling Heather

Stems and Leaves

Brush: #0 or #1
Colors: Green, white and brown

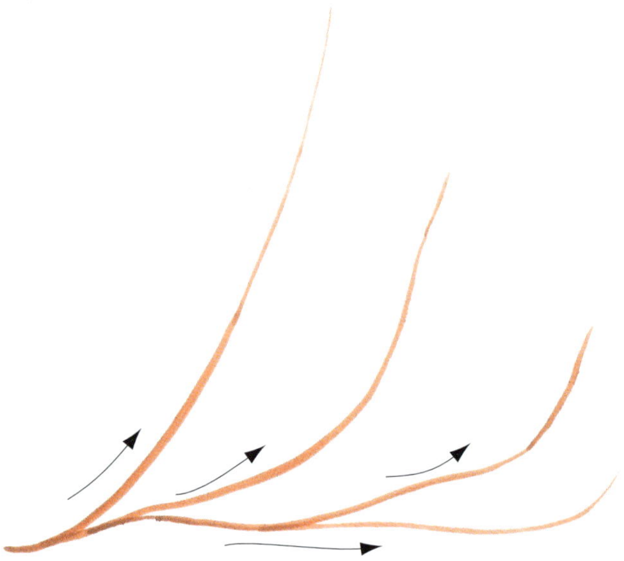

Paint some fine, thin stems.

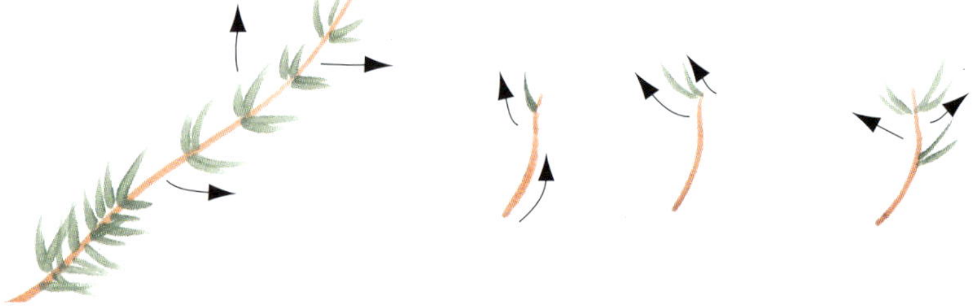

From the stem, make small, fine leaves.
Use the tip of the brush, press down and let up.

The Flower

Brush: #0 or #1
Colors: Green, white, pink and brown

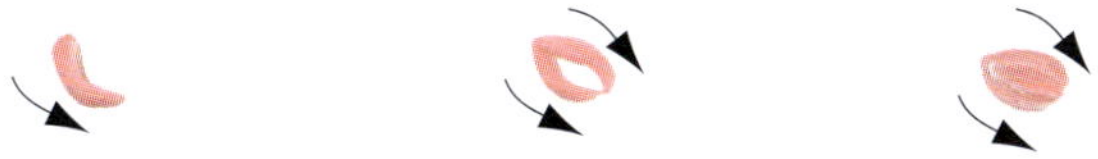

Press down. Follow arrows and fill.

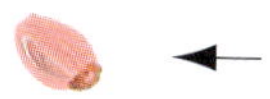

Make a small, fine curve with brown.

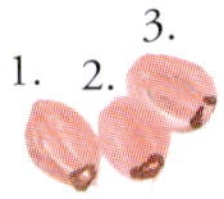

1.

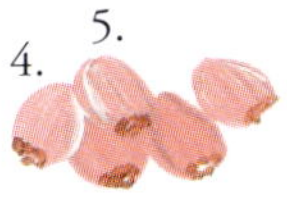

2.

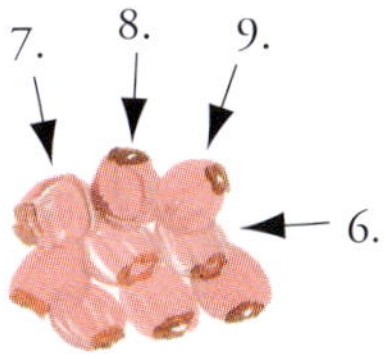

3.

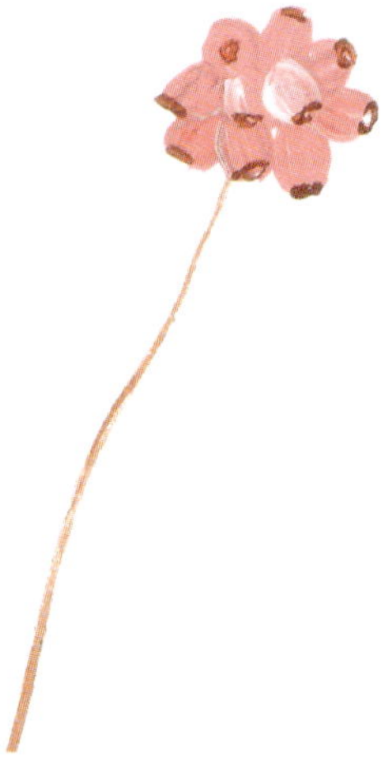

Brown stem with a nice cluster on top.

1. Paint the first three bells. Follow the numbers so that you can build up a nice cluster.
2. Add a little white to the pink.
3. Build up the cluster this way.

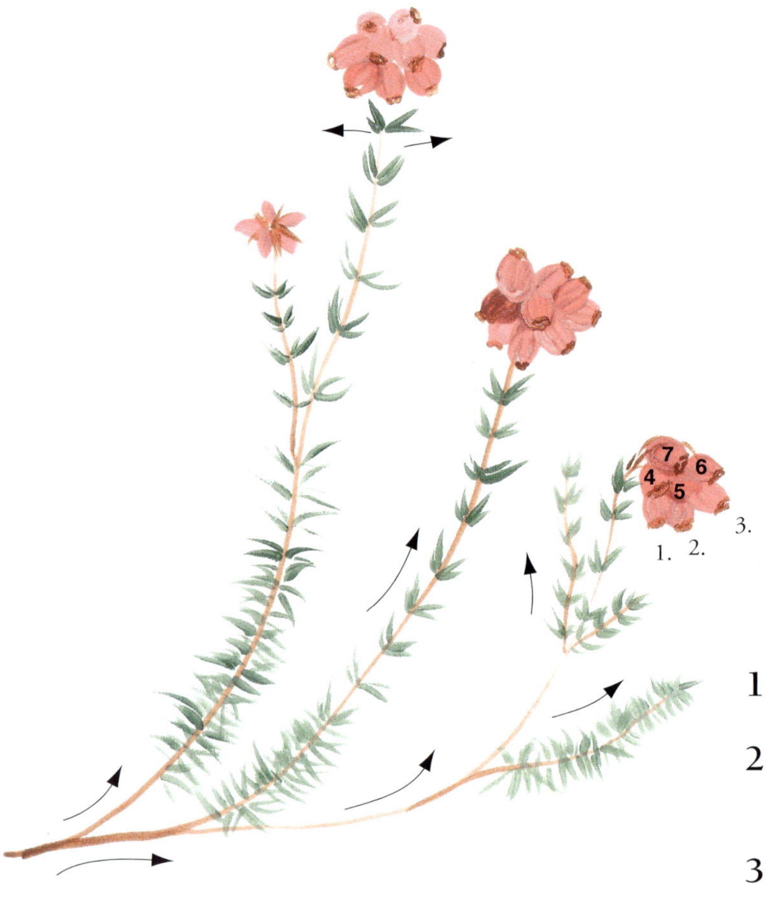

1. Paint some fine stems.

2. Build up a "pouch" — heads on top of each stem.

3. Pull out thin, fine leaves.

Heather

Stems and Leaves

Brush: #0
Colors: Brown, green and white

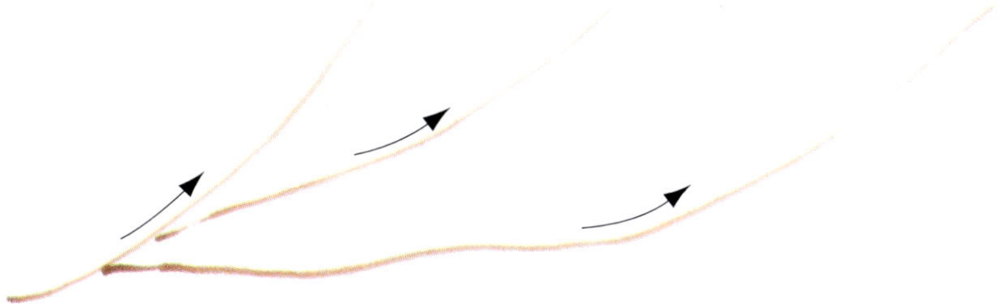

Pull up thin, fine stems with brown.

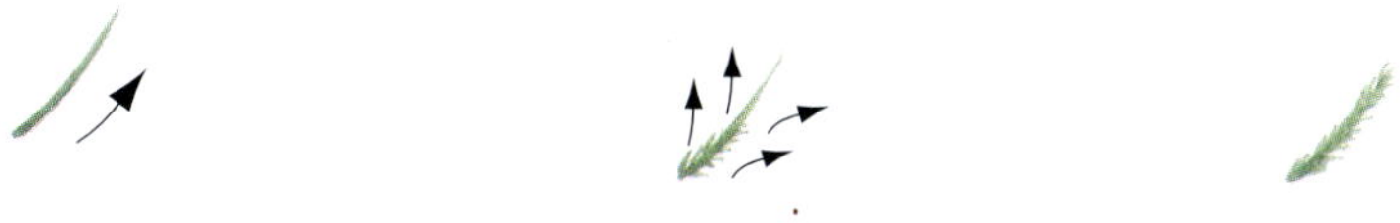

1. **2.**

1. When making leaves for the heather, be light handed. Make a thin, fine stroke.
2. Pull out thin, fine spikes close together. Be light handed.

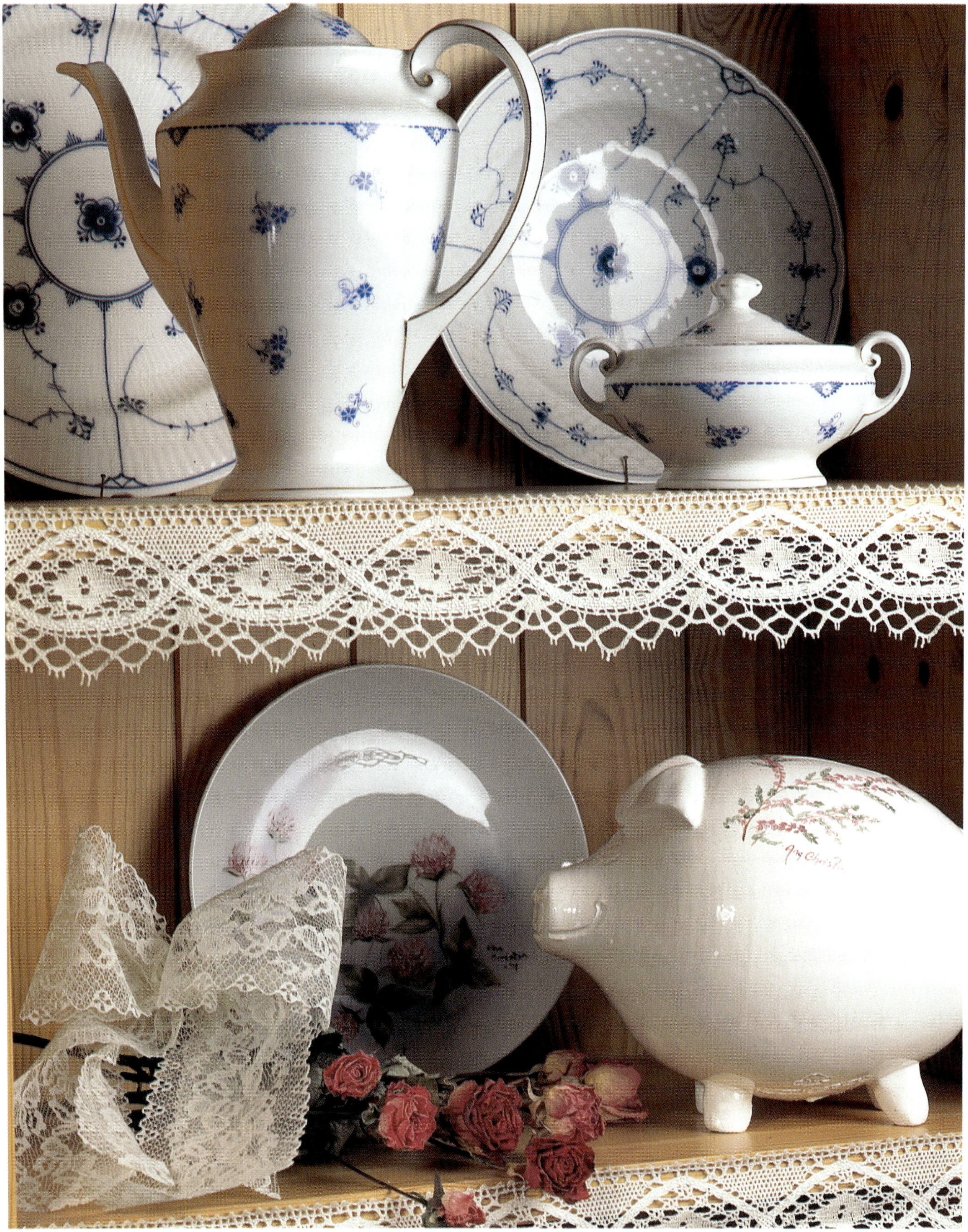

The Flower

Brush: 0 or 1
Colors: Wine red and white

1. **2.** **3.** **4.**

1. Press down and let up.
2. Press down and let up.
3. Make a line in the center.
4. If you want to be realistic, make visible stamens, but it's not necessary.

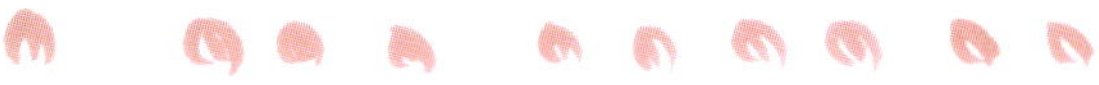

Practice on similar small flowers. Some of the buds can be tight, some divided in half, and some divided into three sections.

1.

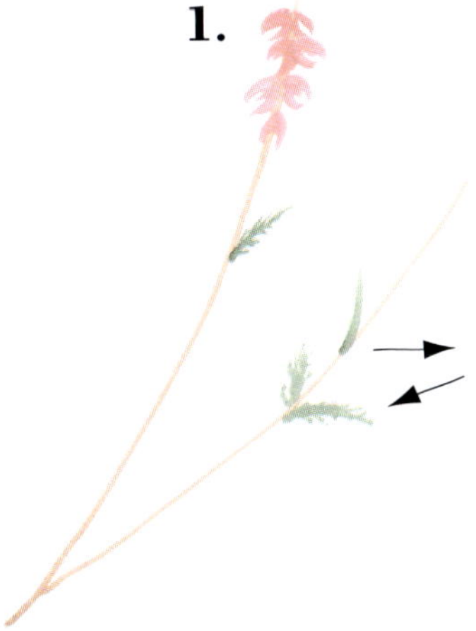

Arrange the flowers close together against the stem. Start at the top.

Paint the leaves.

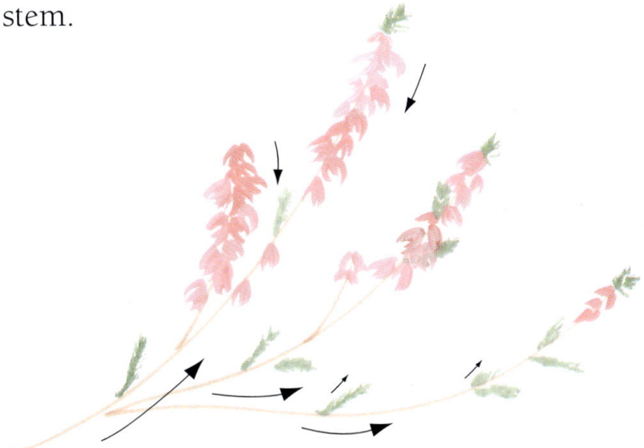

Blue Heather

Stems and Leaves

Brush: #0 or #1
Colors: Green, white, brown and wine red

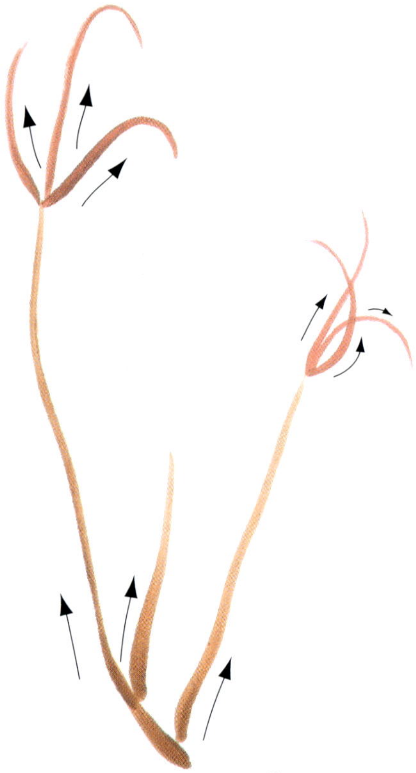

1.

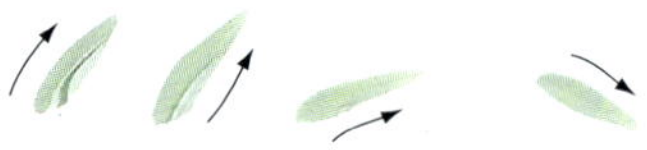

2.

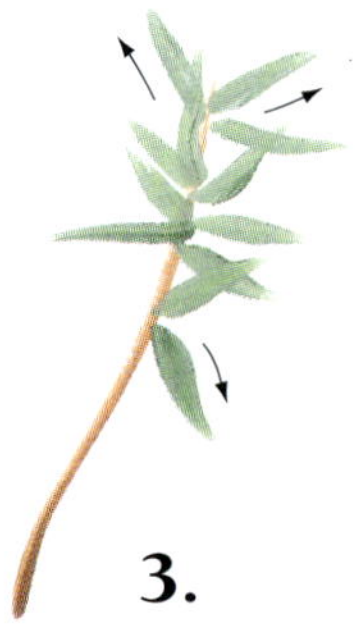

3.

1. Pull up fine stems with brown. The top of the stems are more wine red.

2. Paint small leaves. Press the brush down and let up.

3. Draw up the stem and make some leaves upwards and downwards.

The Flower

Brush: #0 or #1
Colors: Wine red and white

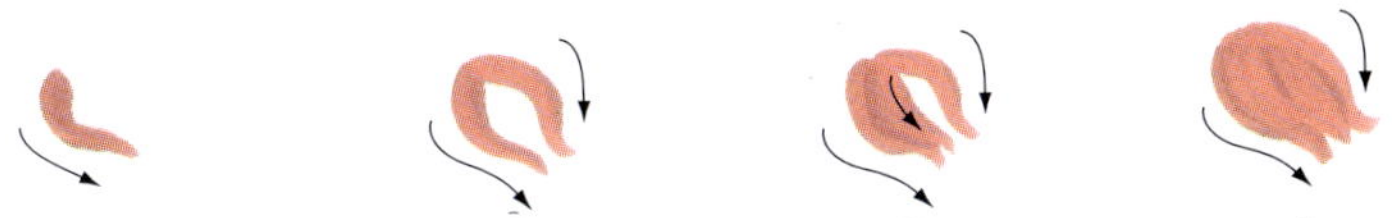

1. **2.** **3.** **4.**

5.

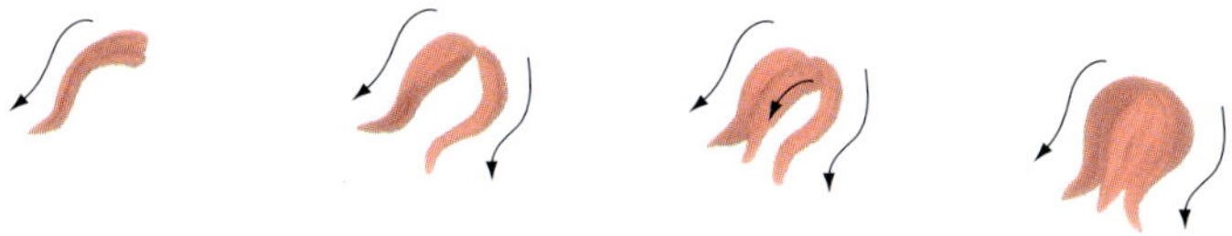

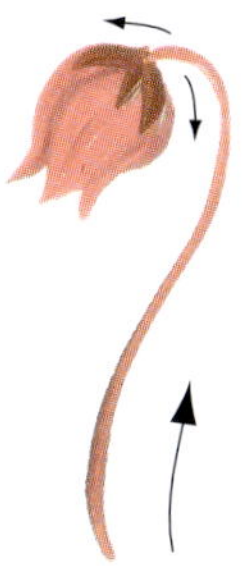

6.

1. Press and pull the brush towards you. Follow arrows.
2. First shape the bell.
3. Fill towards you and draw out the center.
4. Filling towards you adds life to the bells.
5. Paint some bells that turn the opposite way as well.

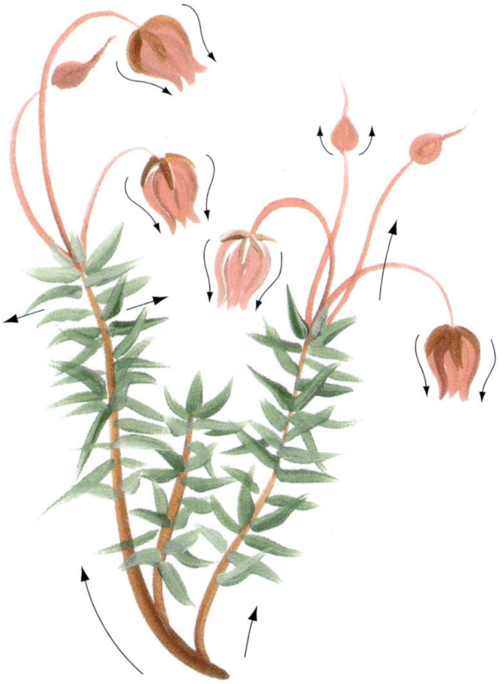

7.

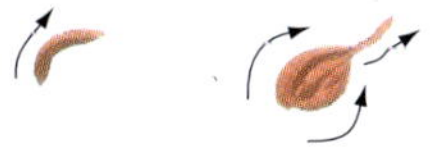

6. On top of the bells you'll find some brown leaves. Pull out three leaves in the direction of the arrows.
7. Add some small buds.

White Heather

Stems and Leaves

Brush: #0 or #1
Colors: Green, white and wine red

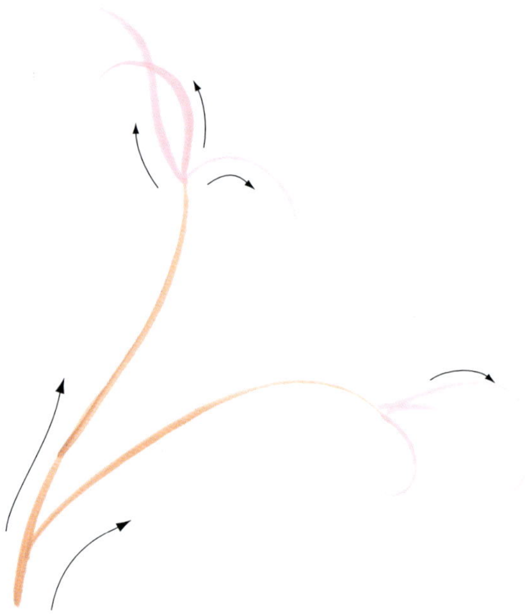

White heather has brown stems. Where the flower sits at the top, the stem is more pink.

Be light handed.

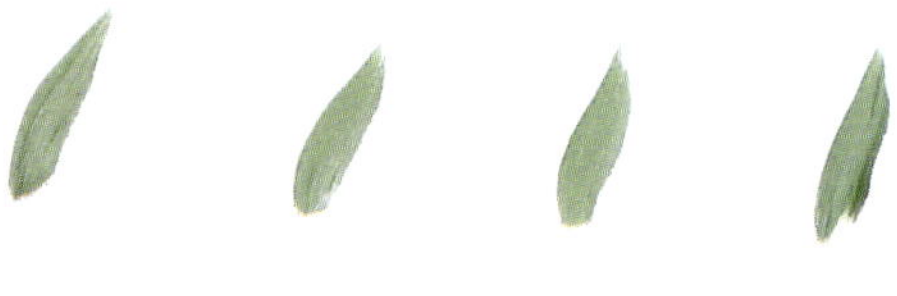

This heather has somewhat larger leaves. Press down and pull up. Use a little white in the green.

The Flower

Brush: #0 or #1
Colors: Green, white and wine red

Make fine bells, follow arrows.
Fill toward you using a pink-shade.

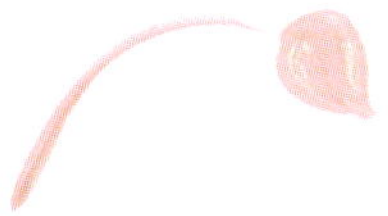

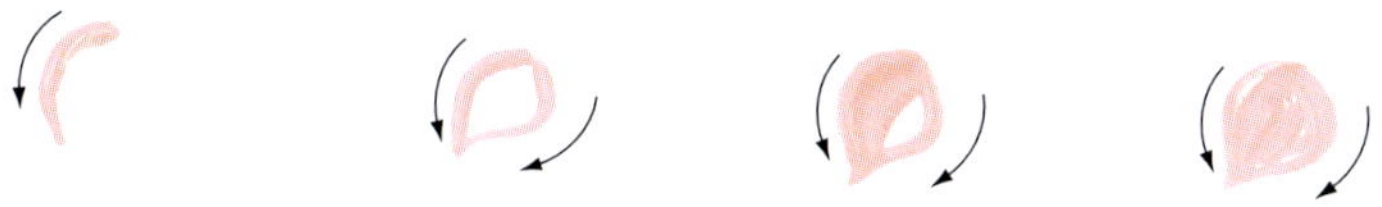

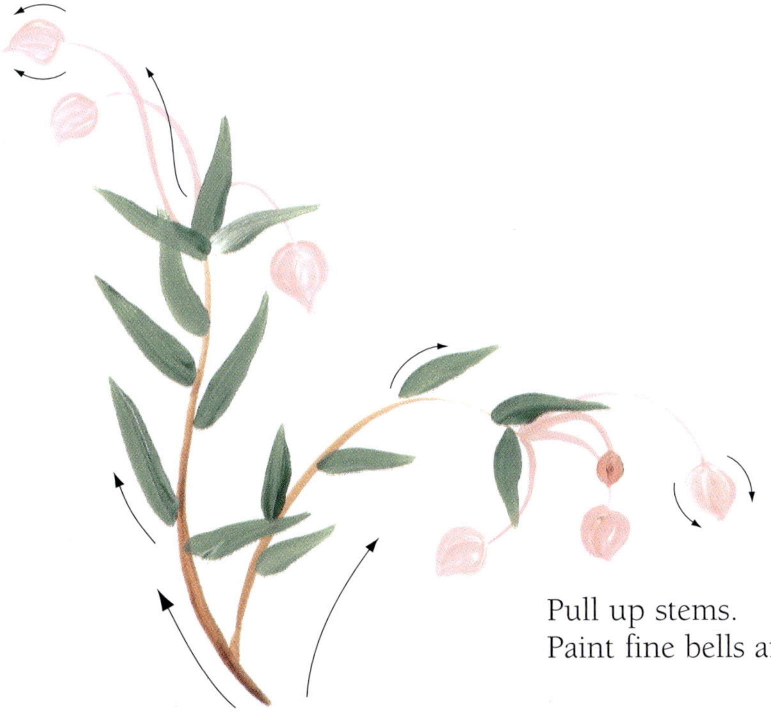

Pull up stems.
Paint fine bells around the tops.

Wild Strawberries

Stems and Leaves

Brush: #0
Colors: Green and white

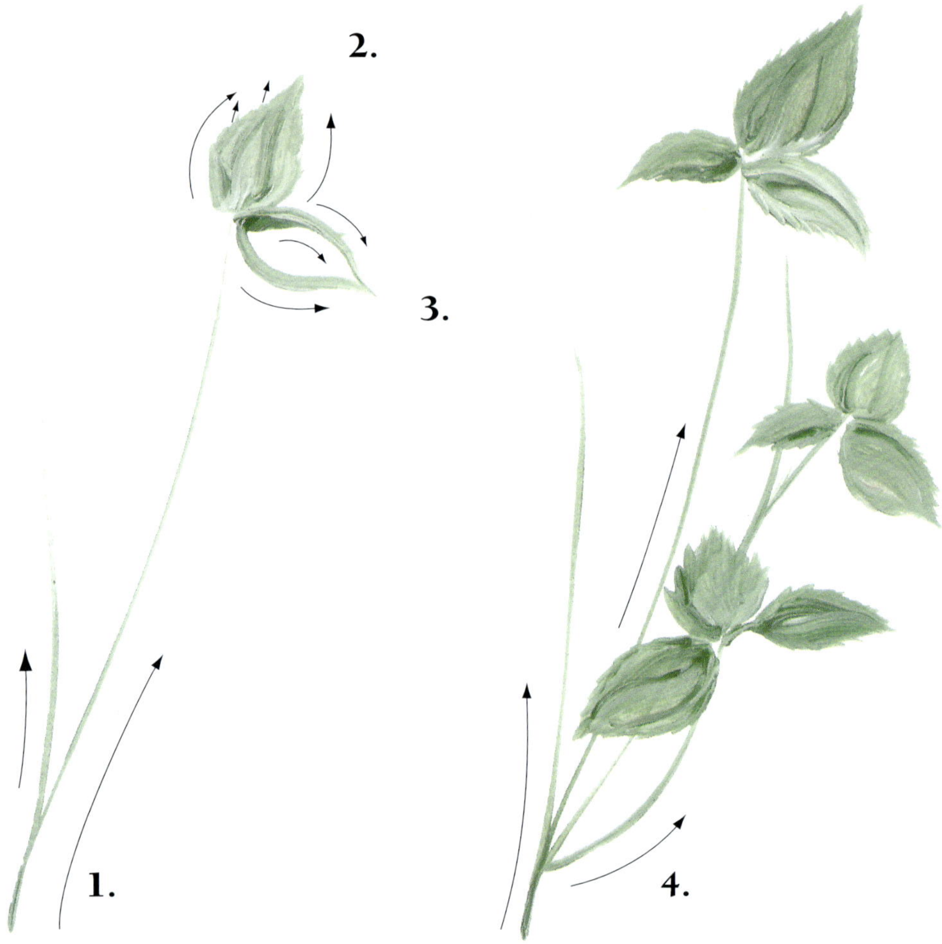

1. Paint thin, fine stems.
2. Make spike leaves *(see description on pages 13 and 21)*.
3. Put leaves together in groups of three.
4. Draw up some stems and paint spike leaves on them.

The Berries

Brush: #0
Colors: Red, white and a little orange

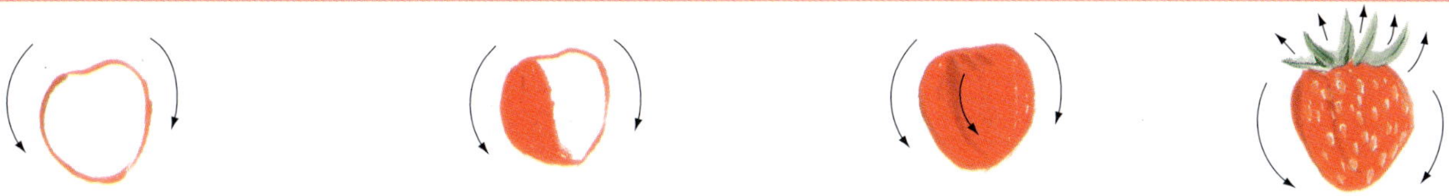

1. 2. 3. 4.

1. Shape berries, note arrows.
2. Fill berries with red — paint towards you.
3. Fill berries completely.
4. Paint small, white strokes on the berries. To soften them a little, you can add some orange to the white. Paint some green stems in the direction of the arrows. When the berries are ripe, they stand up straight.

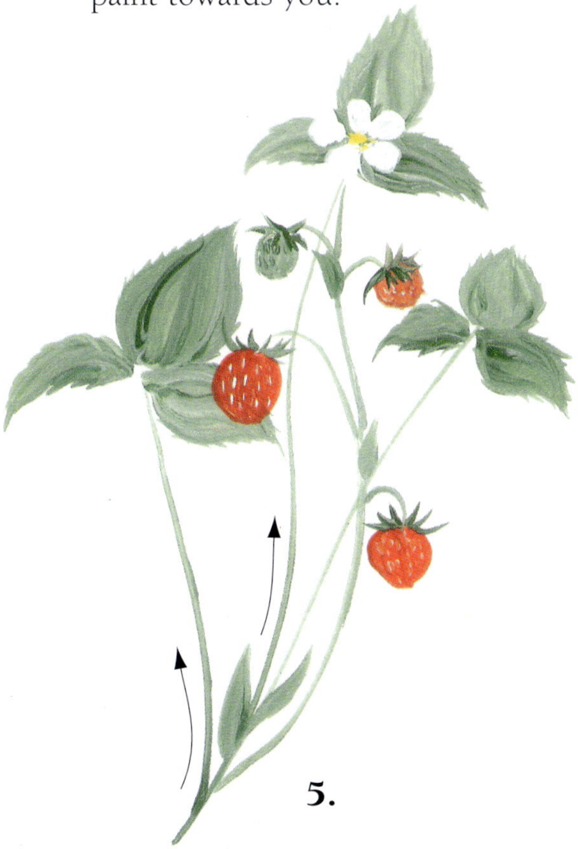

5.

5. Paint some stems and leaves. Paint more berries. Some can be green (before they ripen). Paint a flower such as the blackberry flower. Paint a jack-in-the-box flower described on page 39, and remember the small green leaf under the flower afterwards.

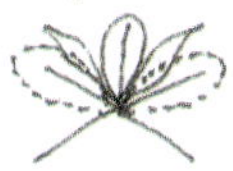

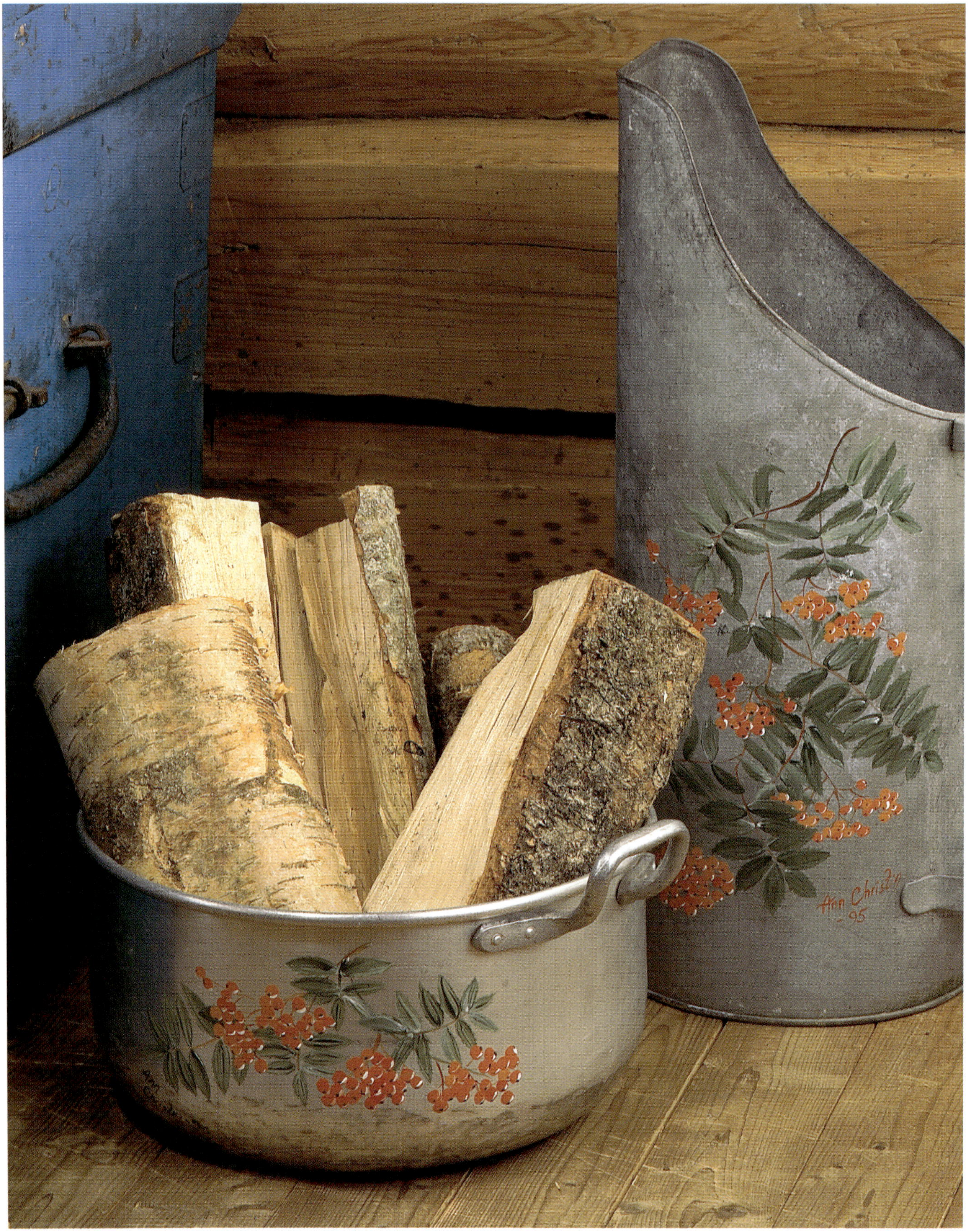
Ann Christin
-95

Rowan Berries

Stems and Leaves

Brush: #0 or #1
Colors: Green, white and brown

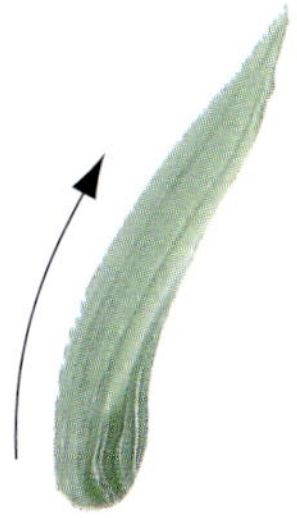

Press down and pull up.

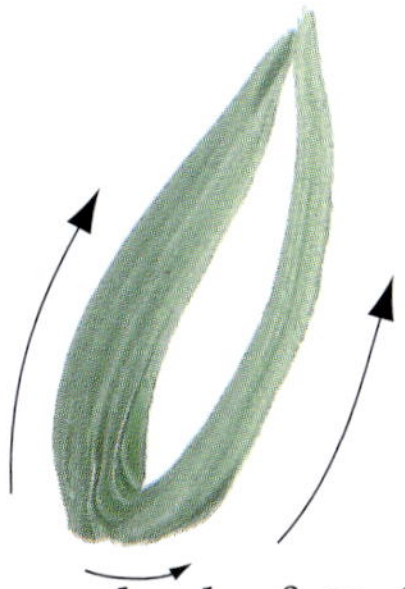

Shape the leaf. Pull up on the opposite side for a nice leaf.

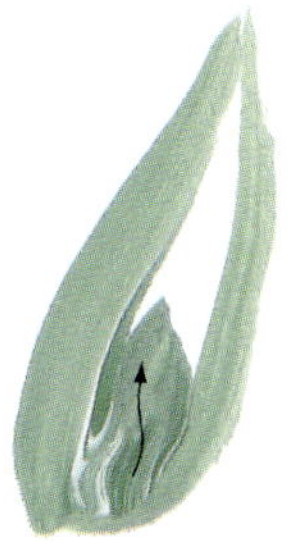

Fill the leaf.

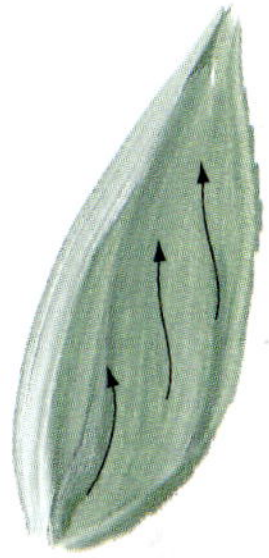

Note arrows to make a nice curve on the leaf.

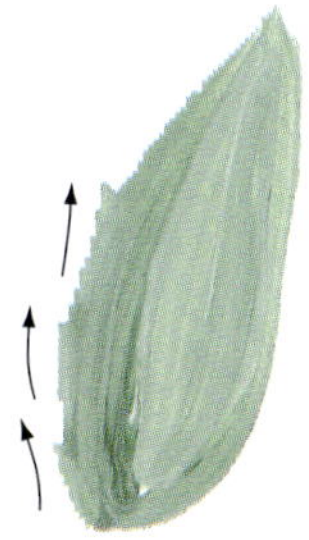

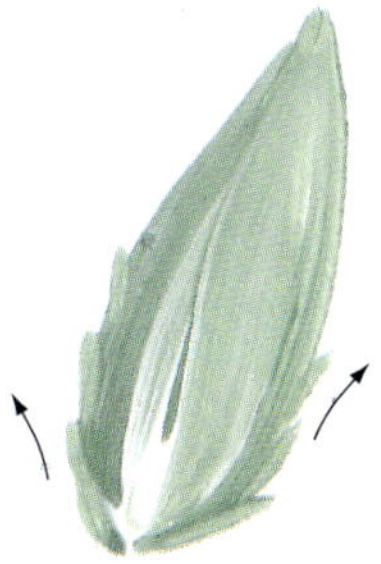

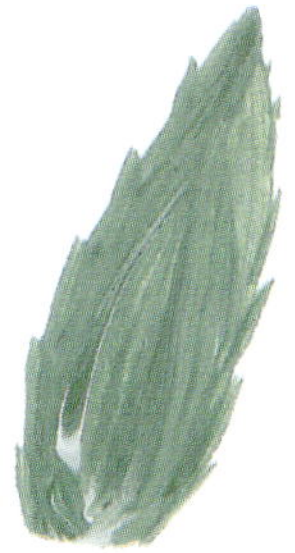

The rowan berry leaf has spikes. While the leaf is damp, pull out small spikes on both sides of the leaf *(See page 21)*.

Remember to use white in the leaf. (The mixture of green and white is made on your palette to create nice natural shading.)

Stems and Leaves

Brush: #0 or #1
Colors: Green, white and brown

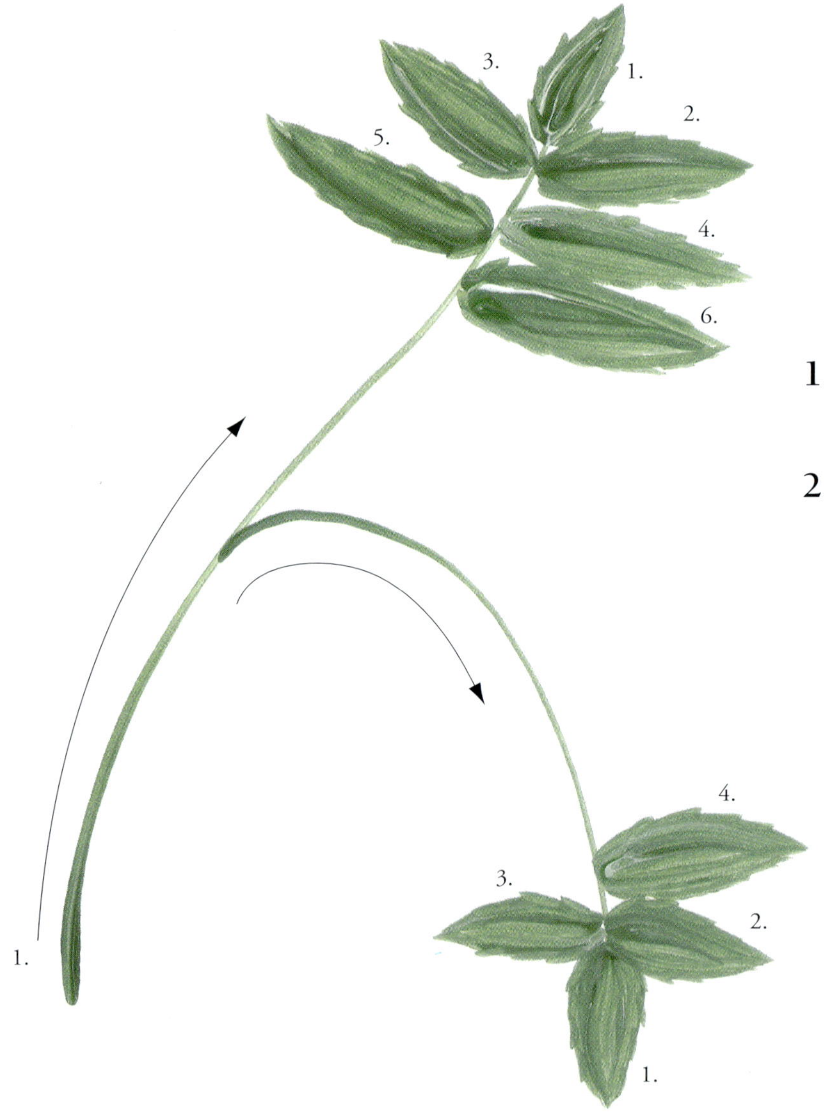

1. Paint thin, curved stems, be light handed.
2. Build up leaves according to description on previous page.

The Berries

Brush: #0 or #1
Colors: Red, orange, white and black

1. Turn your brush upside down and use the handle. Dip the tip in paint and make a dot.
2. While the berry is damp, make a small, white stroke towards you.
3. Make a black dot on the berry.

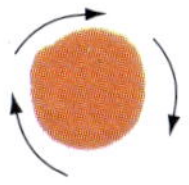

1.

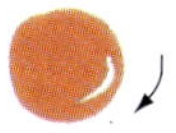

2.

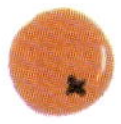

3.

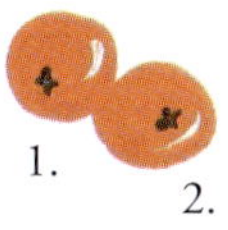

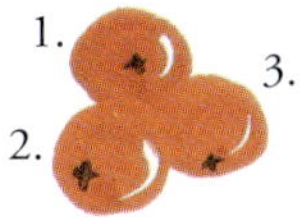

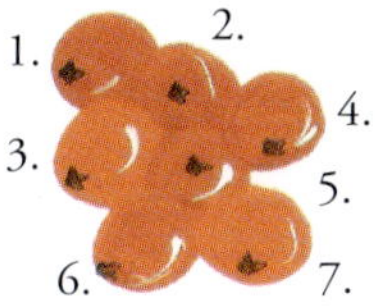

Build up clusters of rowan berries by putting the berries on top of each other. Paint a small, white highlight towards you to add life to the berries. Finally, add a small, black dot.

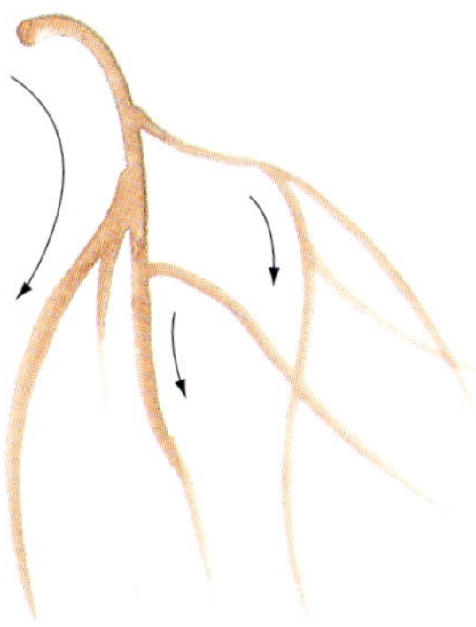

Make twigs that the rowan berries will hang from. Paint the stems toward you.

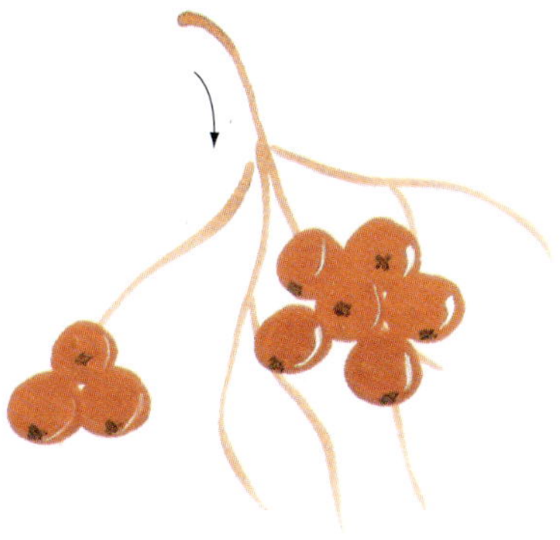

Hang clusters of berries on the twigs.

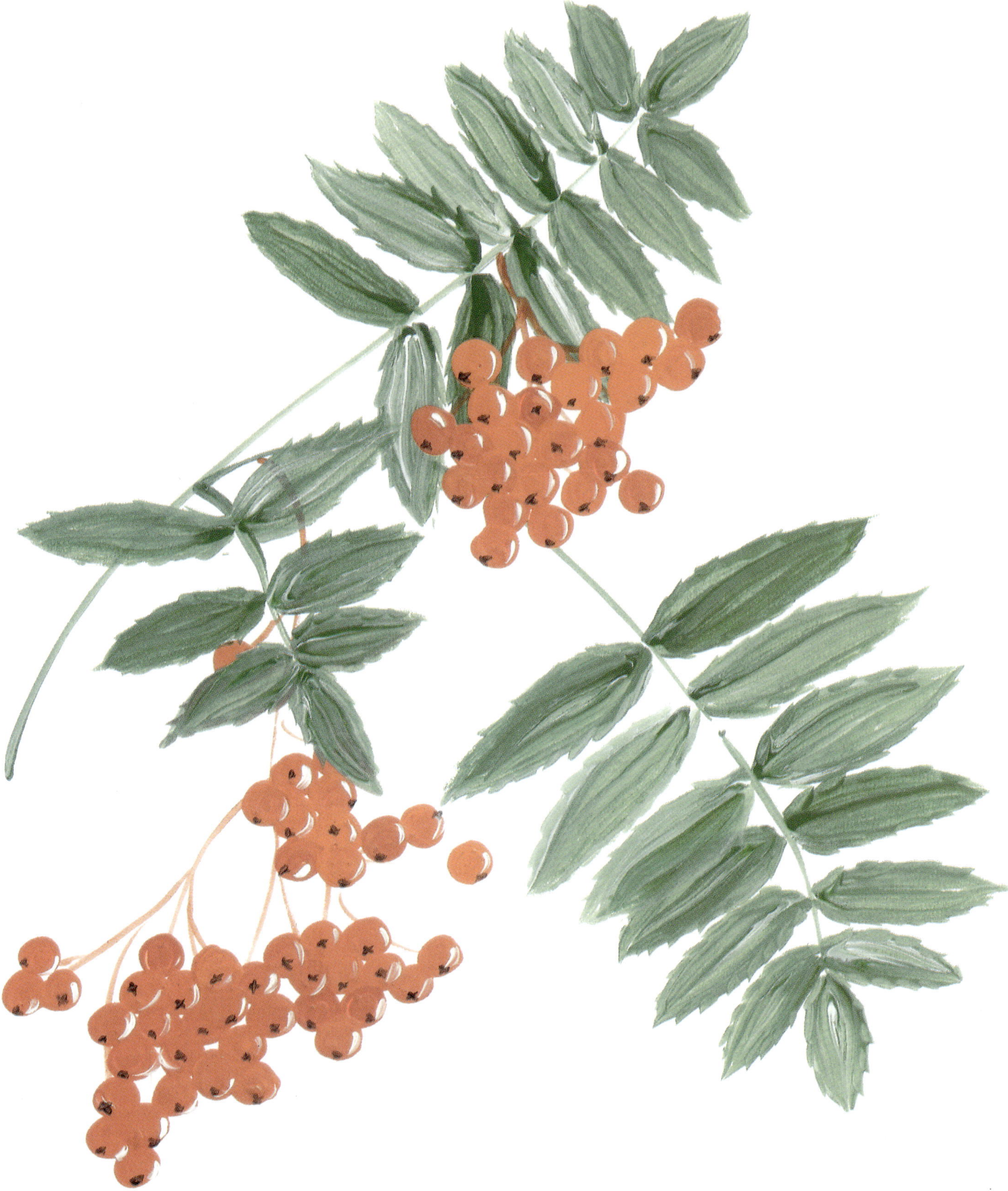

Black Berries

The Flower

Brush: #1
Colors: Green and white

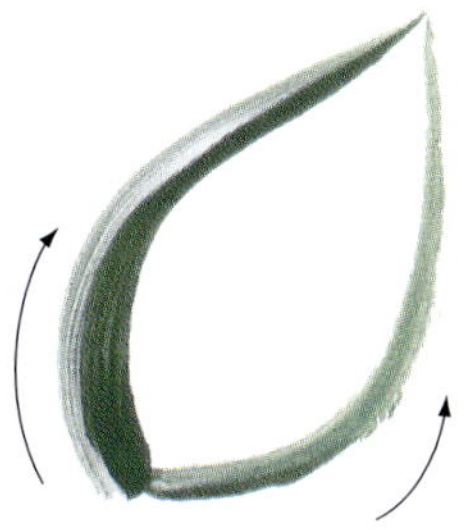

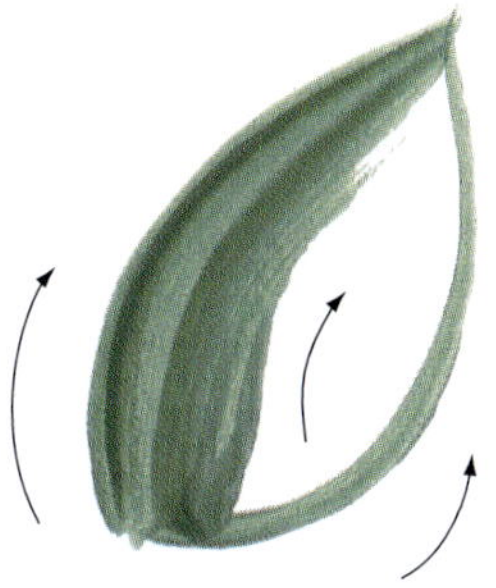

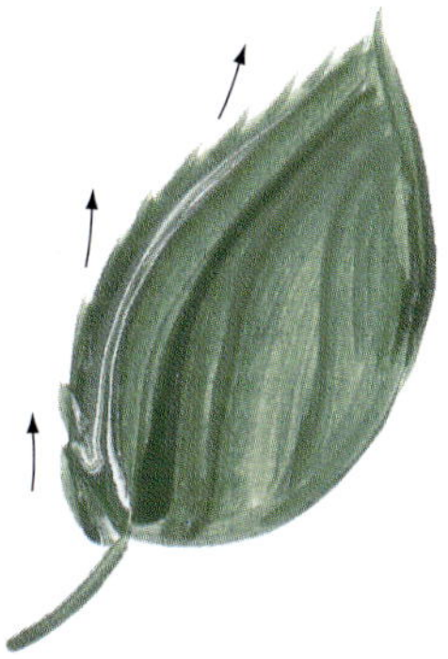

Shape some large, fine-spiked leaves. Follow arrows.

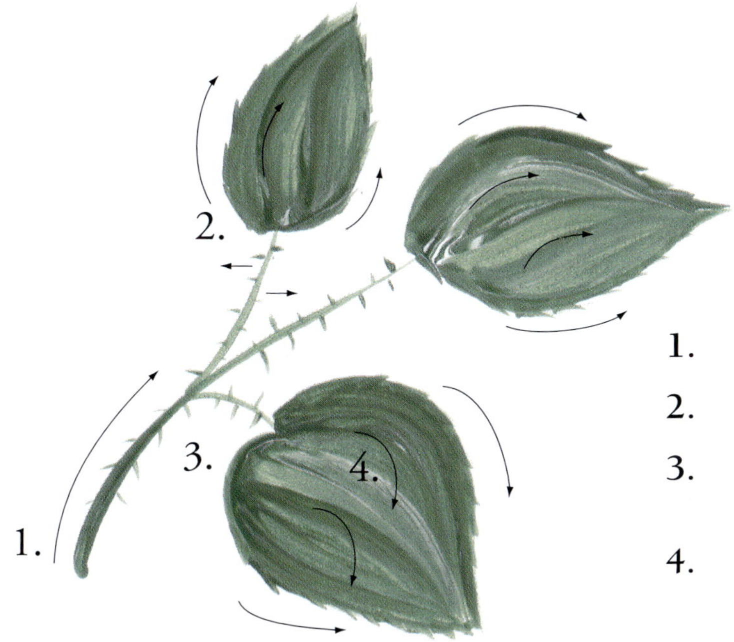

Several leaves hang on twigs that have thorns.

1. Draw up a stem.
2. Paint leaves with spikes *(See pg. 21)*.
3. Make small thorns by pulling out small stems from the stalk.
4. Fill leaves in the same direction for a more natural effect.

The Berries

Brush: #0 or #1
Colors: Black and white

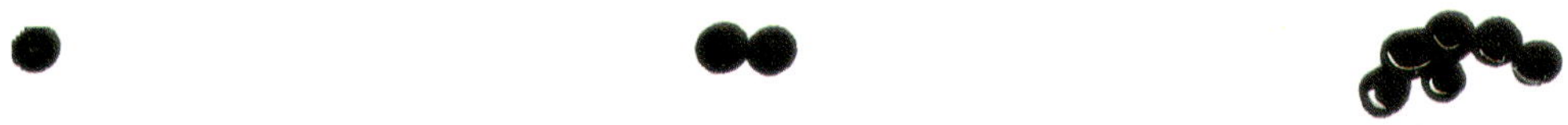

1. 2. 3.

1. Turn your brush upside down and dip the handle in black paint, make a dot.
2. Put several dots together to make one berry. Keep in mind the shape and size of the blackberry.
3. Note how I keep building up the small dots to form a nice berry.
4. Paint a green leaf from inside to out. The stem also has small thorns.

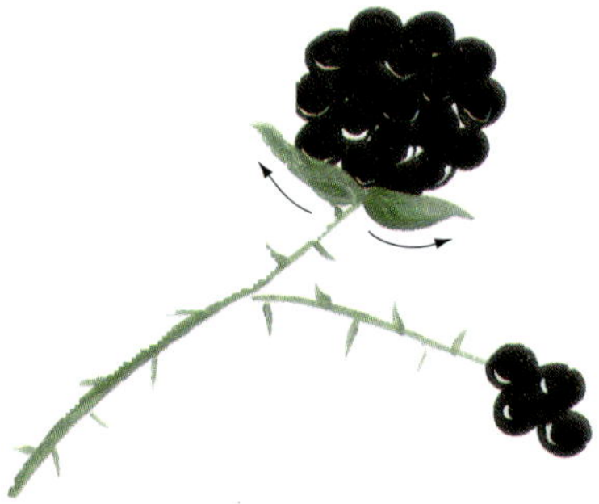

5. Make some small white lines in some of the berries. This makes the berry stand out and look more alive.

The Flower

Brush: #0
Colors: White, green, brown and yellow

1.

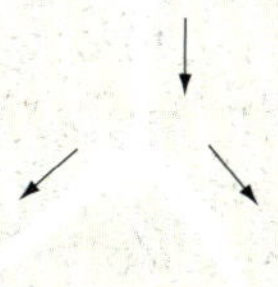

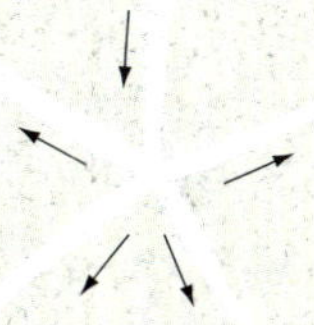

1. Paint a jack-in-the-box with five arms. Note arrows.

2.

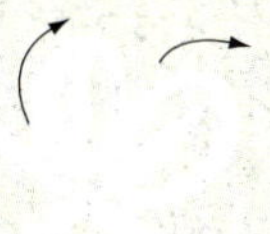

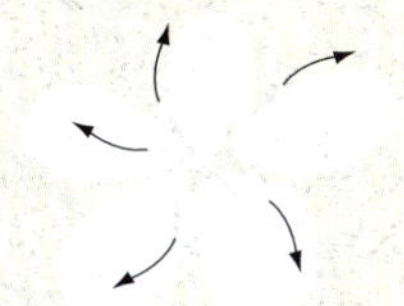

3.

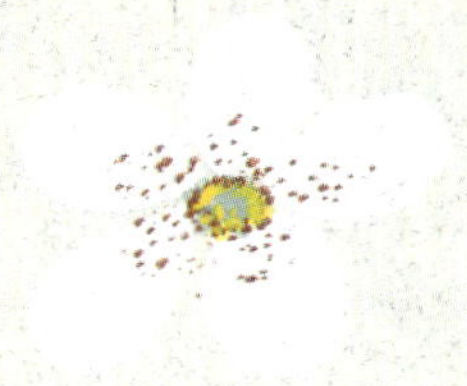

2. Then outline fine, round petals and fill. Remember to fill in the same direction for a more natural effect.

3. Add a little green in the center along with some yellow. Use the tip of your brush and make several small stamens with brown paint.

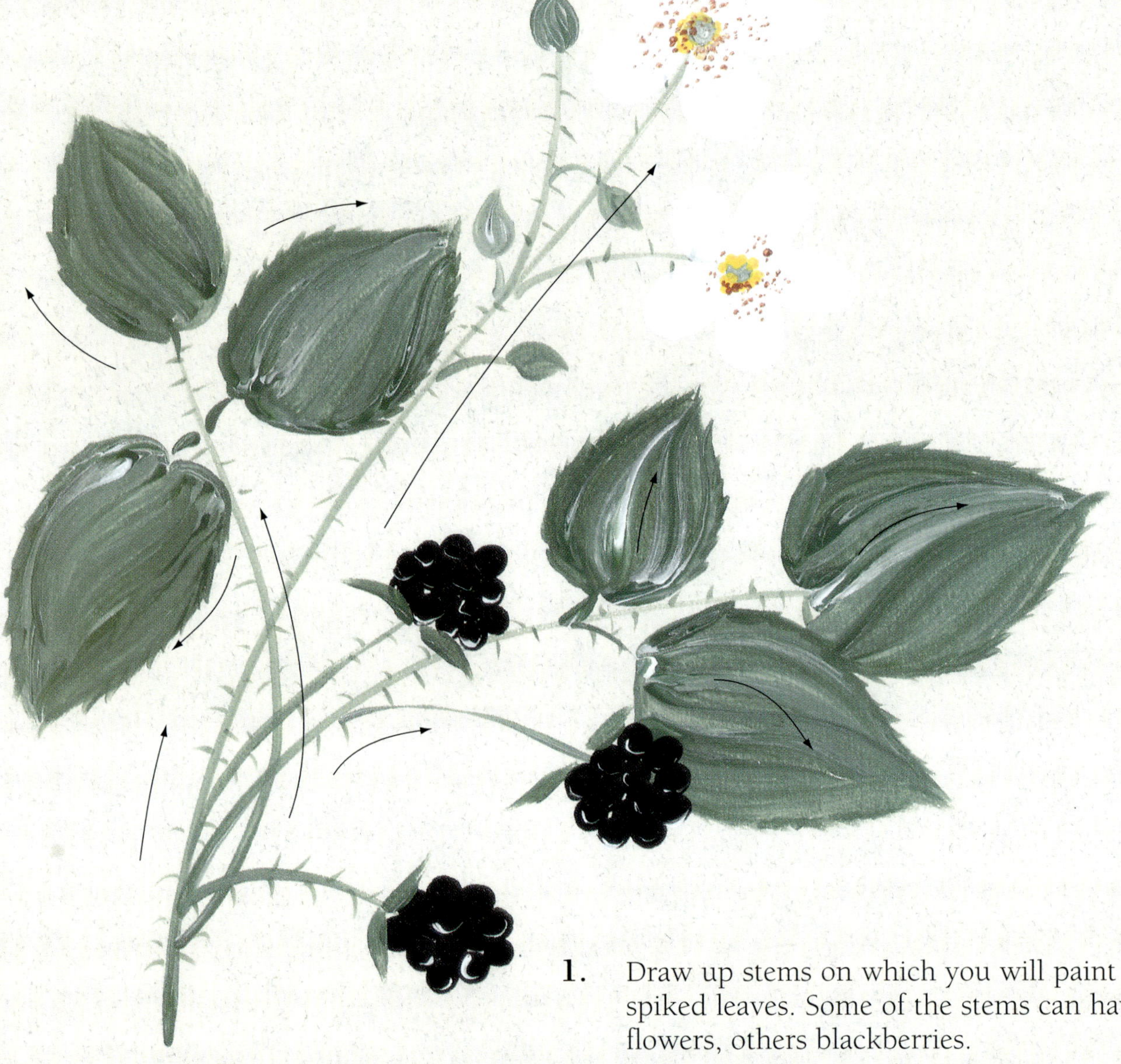

1. Draw up stems on which you will paint spiked leaves. Some of the stems can have flowers, others blackberries.

2. Sketch a jack-in-the-box as a guide for the flowers.

Blueberries

Stems and Leaves

Brush: #0 or #1
Colors: Green, white and brown

1.

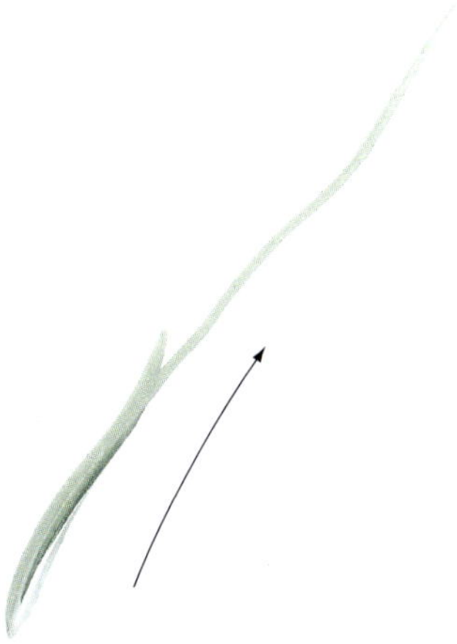

2.

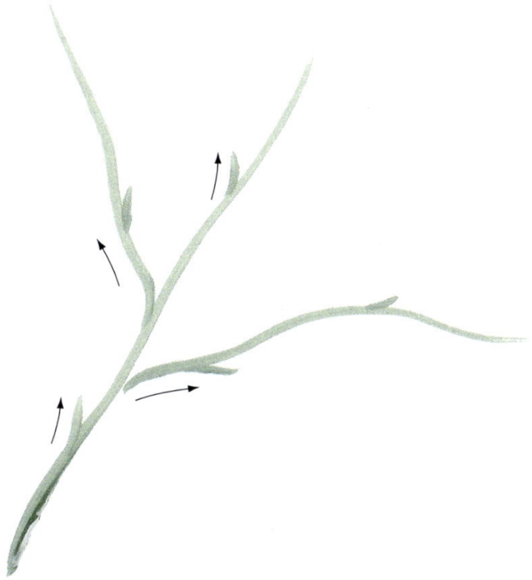

1. Paint a stem with fine shading of green and white.
2. Paint twigs.

1.

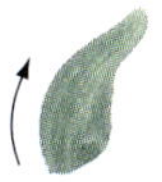

2.

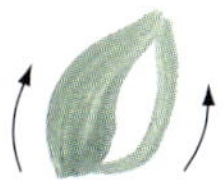

3.

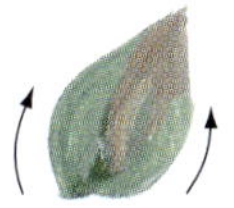

1. Press down brush filled with green paint.
2. Shape the leaf.
3. Fill leaf from bottom up. Mix a little brown in the green paint. Leaves are a little brownish.

Stems and Leaves

Brush: #0 or #1
Colors: Green, white and brown

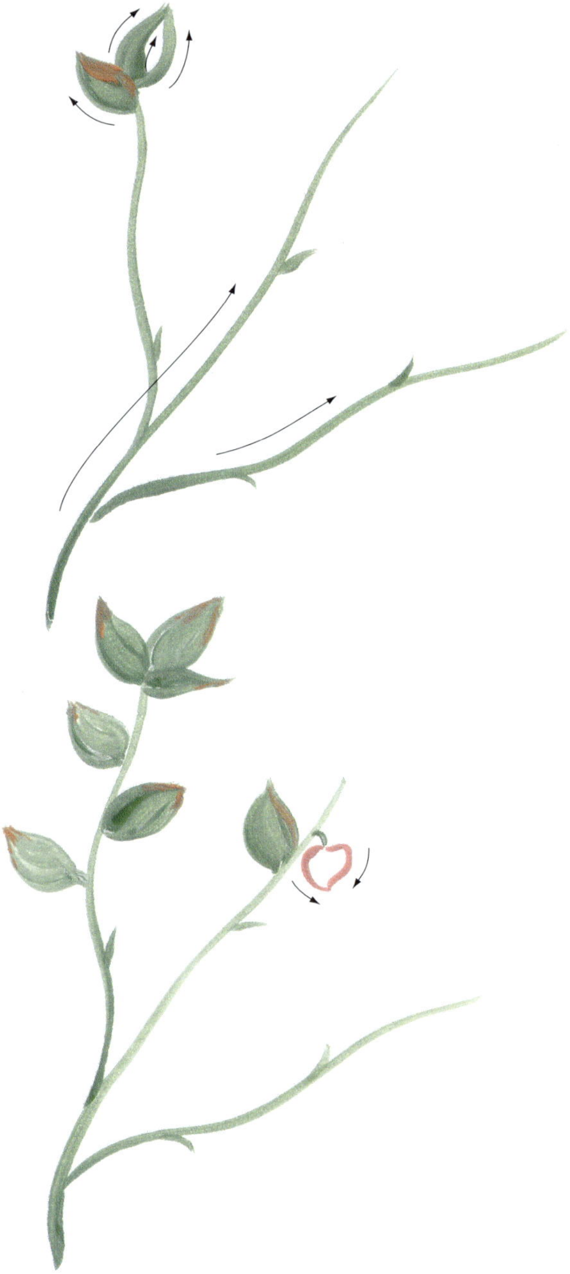

1. Paint the stems.

2. Paint leaves "here and there" on the stems. Add a little brown to the leaves.

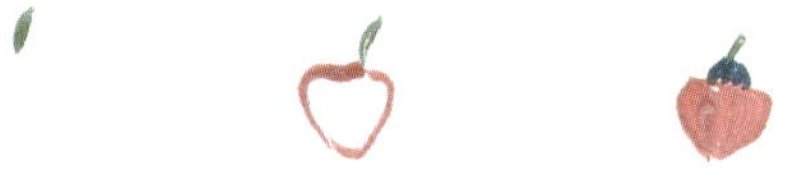

1. **2.** **3.**

Do you want to paint some blueberry twigs with flowers? They make a nice decoration.

1. The flower head (which later turns into a blueberry) hangs down from a small stem.

2. Outline the "head."

3. Fill "head" and paint a small blue top on the flower head, see arrows.

The Berries

Brush: #0 or #1
Colors: Dark blue and white

1. Turn brush upside down and dip handle in paint. Make a dot.
2. Turn brush and hold the correct way again. Use a little white and push aside some of the paint on the berry so that its forms a small curve.
3. Using the tip of the brush, make small dots with blue.
4. Add a small white line in the berry. Look how great it looks!

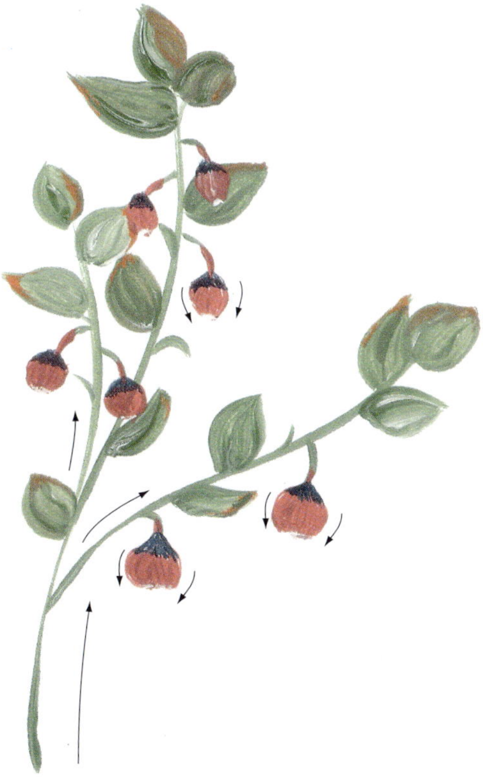

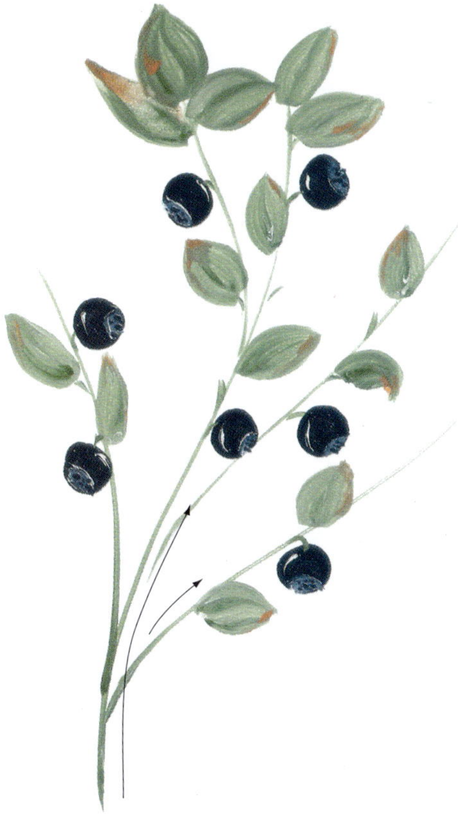

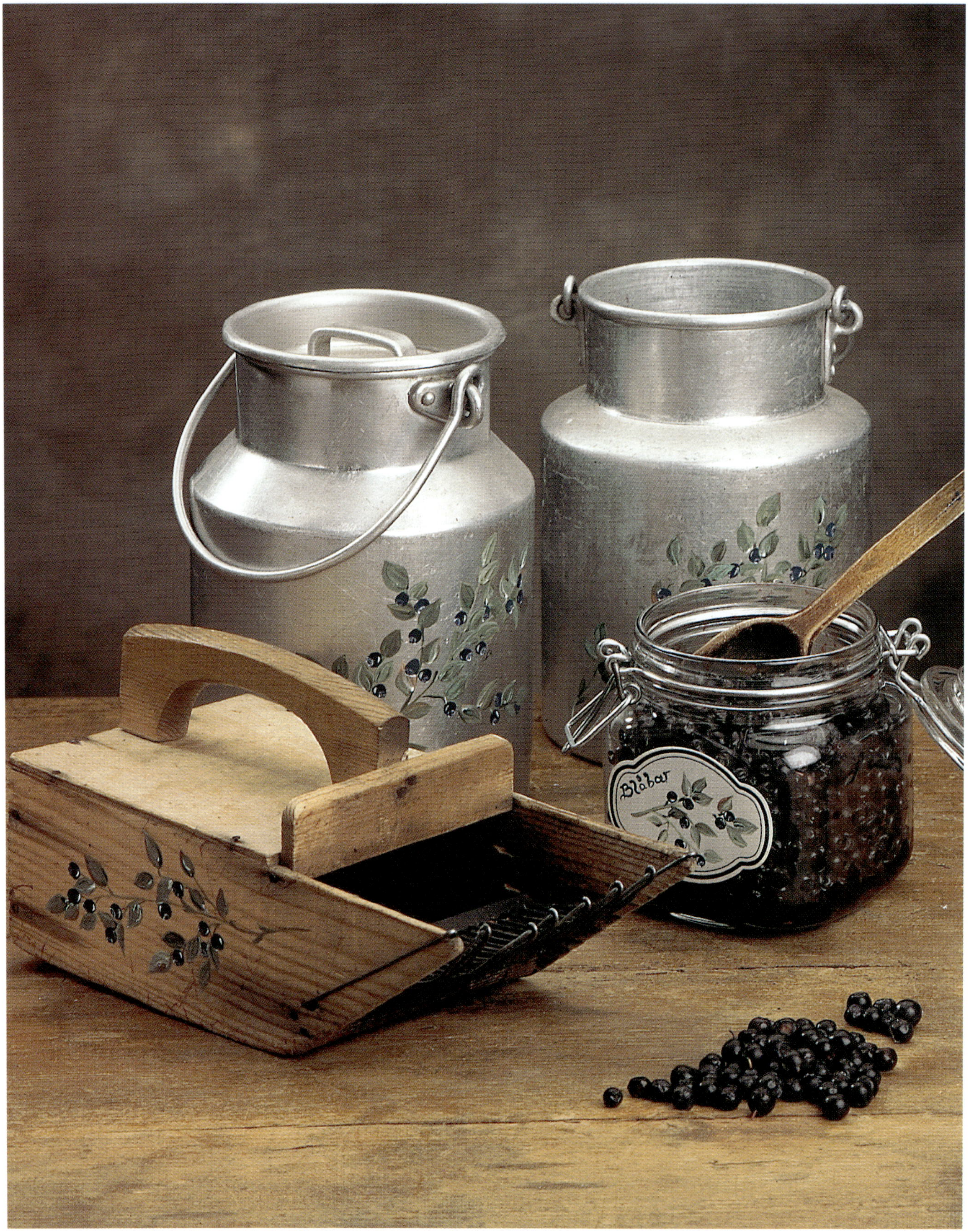
Blåbær

Mountain Cranberries

Stems and Leaves

Brush: #0 or #1
Colors: Green and white

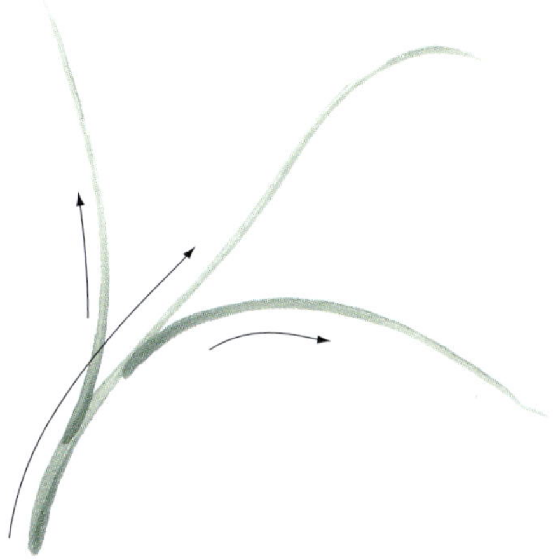

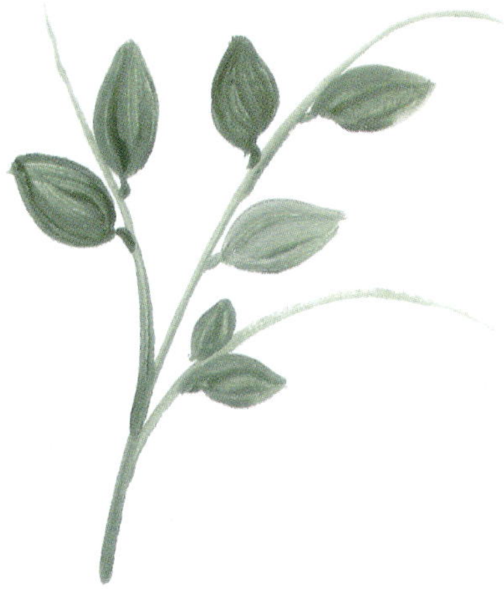

Paint fine stems for cranberries. Paint leaves around the stems.

Leaves are shaped like this:

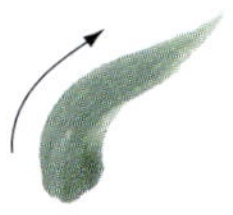

1.

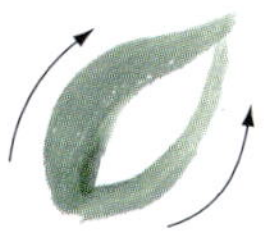

2.

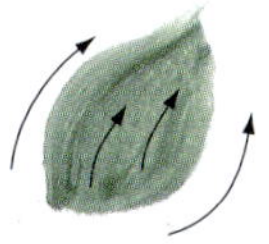

3.

Press down and pull up a leaf in the size you want.
Fill in the same direction.

The Berries

Brush: #0 or #1
Colors: Red and white

Berries are made as shown on the previous pages. Berries sit in clusters that you build up with several dots.

Always add small, white highlights on the berries. This adds "life" and creates definition.

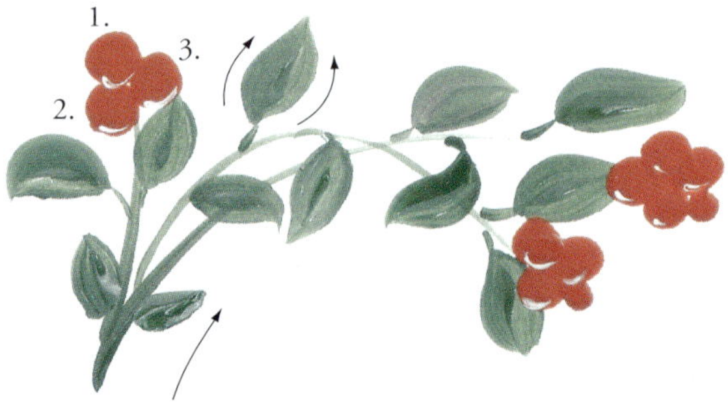

1. Paint the stems.
2. Paint the leaves.
3. Build up clusters of berries.

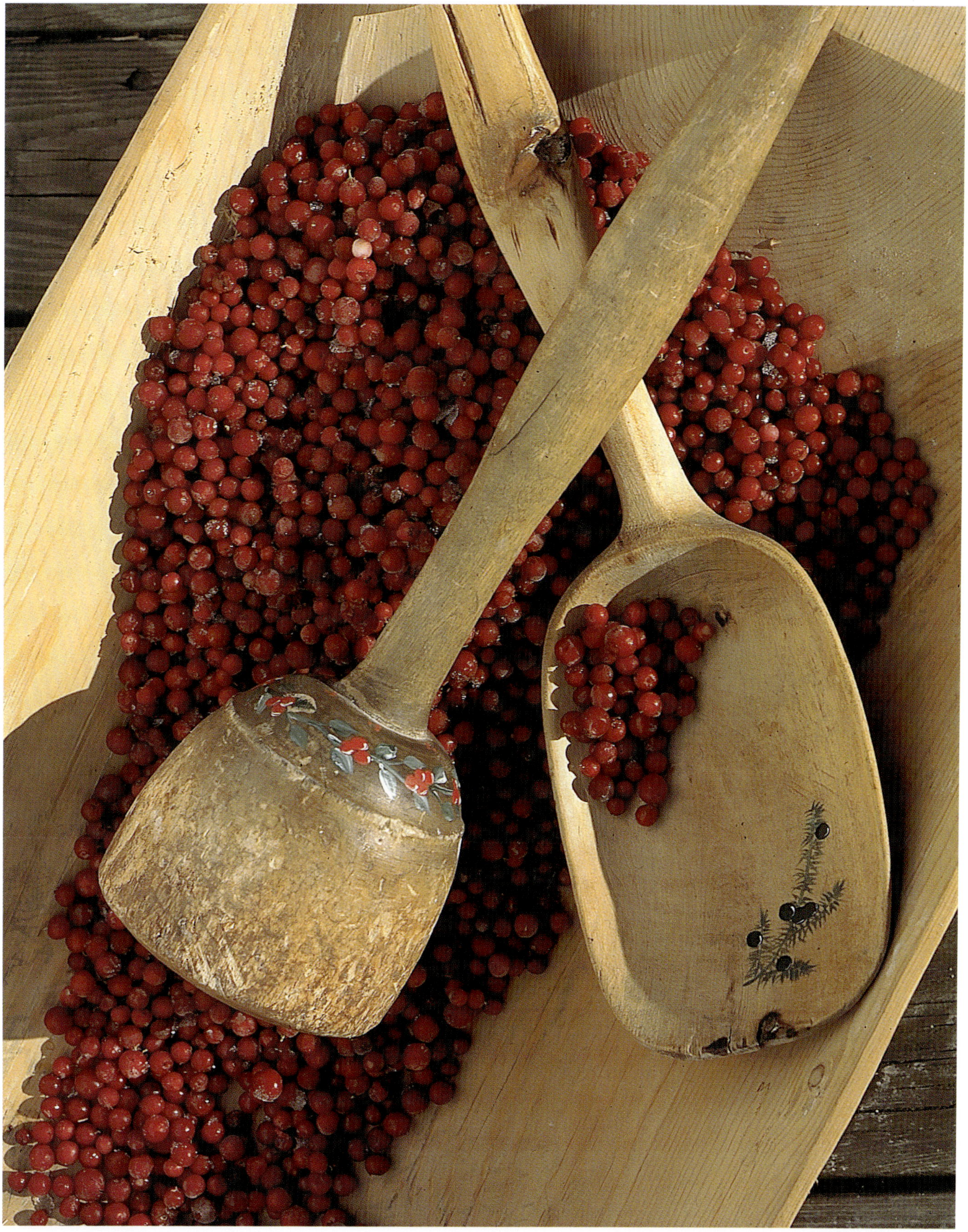

Cowberries

Stems and Leaves

Brush: #0 or #1
Colors: Green, white and brown

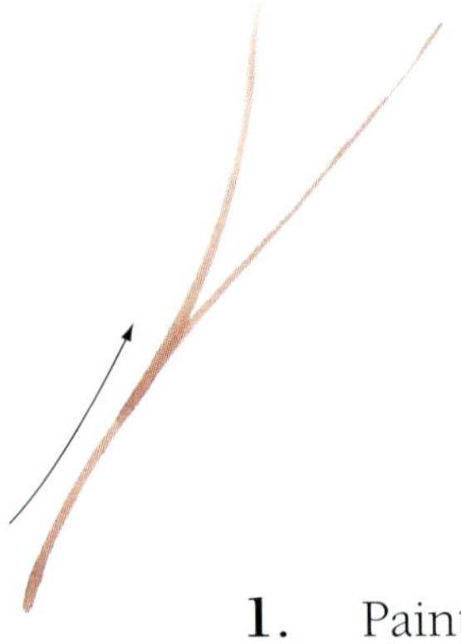

1. Paint fine stems with brown.

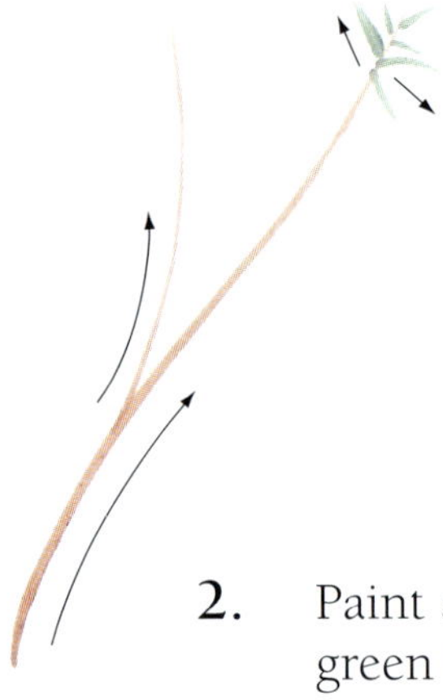

2. Paint some thin, green leaves.

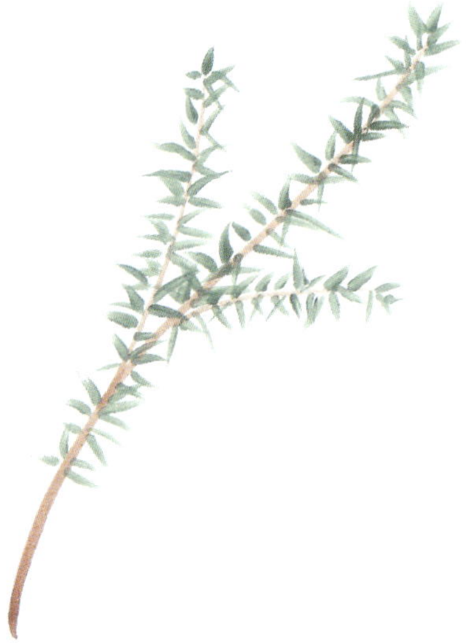

3. It's fun to paint these leaves. Be light handed using a swift motion.

The Berries

Brush: #0 or #1
Colors: Black and white

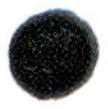
1.

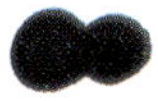
2.

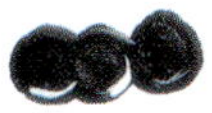
3.

Paint cowberries the same as other berries, by turning the brush upside down and using the handle. Cowberries grow both individually and in clusters on the stems.

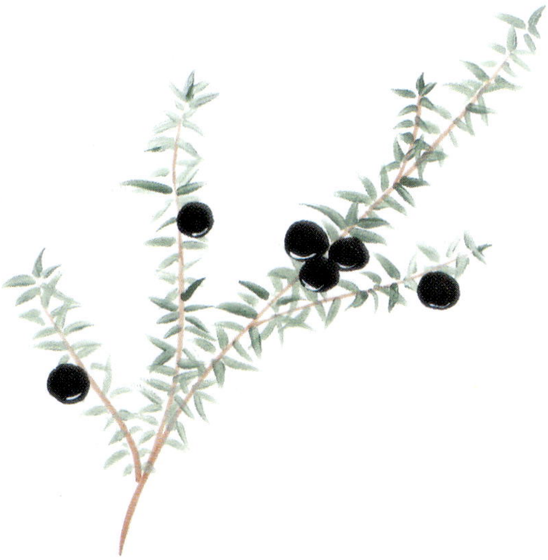

Cloud Berries

Stems and Leaves

Brush: #1
Colors: Green and white

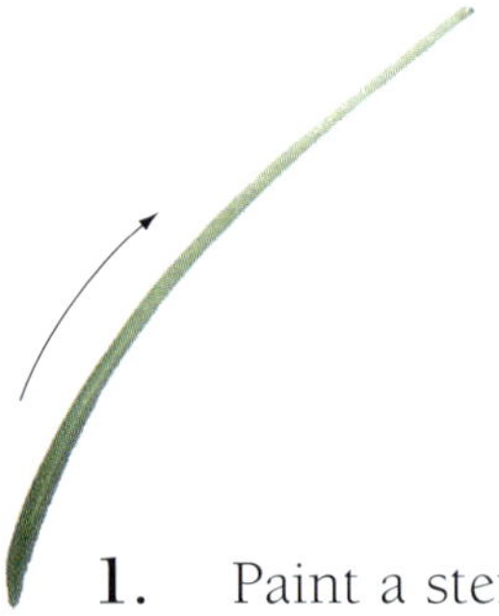

1. Paint a stem.

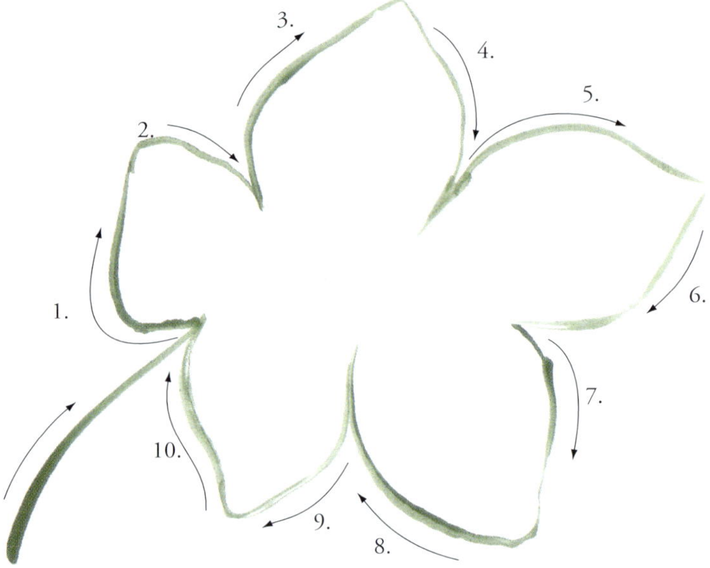

2. Shape leaf following the arrows.

3. Leaves are somewhat spiky.

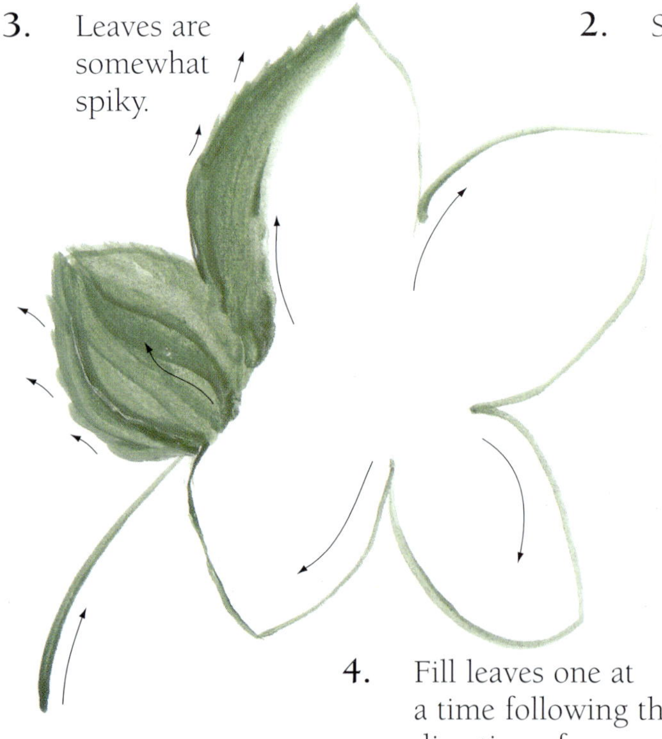

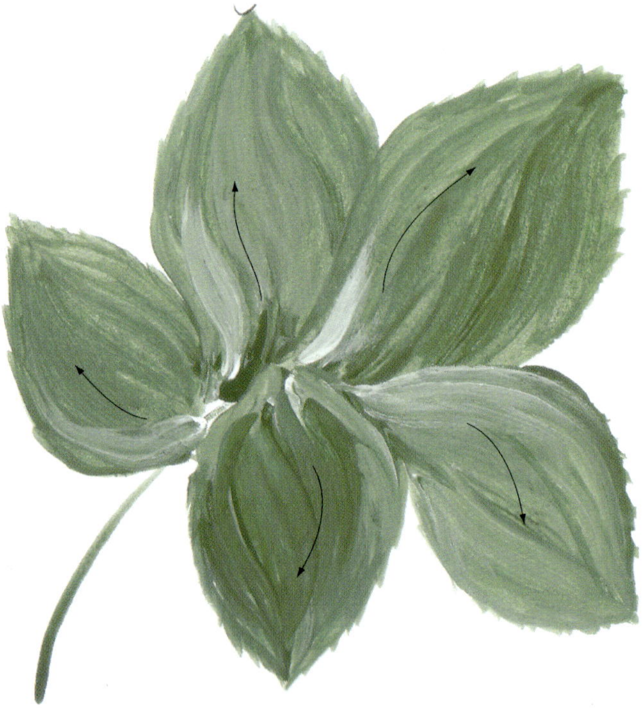

4. Fill leaves one at a time following the direction of arrows.

The Flower

Brush: #0 or #1
Colors: White, yellow and green

1.

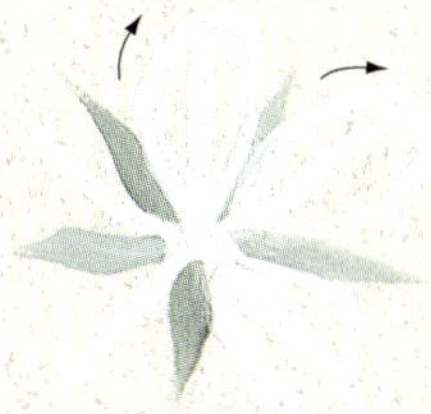

2.

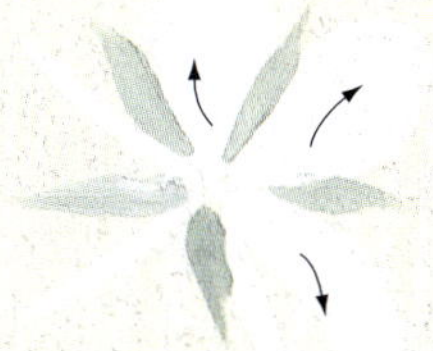

3.

See description of jack-in-the-box flower on pg. 39.

1. Make five arms from the dot.

2. Paint a green leaf between each line. It is hard to paint the leaves after you have finished painting the flower. The leaves lies under the flower head. Make a leaf by pressing down on the brush lightly, pull and let up.

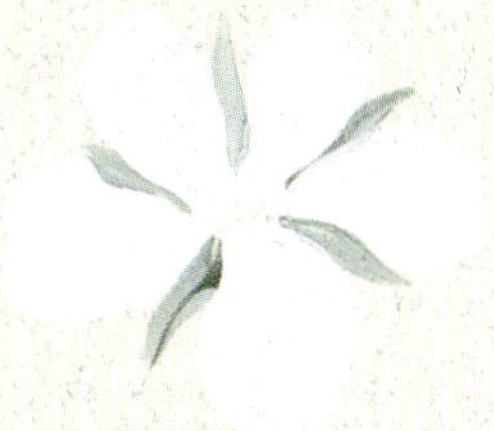

4.

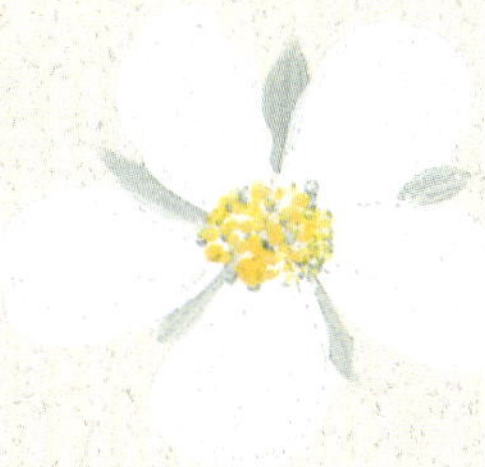

5.

3/4. Fill petals in the same direction, see arrows.

5. Paint some green dots in the center, then some yellow ones.

Finish painting a leaf and let it dry. Then paint a flower on top of the leaf. This is not necessary, but it adds a nice touch.

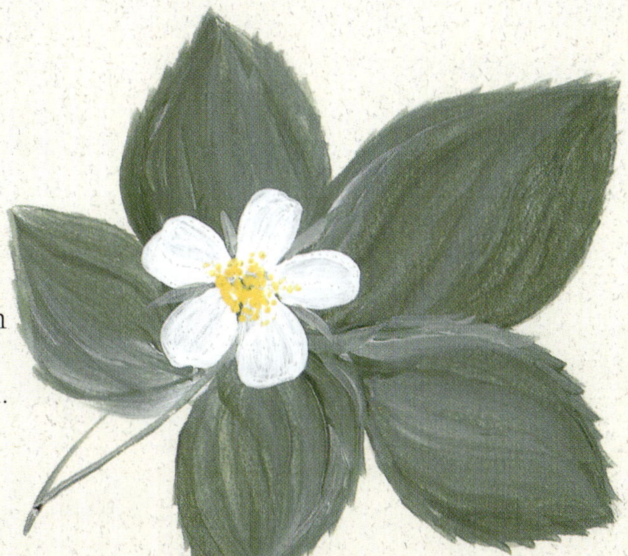

The Berries

Brush: #0 or #1
Colors: Orange, red and white

1. Make a small round curve that you fill.

2. Build up cloud berries until it looks like a cluster.

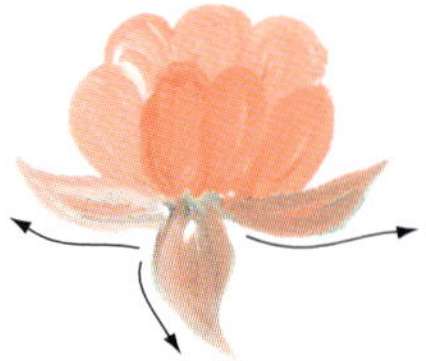

3. Lighten with a little white, darken other areas to make it look more natural.

4. Make three leaves under the berry that have gold tones. Press brush down and let up. Note arrows.

Make some red cloud berries — unripe — and remember these must not be picked even if they look very tempting.

Rosehips

The Flower

Brush: #0 or #1
Colors: Green and white

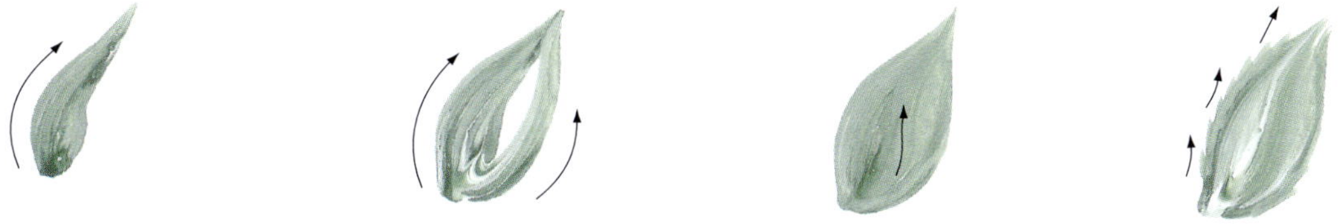

Paint the leaf with spikes as you have learned previously.

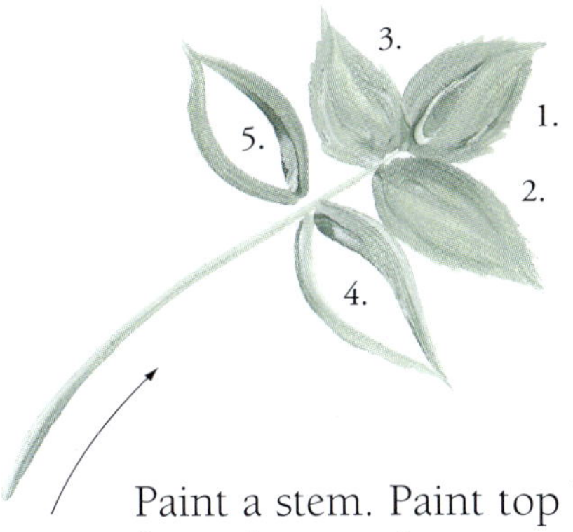

Paint a stem. Paint top leaf first, then work your way down the stem.

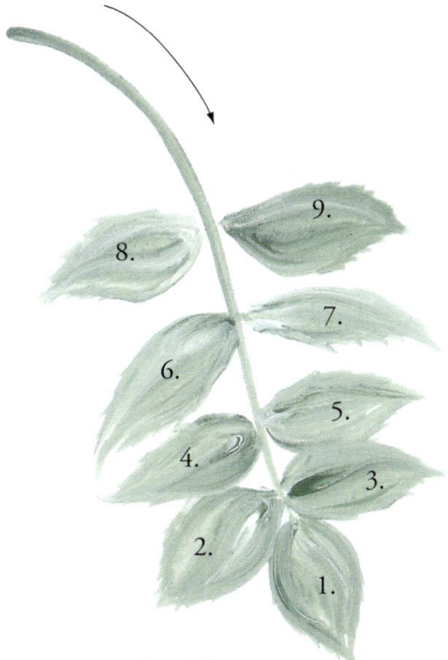

Make a stem that hangs and add several leaves. If it is difficult to paint towards you, turn your project.

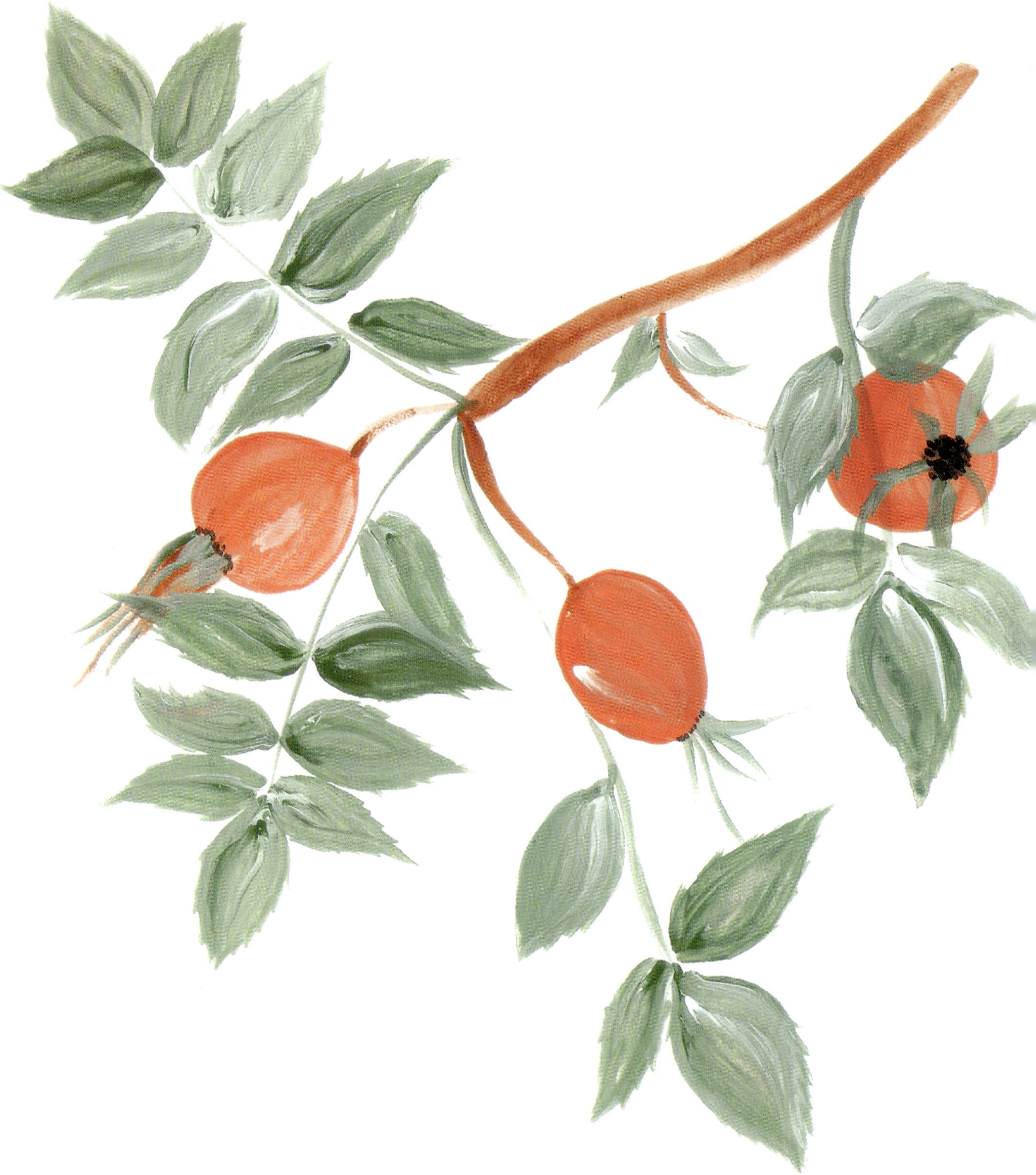

Dog Rose

Brush: #0
Colors: Pink, white, yellow and green

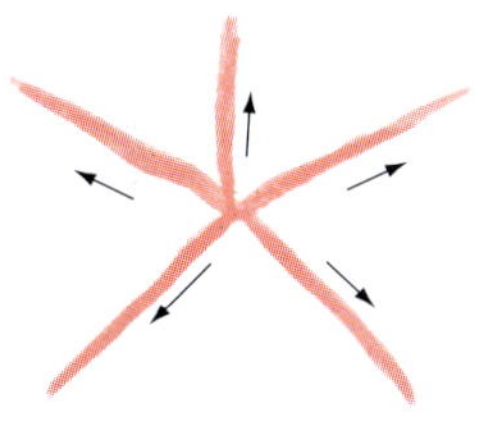

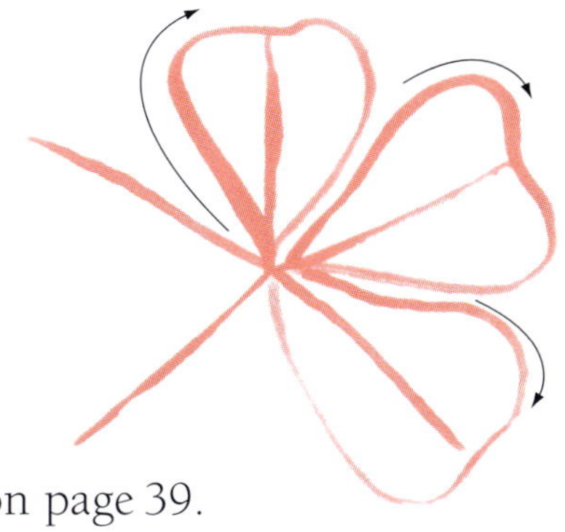

Paint a jack-in-the-box flower as described on page 39.

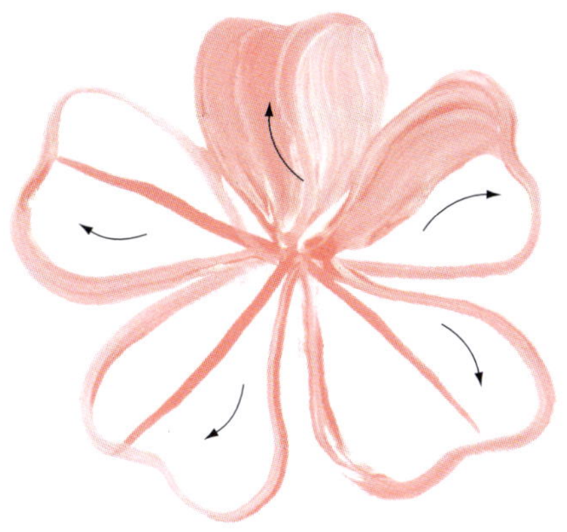

Fill petals from the center to the outside.
Remember to fill in the same direction.
Use pink and white for natural shading.

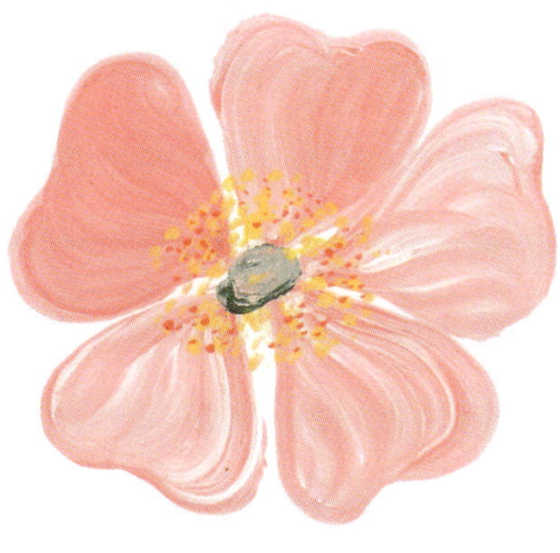

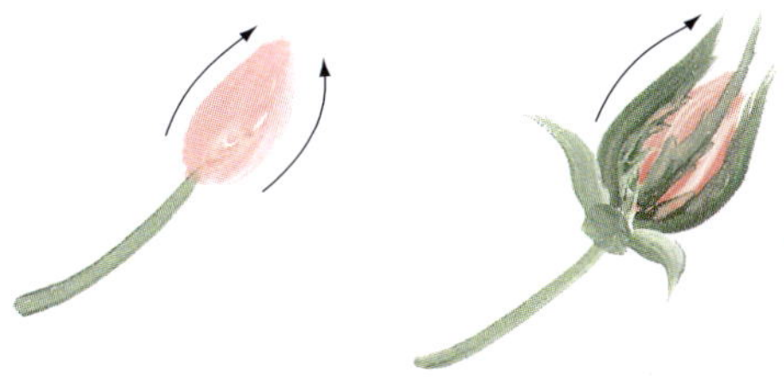

The Bud

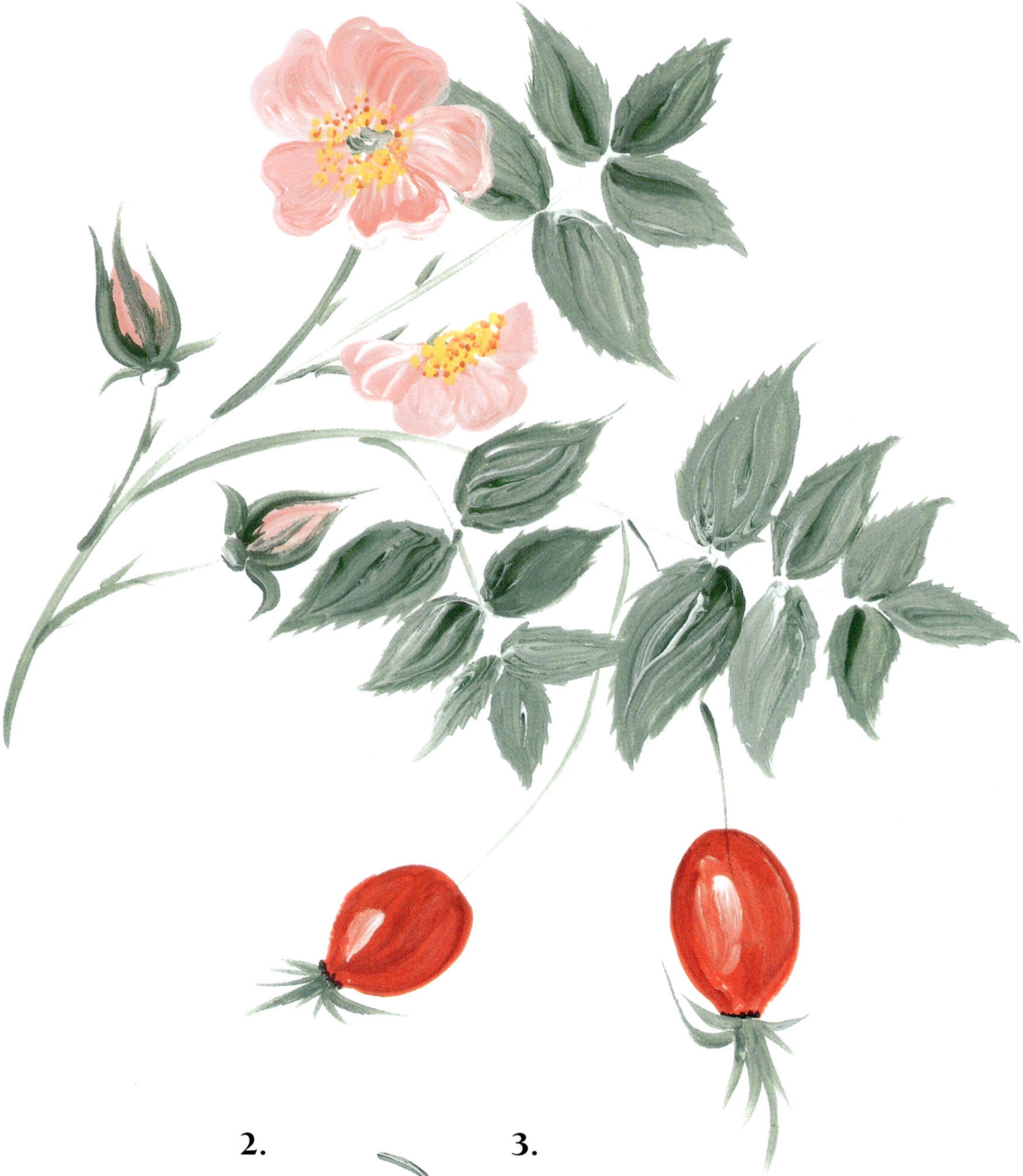

1. 2. 3.

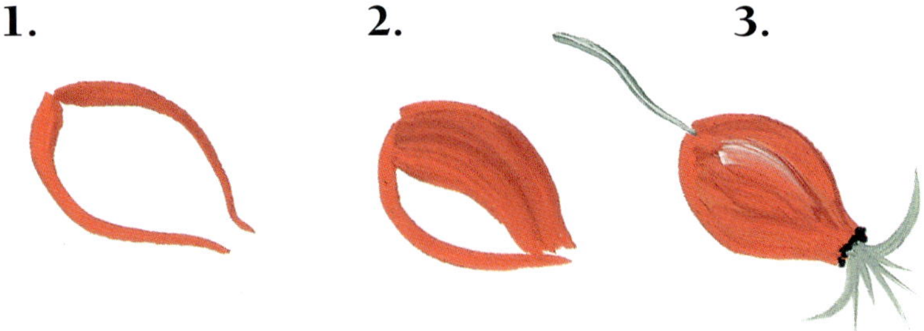

1. Paint outline of the rosehip.
2. Fill the rosehip with red (you can mix in a little orange).
3. Add some white while the paint is still damp.

Dip your brush in black and make some small dots. Finally, make some green stems (or brown) coming out of the rosehip.

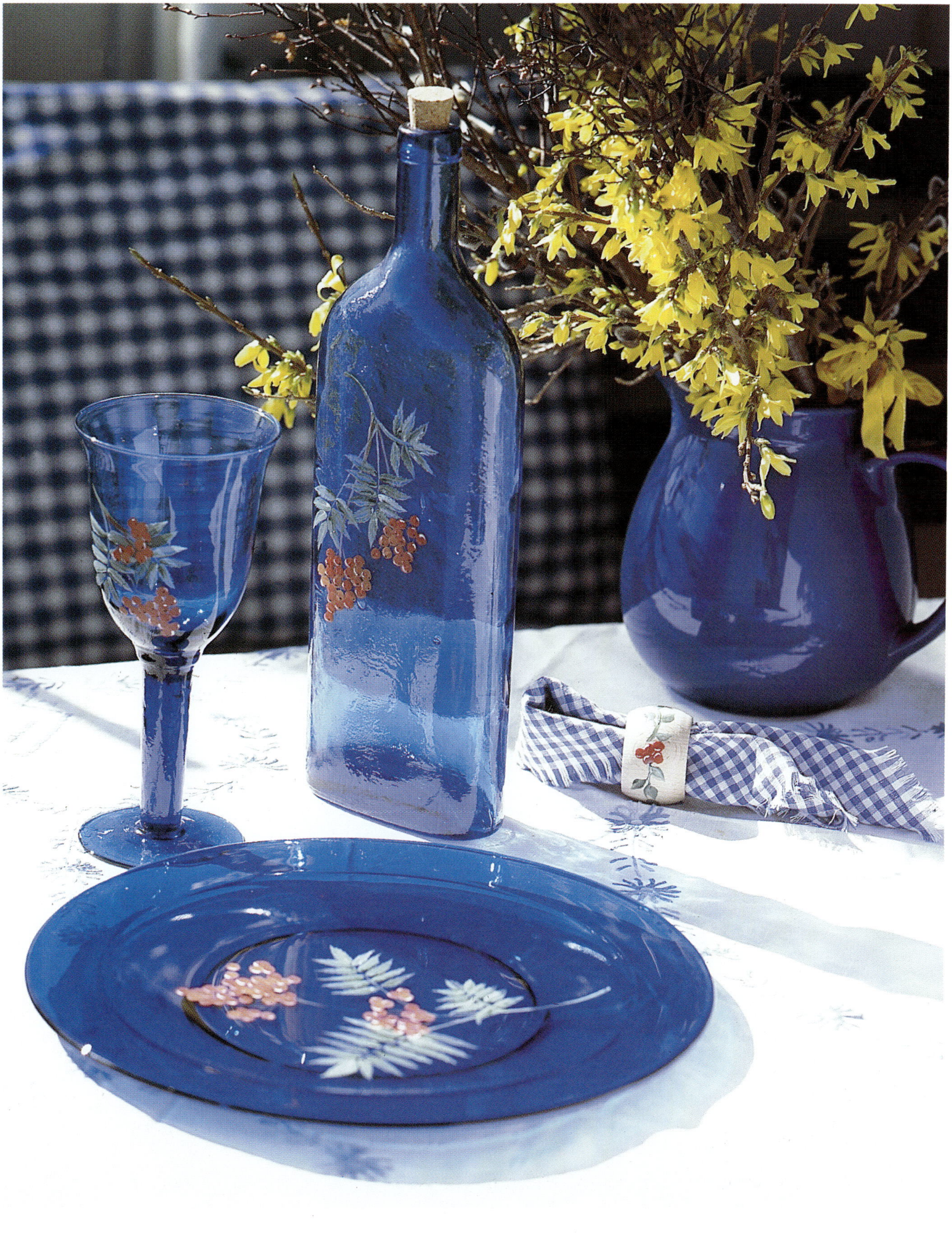

Painting Mushrooms

It's fun to paint mushrooms. We know there are about 12,000 different varieties of mushrooms, and I will show you how to paint a few of them. You can paint a mushroom basket to bring along on a picnic — or perhaps on a little mushroom gathering walk.

Remember, when gathering mushrooms, never pick them unless you are absolutely sure they are edible. You cannot tell just from looking whether a mushroom is poisonous or not. Pick mushrooms in dry weather — or paint them outside in dry weather. That's when the colors are best, and they are not as watery if you pick them.

1. When you paint mushrooms, use a fine brush for outlining. Try to use the colors of the mushrooms, whatever they may be.
2. Old worn brushes come in handy. They are good to use when filling in the mushroom. Dip the brush in paint and drag it back and forth until it is filled with color. You may want to add a little water to the paint to make it glide more easily, and this creates fine shading when the paint is dry. Adding colors (white or other colors) while the paint is damp, creates natural looking shading and adds vitality to your mushrooms.

Sometimes mushrooms look sad by themselves. Therefore, add some grass around the mushroom or perhaps some wildflowers. A small titmouse works wonders in a design.

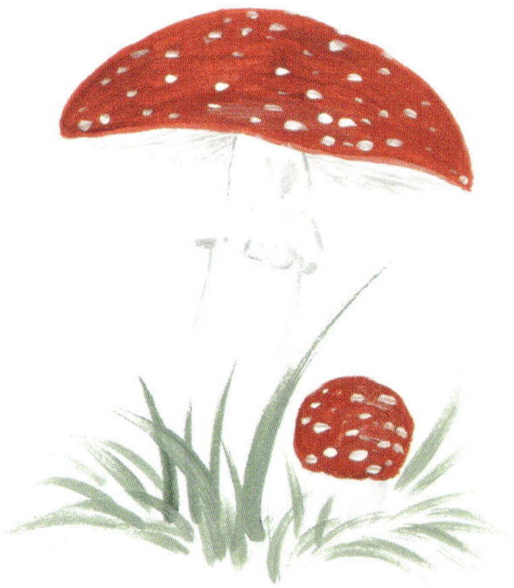

Red Toadstools

Brush: #1
Colors: Red, white and gray

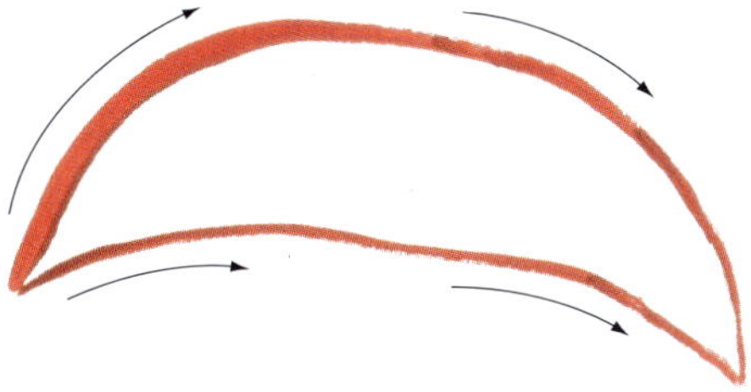

Outline the toadstool cap with red.

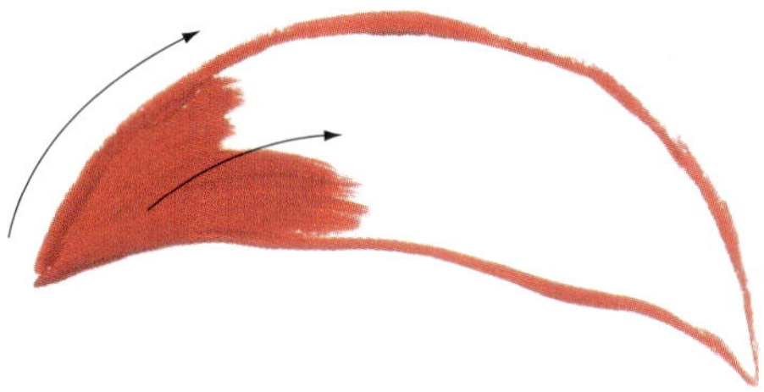

Fill in the cap with red paint using an old worn brush.

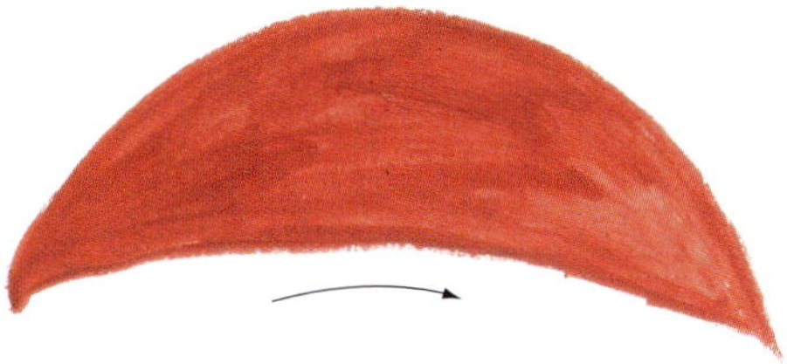

Mix a little water in the paint to make it glide easier and to add texture. If desired, use a little white for shading.

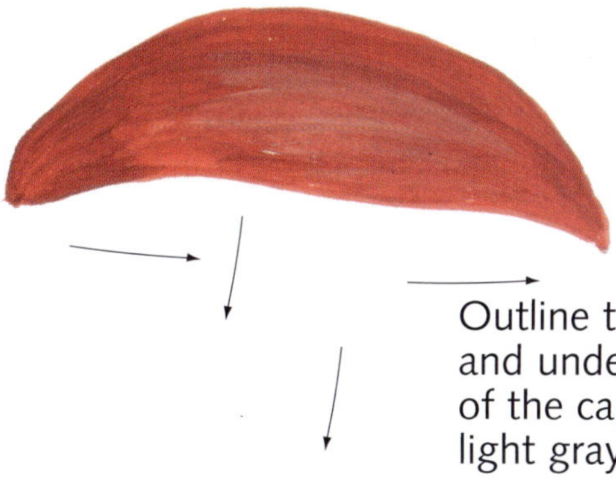

Outline the stem and underside of the cap with light gray.

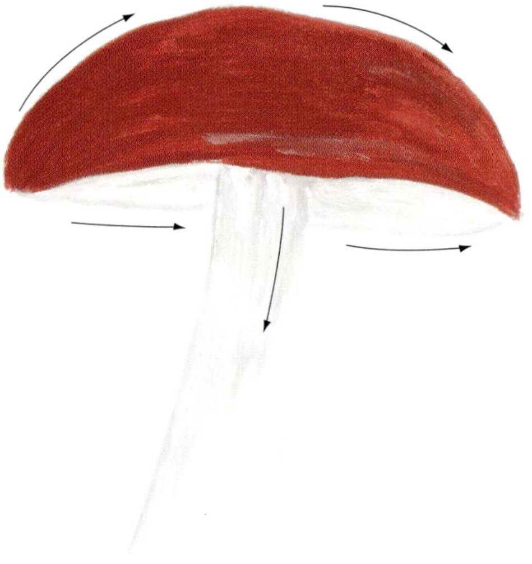

Fill the stem and underside of the cap with white and light gray. See below.

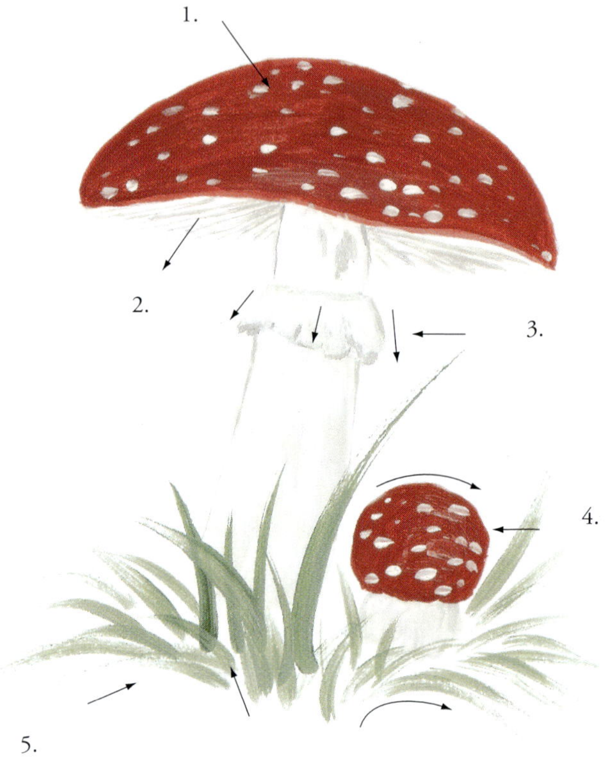

1. Dip your brush in white and paint small skin cells on the cap with the tip of the brush. Press down and let up.

2. Make the layers or "slices" with light gray.

3. With a slightly darker shade, paint the ring that identifies this mushroom.

4. Paint small mushrooms next to it for a pleasing design.

5. Paint some grass around the mushroom. Press down on the brush and draw up to create fine, thin blades.

Steinsopp

Brush: #1
Colors: Brown, yellow and white

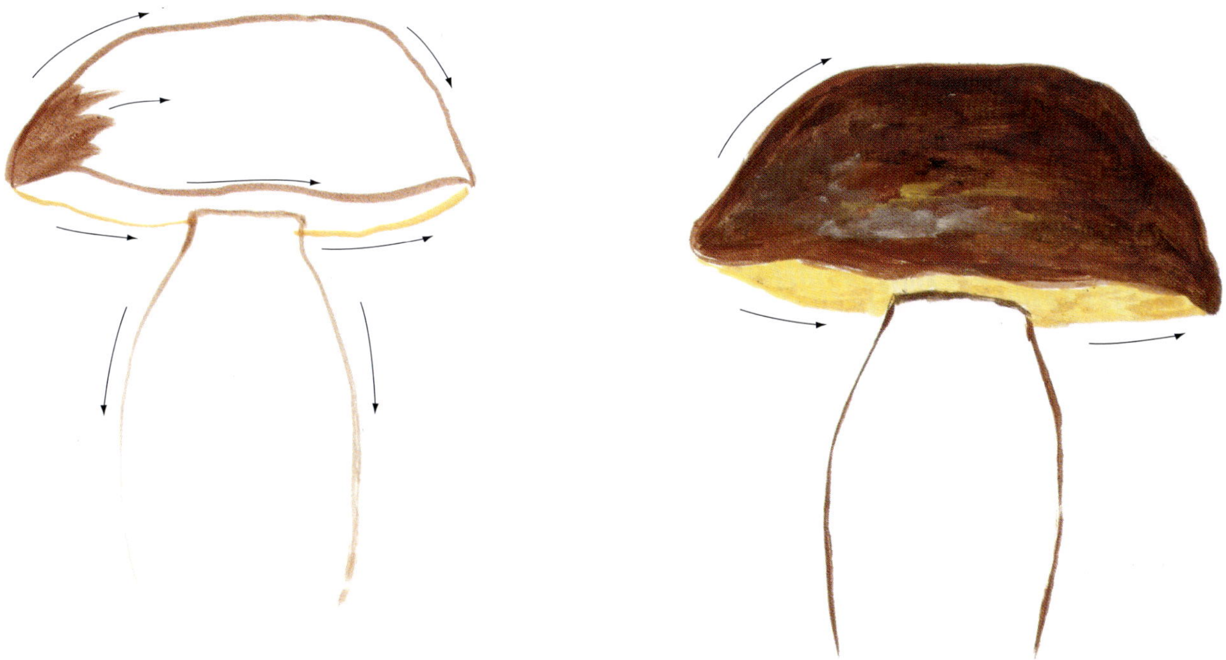

Paint this mushroom the same as you did the red toadstool.

1. Outline the cap with brown and fill. You can add a little water to the brown, and some yellow paint. This makes nice shading.

2. Fill underside of the cap with yellow.

3. Outline the stem with brown.

Remember to use an old, worn brush to fill the cap.

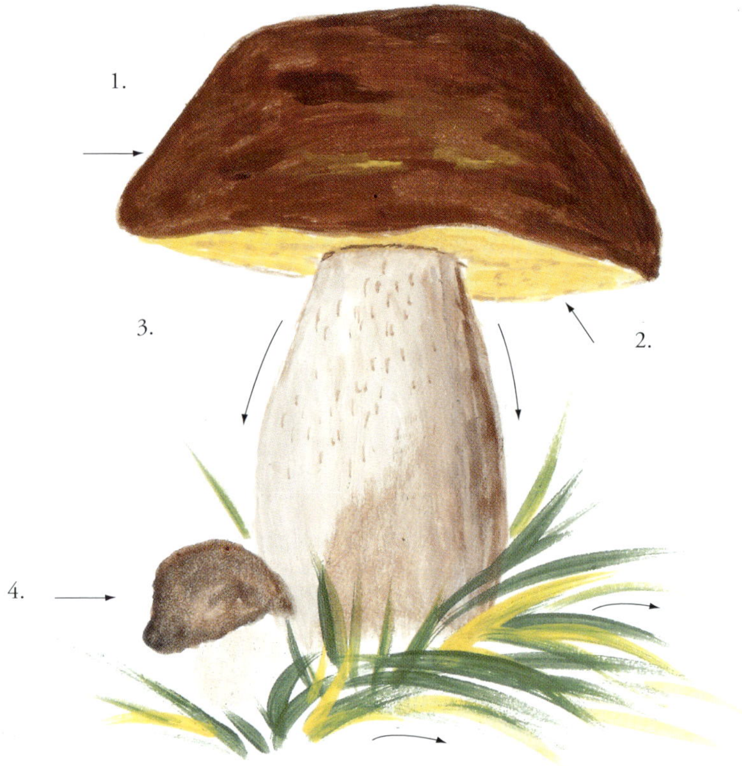

1. Fill in the cap so the shading has a natural, uneven texture.

2. Paint the underside yellow with light brown dots that you make with the tip of your brush.

3. Fill the stem with light brown and white. Additional shading on the stem is necessary because of the shadow created by the large cap. Paint small brown lines on the stem using the tip of your brush.

4. Paint a small mushroom next to the other one, and finish by painting some grass.

The "steinsopp" is known for being the best of all edible mushrooms, It is large and solid. The cap is a dull, dark brown on top, and yellow or cream colored underneath.

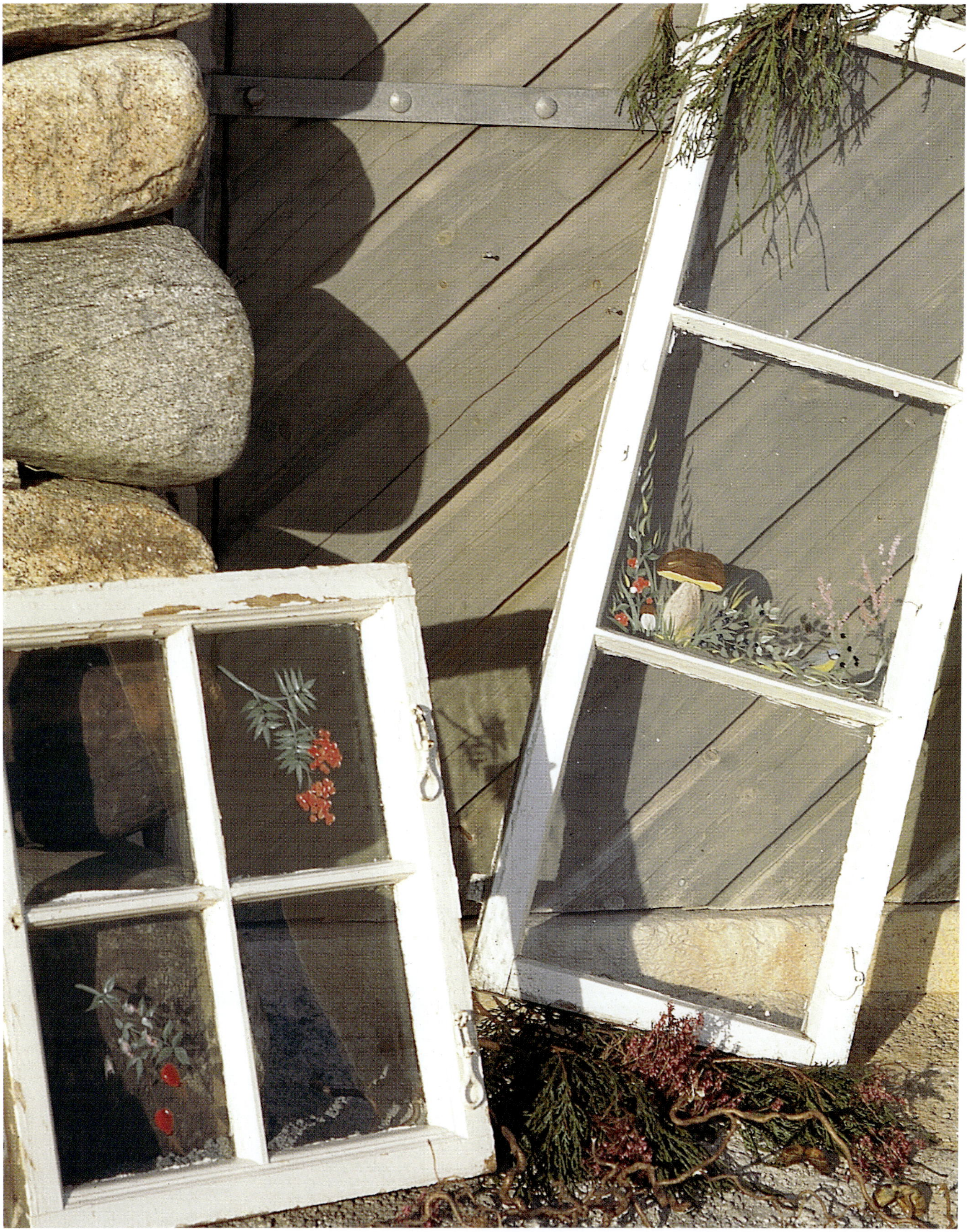

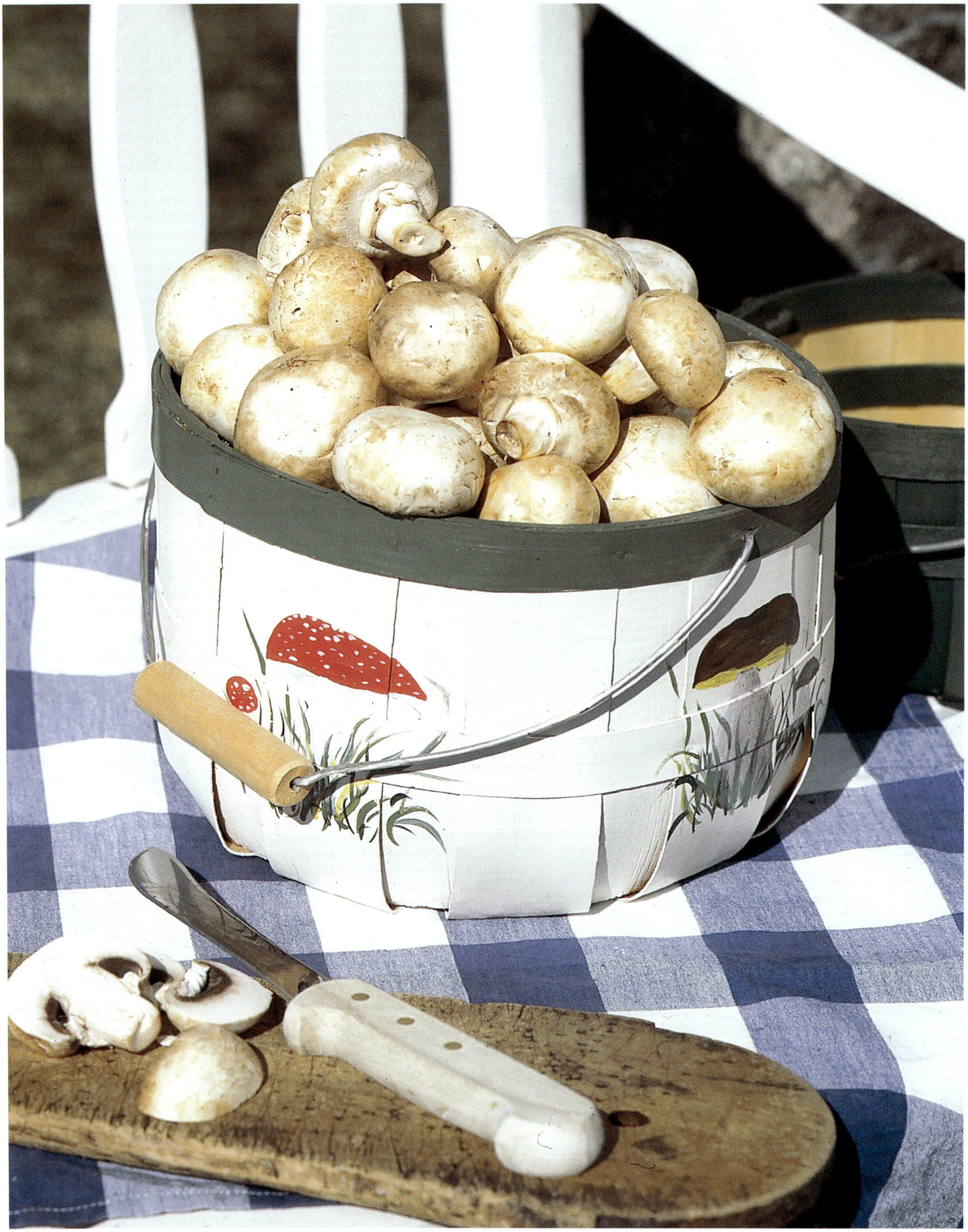

Matriske

Brush: #1
Colors: Orange, white, brown and green

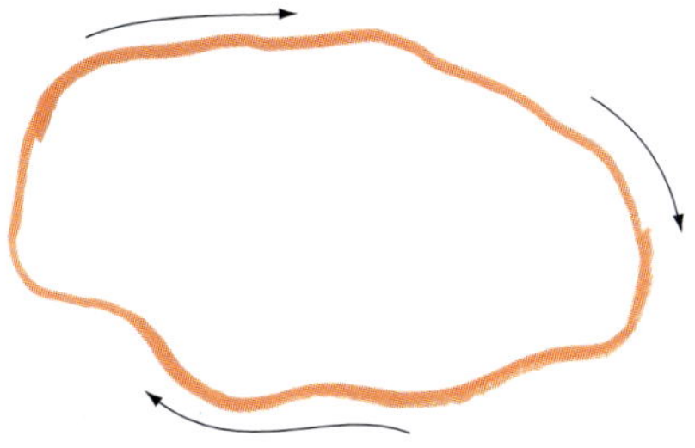

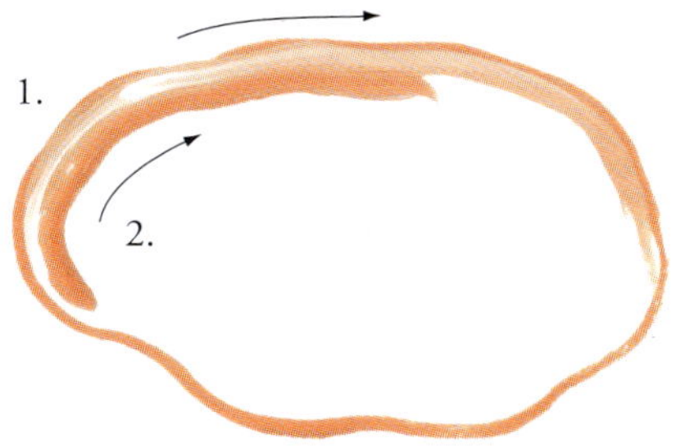

Outline the carrot colored cap. This cap also has green spots (see following page) and a circular design. This is how you build up the circular design: First paint one circle lightened with white, then paint a darker circle.

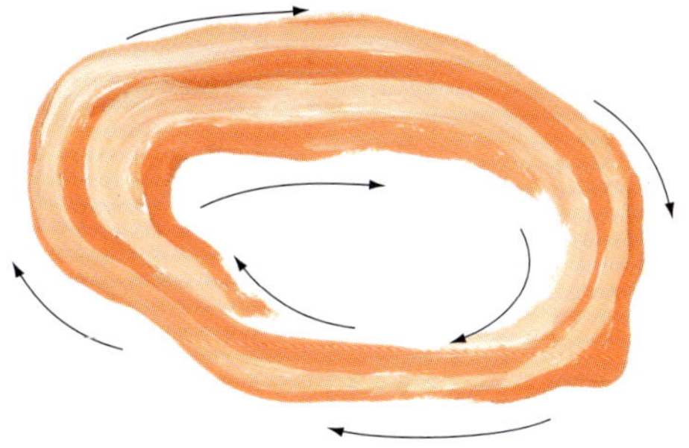

1. Paint circles of the mushrooms, fill in completely.
2. Put a little brown in the middle to enhance the depression in the mushroom.
3. The lowest part of the stem is smooth. Place some green spots around the mushroom and the stem.

Finally, paint a smaller mushroom and add some green grass.

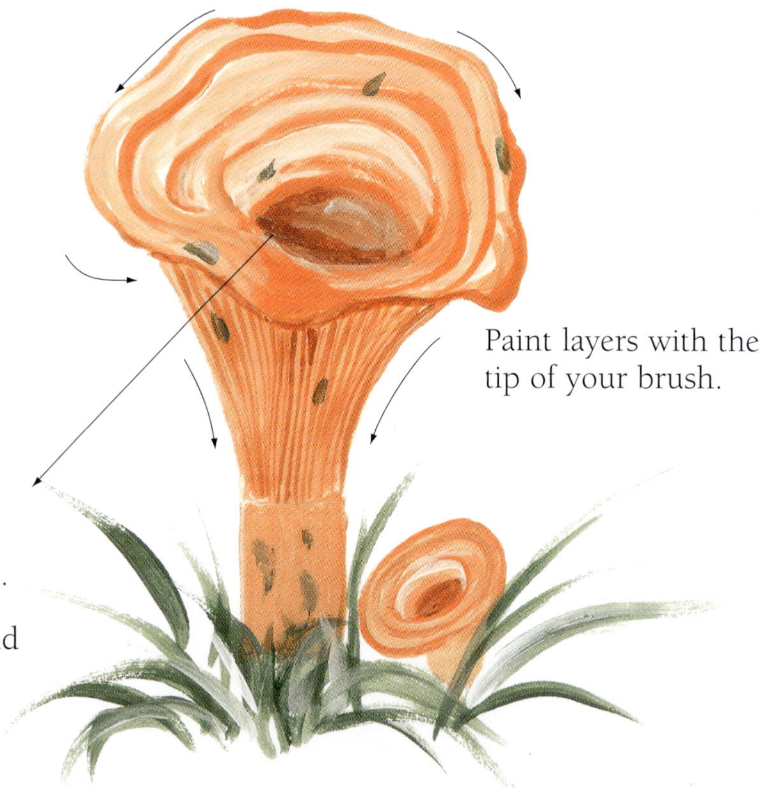

Honey Mushroom

Brush: #1
Colors: Brown, yellow, black and white

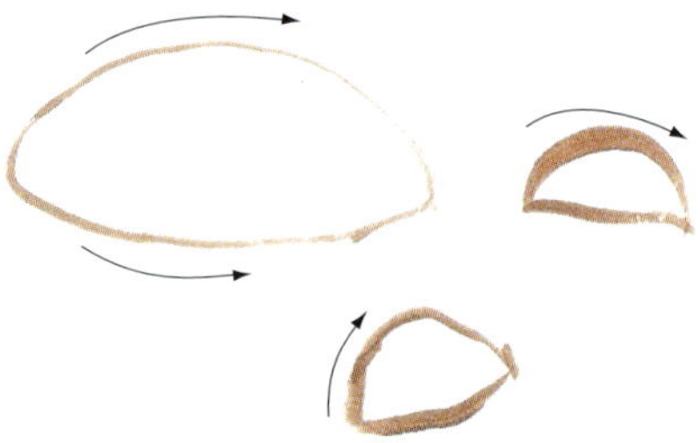

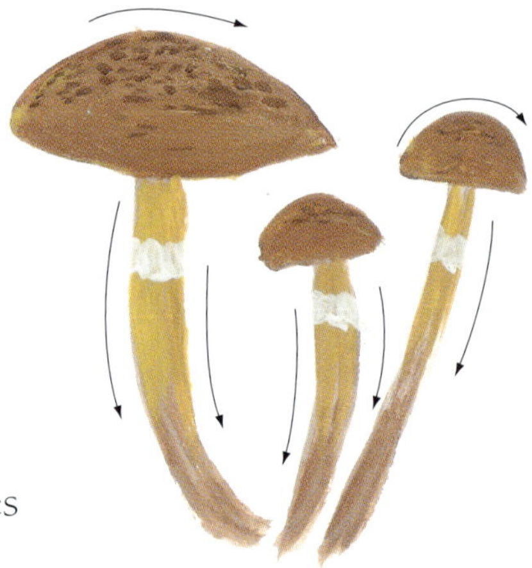

Outline some caps for the "honey mushroom."

This mushroom grows in large clusters on tree stumps and roots. The caps are brown on the top, and the stripes or discs underneath are lighter and more yellow.

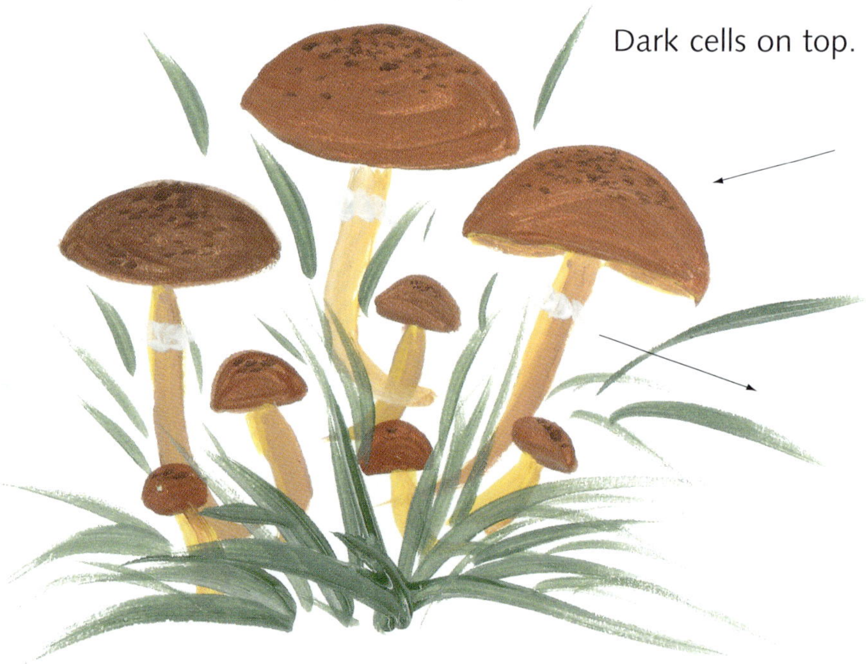

Dark cells on top.

Several "honey mushrooms" make a nice design. Mix a little yellow in the stems. On top of the caps make dark cells by using the tip of the brush. Mix in a little black for a darker shade of brown.

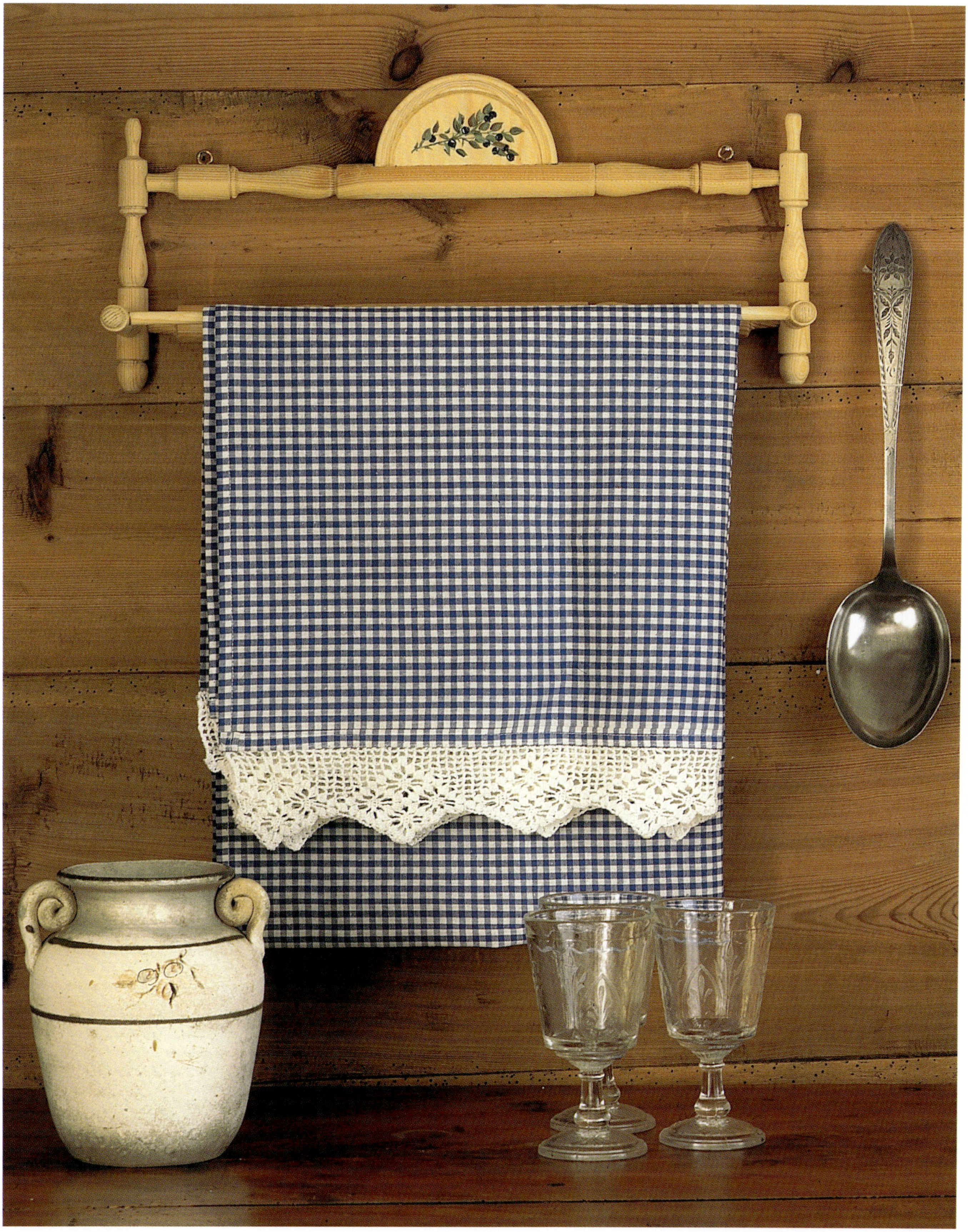

Blue Titmouse

Brush: #0
Colors: Blue, white, black and yellow

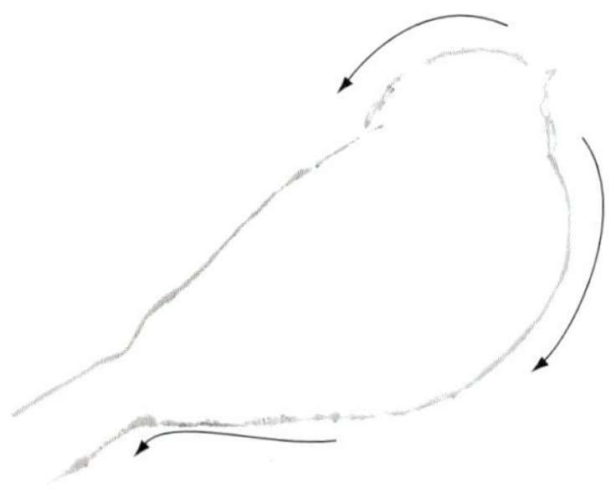

1. Outline the bird with a little black mixed with white for a gray shade.

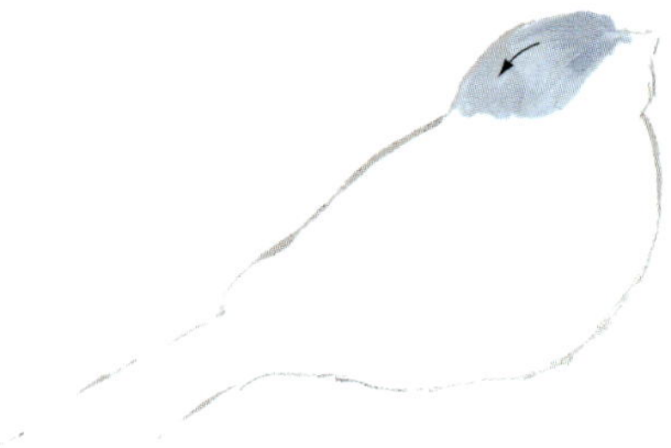

2. Paint the head blue.

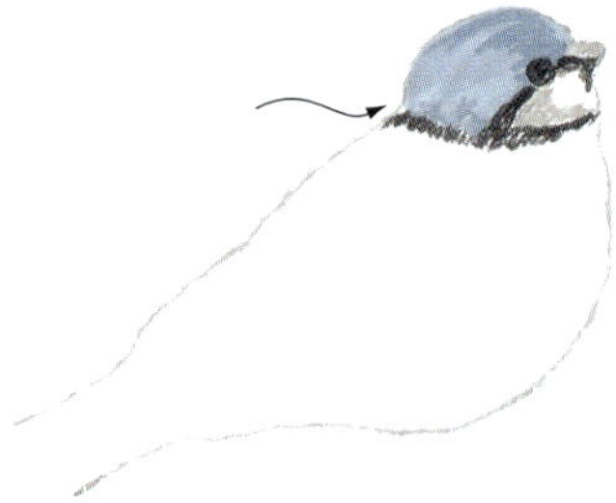

3. Paint a black eye and a small black "collar."

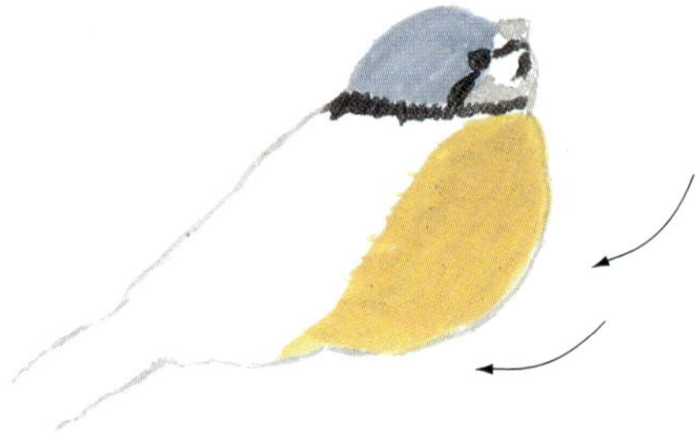

4. Paint the breast yellow from outside to in. Remember how the feathers lie on the bird.

5. Fill the back. (You can look in a bird book to find the correct colors.) Start the same way for other birds.

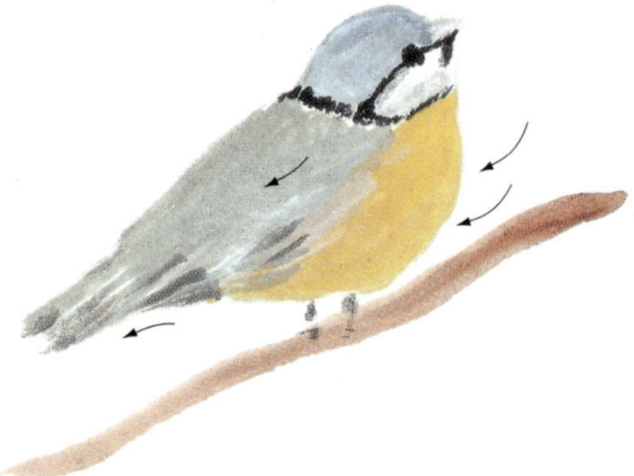

Bullfinch

Brush: #0
Colors: Black, blue, white and red

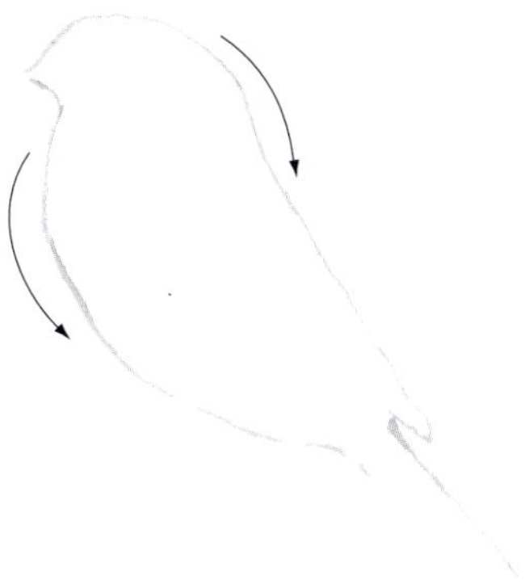

1. Paint the outline of the bird.

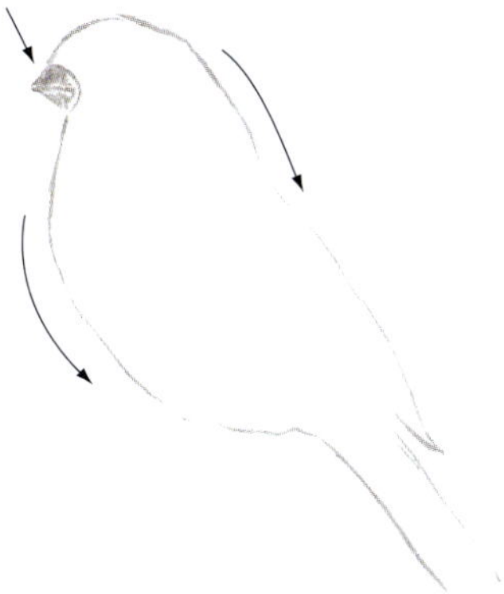

2. Make the beak more prominent with gray.

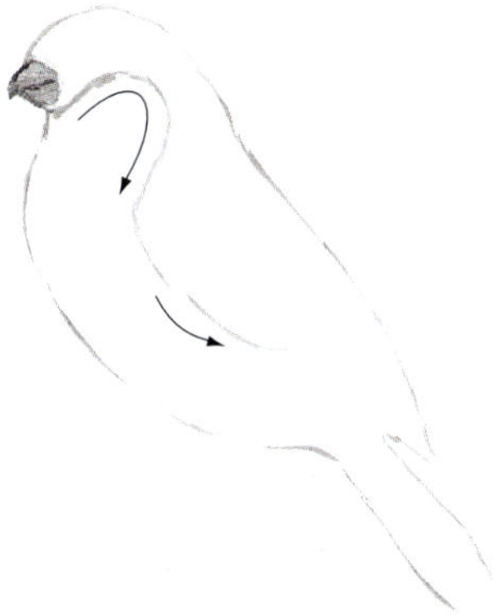

3. Paint the curve for the red breast.

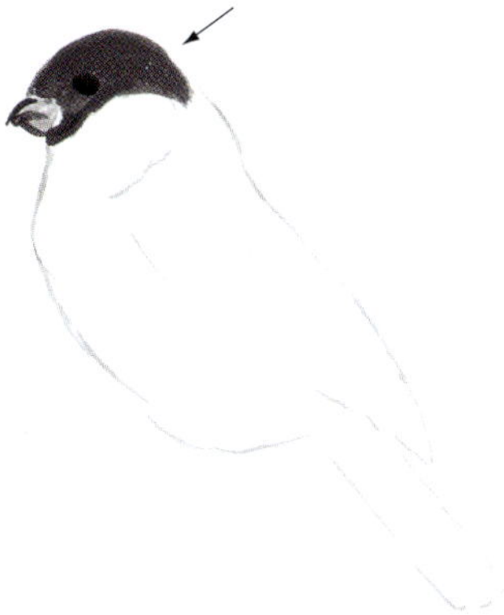

4. Paint the head dark gray with a black eye.

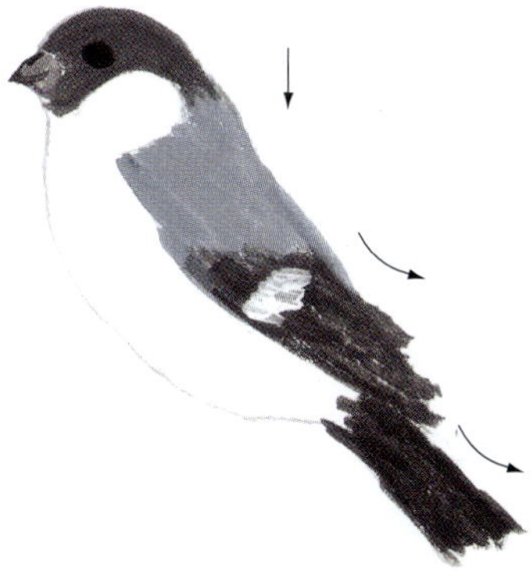

5. Paint the back blue and black, see arrows.

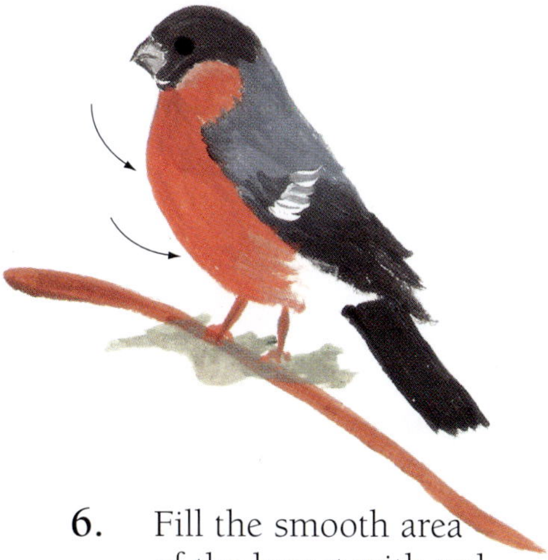

6. Fill the smooth area of the breast with red from outside to in.

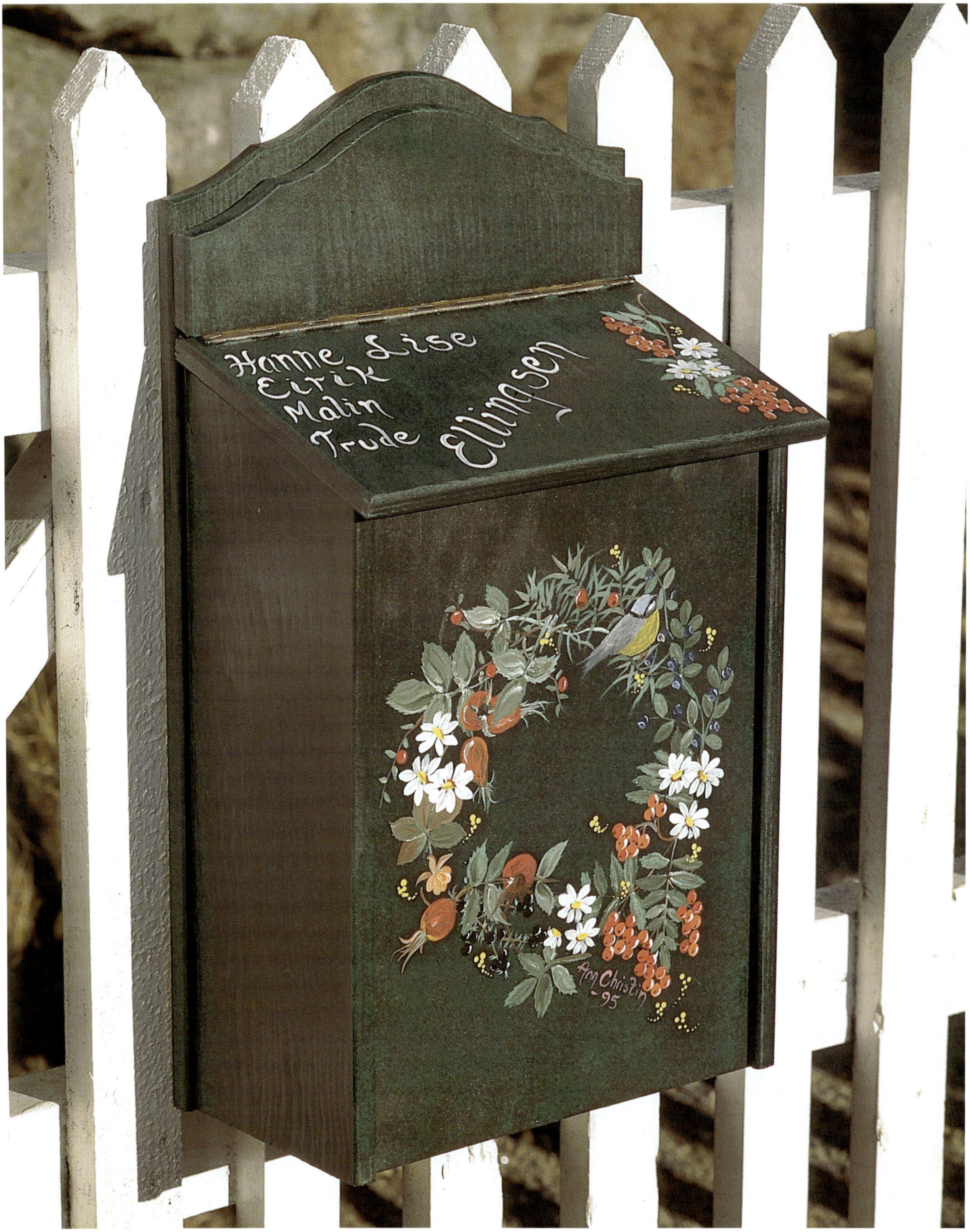
Hanne Lise
Eirik
Malin
Trude
Ellingsen
Ann Christin
-95

Composite Designs

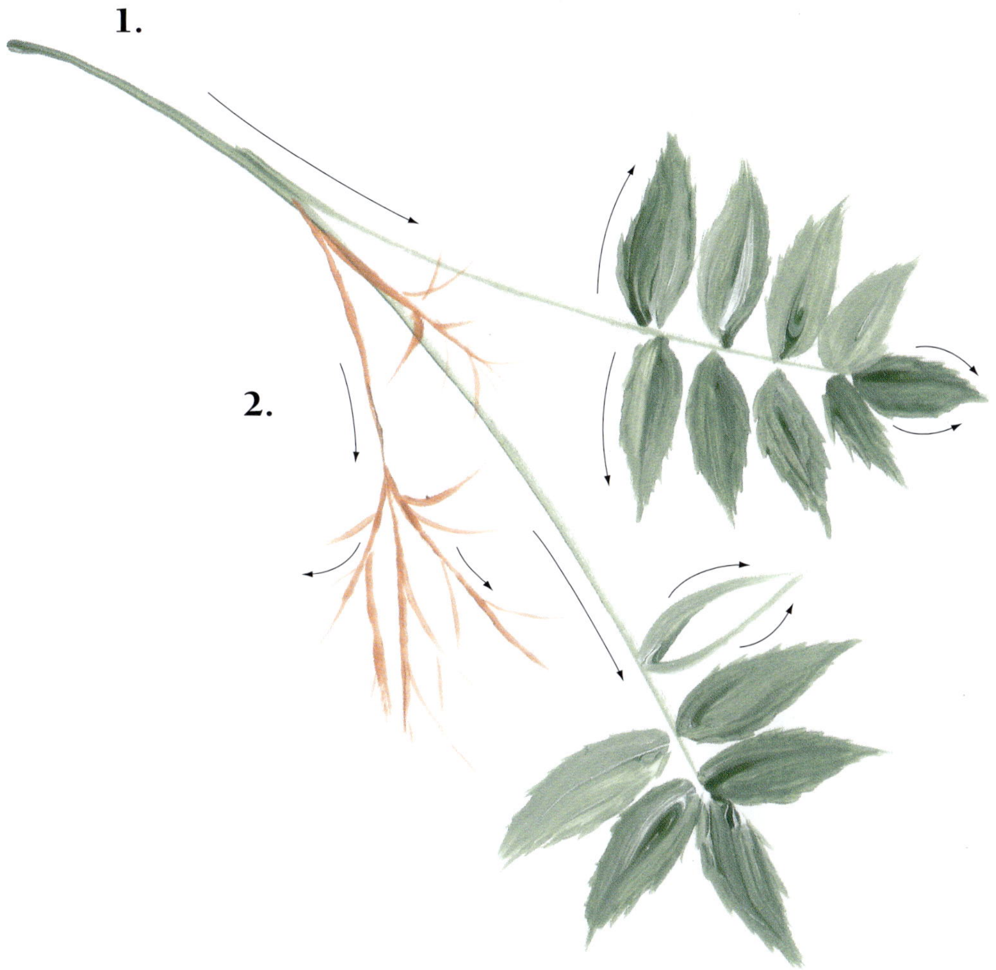

1. Paint some rowan berry stems with green. Then paint the leaves. Remember to mix a little white in the green to make the leaves more natural and lifelike.
2. Paint some brown stems for the berries to hang from. Follow direction of the arrows.

Composite Designs

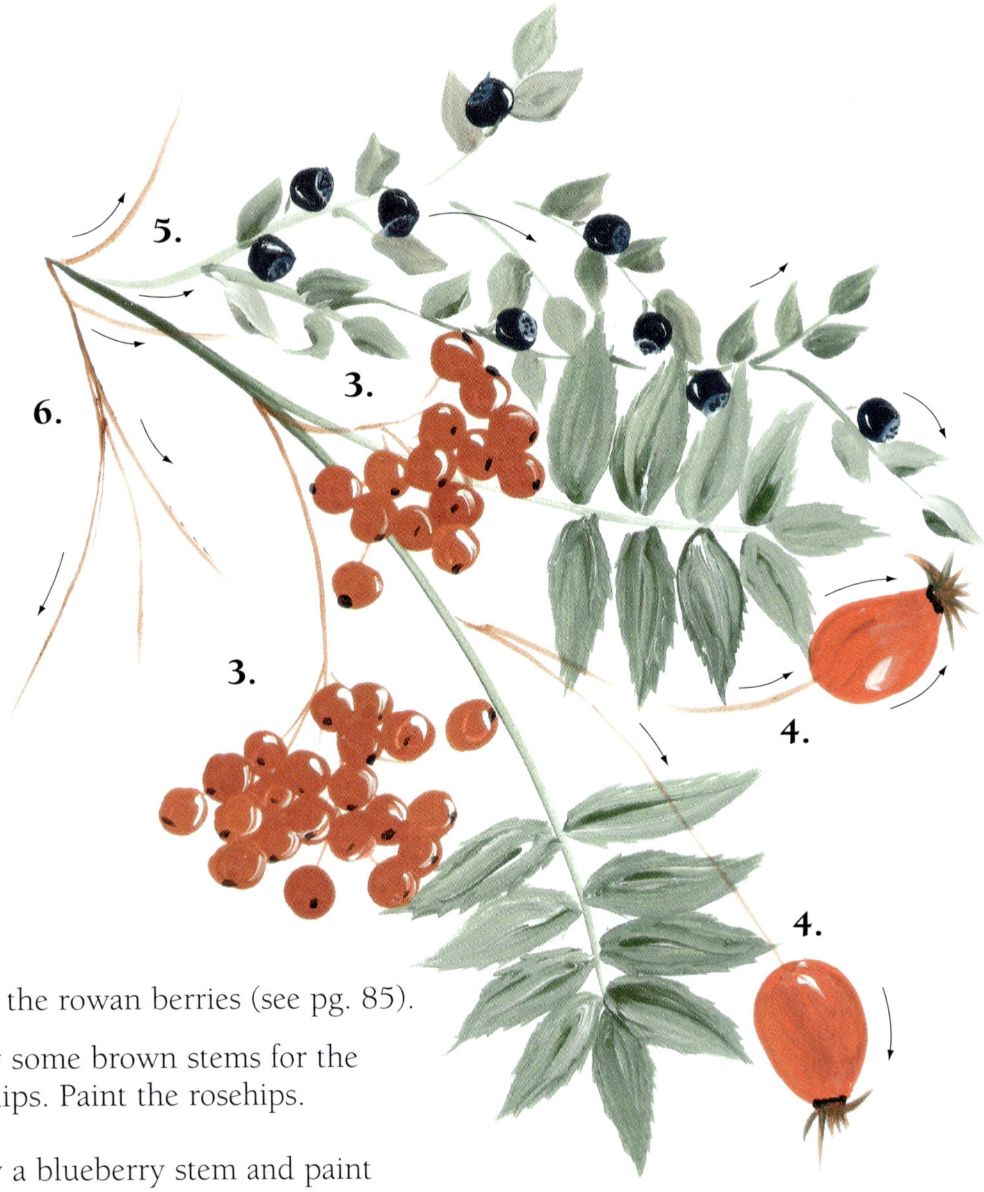

3. Paint the rowan berries (see pg. 85).
4. Draw some brown stems for the rosehips. Paint the rosehips.
5. Draw a blueberry stem and paint some blueberries.
6. Draw twigs for cowberries.

Composite Designs

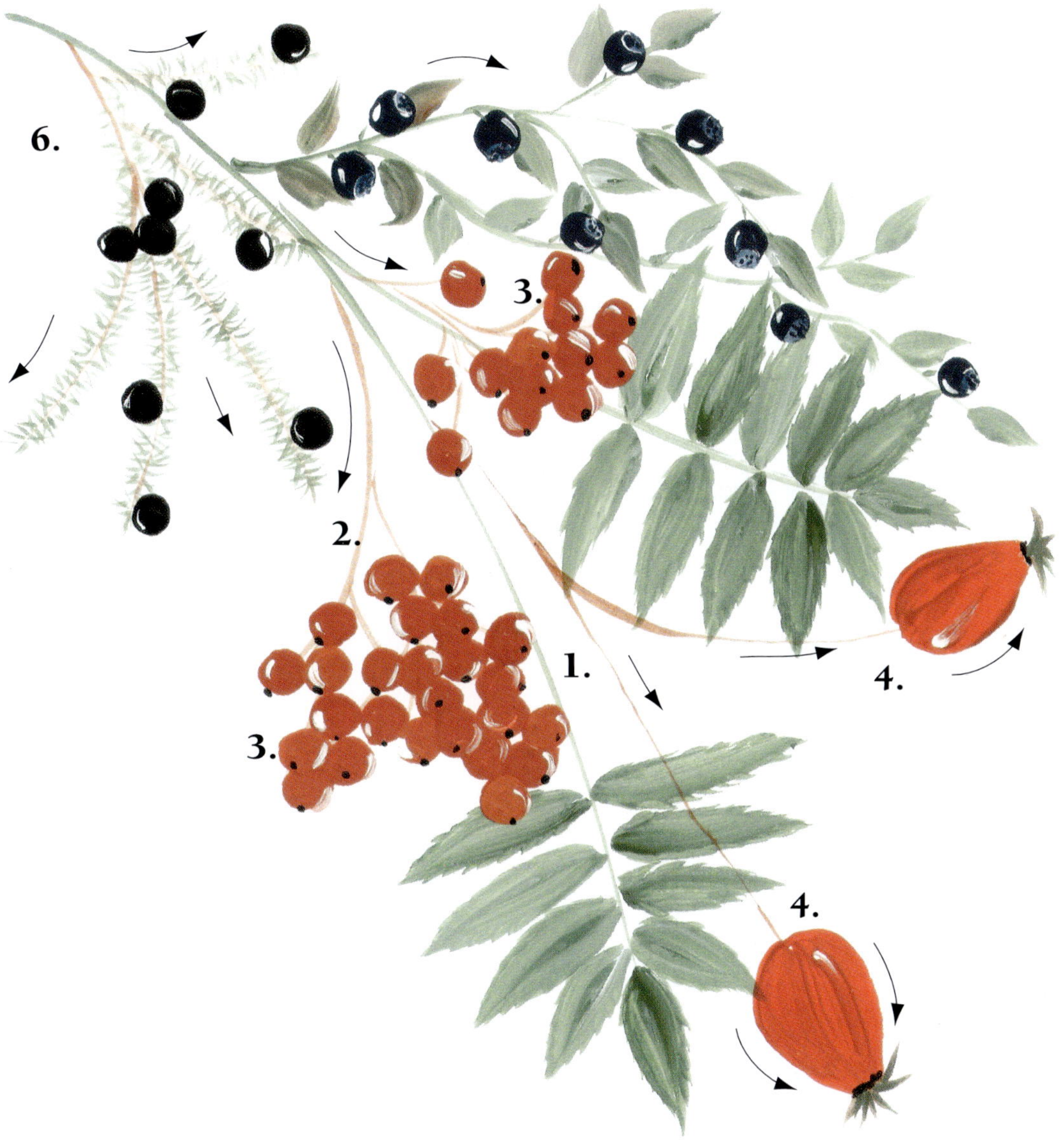

Paint small green leaves for the cowberries. Paint the berries and remember the small white "highlight" lines which emphasize the berries.

Now you have a basic composition that you can build on as you wish.

Composite Designs

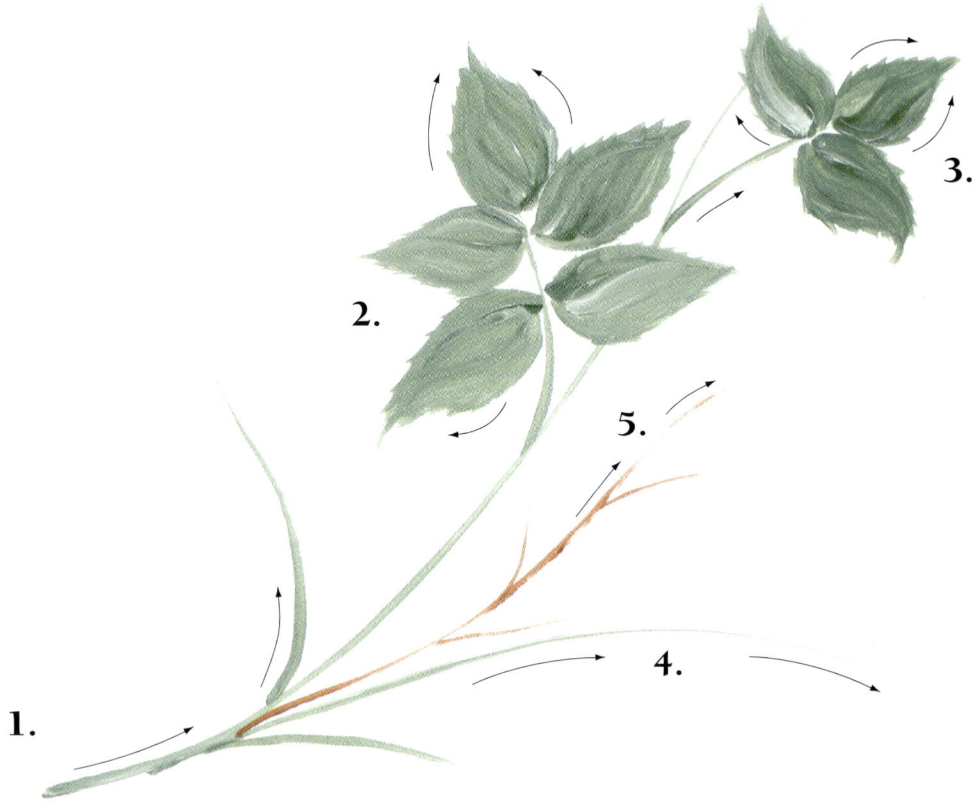

1. Paint stems for a rosehip flower (or dog rose).
2. Paint the leaves; fill from inside to out. Remember to mix white in the green.
3. Paint more leaves.
4. Paint a stem for the blueberries.
5. Paint a stem for the heather.

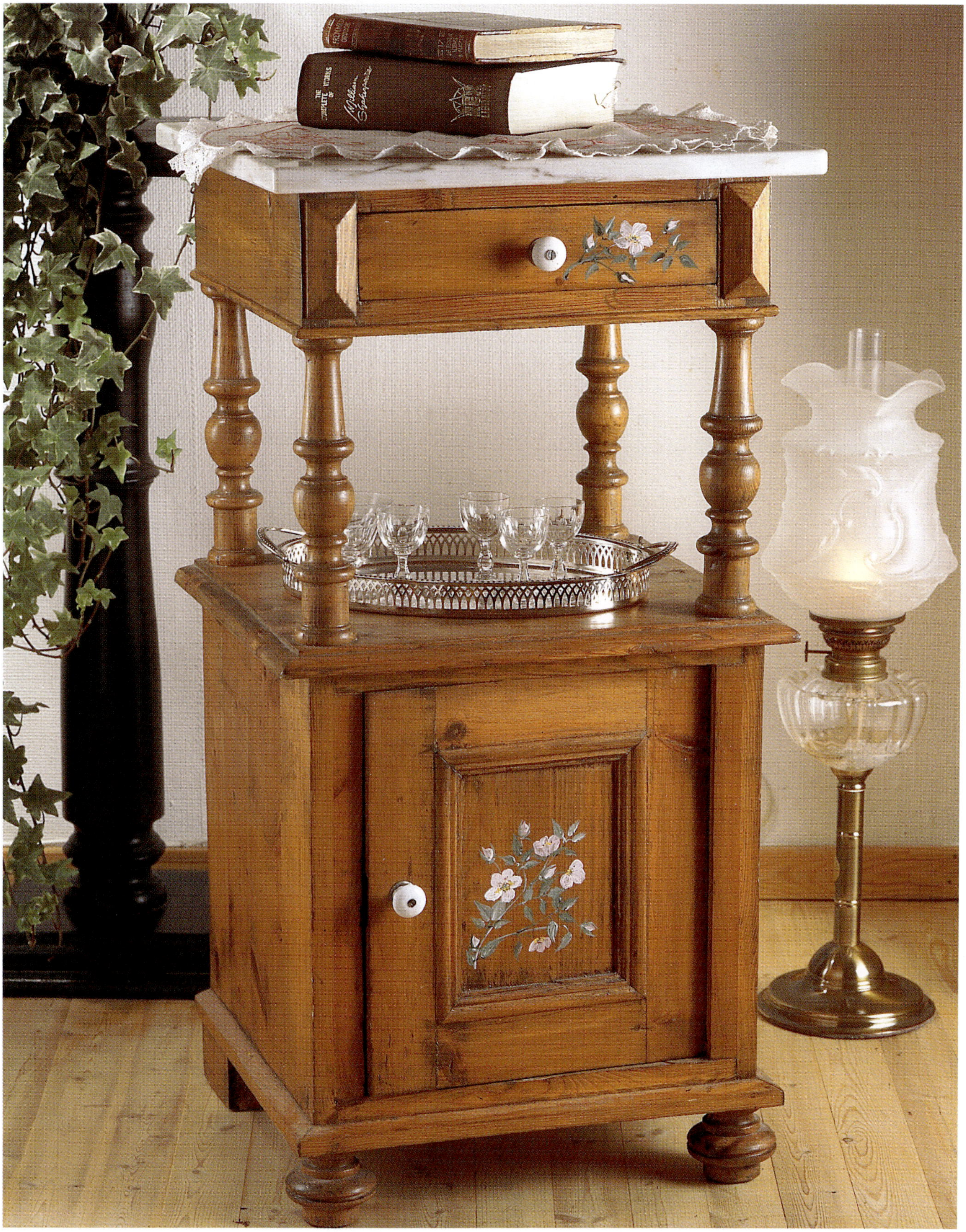

Composite Designs

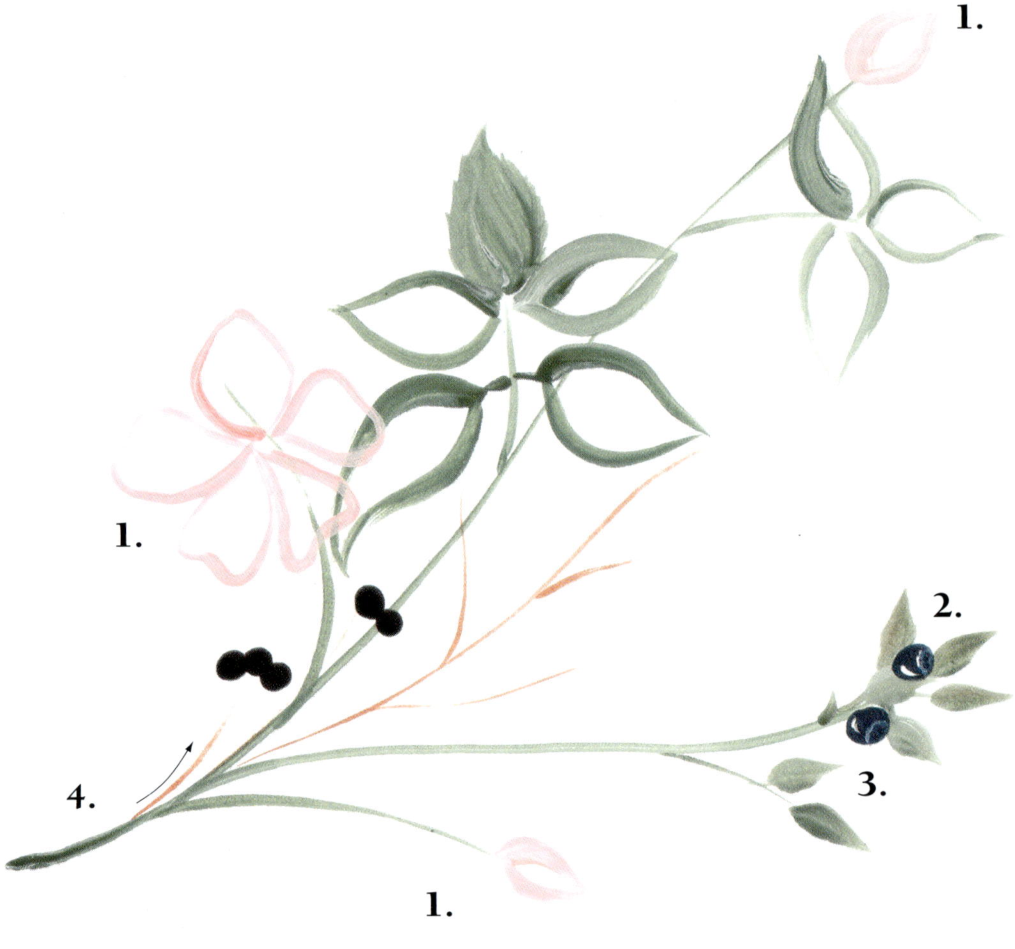

This is an example of creating a "mixed" design.

1. Paint a rosehip flower (or dog rose) and some buds.
2. Paint leaves on the blueberry stem.
3. Then paint the blueberries.
4. Paint a stem for the blackberries.

If you are not sure how to paint the different items, check back in the book and read the instructions.

Composite Designs

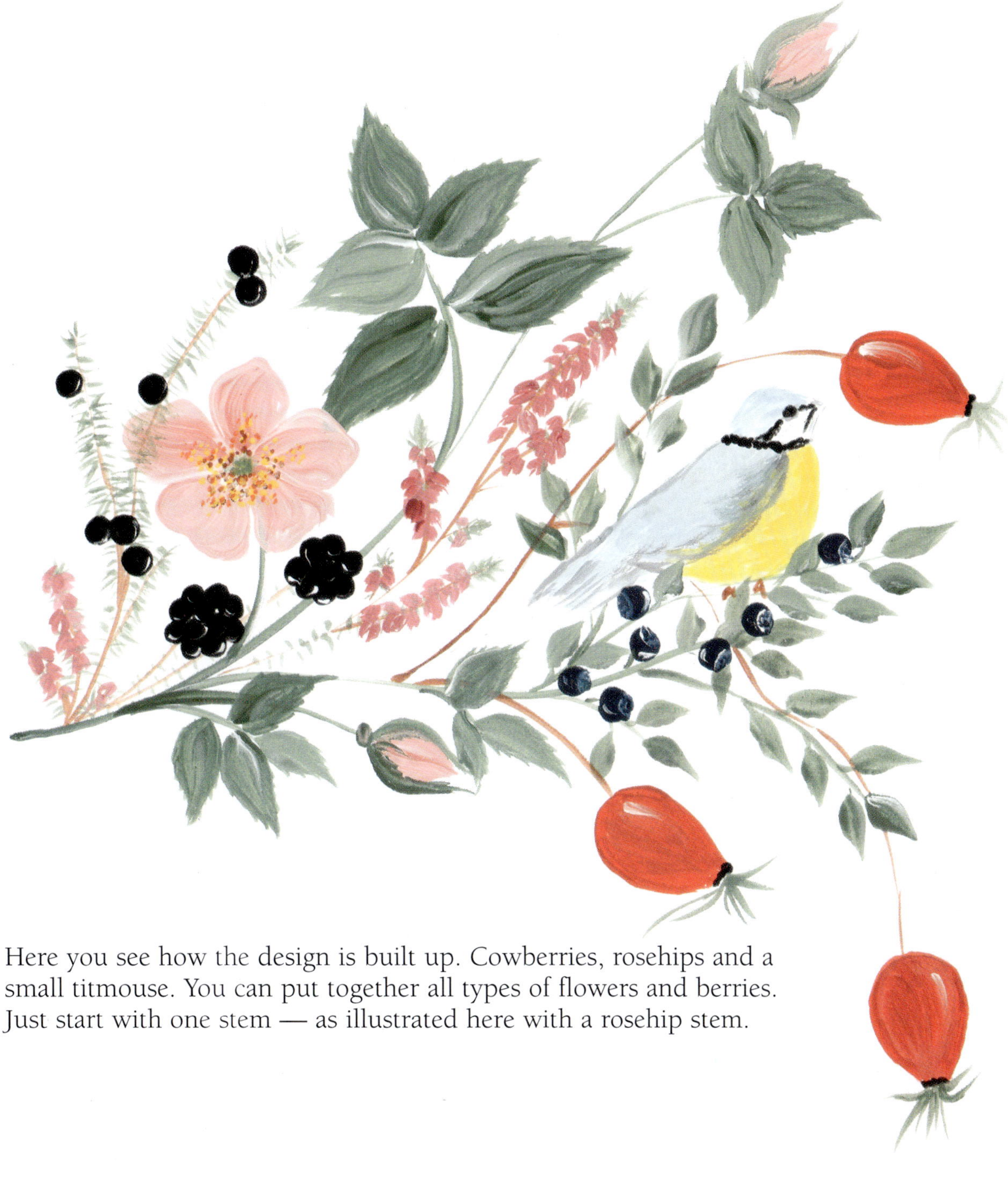

Here you see how the design is built up. Cowberries, rosehips and a small titmouse. You can put together all types of flowers and berries. Just start with one stem — as illustrated here with a rosehip stem.

Index

List of Suppliers

The Artist's Club
13118 NE 4th Street
Vancouver, WA 98684
TEL 360-260-8877

Cabin Craft
1500 Westpark Way
Euless, TX 76040
TEL 817-571-3837
FAX 817-571-4925

Christopher S. Burch
216 W Hyde Park Place
Tampa, FL 33606
TEL 813-251-1522

CLC Designs Inc.
6204 Edith NE
Albuquerque, NM 87111
TEL 800-745-8707
FAX 505-344-4700

Covered Bridge Crafts
449 Amherst Street
Nashua, NH 03063
TEL 603-889-2179
FAX 603-882-5240

Decorative Artist's Workbook
1507 Dana Avenue
Cincinnati, OH 45207
TEL 800-283-0963

Decorative Artist's Book Club
1507 Dana Avenue
Cincinnati, OH 45207
TEL 513-531-8250

Gail's Brush & Palette
4159 S 76th Street
Milwaukee, WI 53220
TEL 414-321-6611

Grant Allison Decorative Painting Inc.
20 W 20th Street
New York, NY 10011
TEL 212-675-2286
FAX 212-675-2286

Homecraft Express Inc.
PO Box 24890
San Jose, CA 95154
TEL 800-301-7377
FAX 800-528-4193

The Paint Box
1540 NE 172nd Street
Portland, OR 97216
TEL 503-255-8560

Patty's Country Sampler
1931 N 3rd Street
Terre Haute, IN 47804
TEL 812-235-6896

Pitter Patter Pigtail Girls
2210 Silver Lane #308
Saint Paul, MN 55112
TEL 218-463-1984

Plain and Fancy
600 Baxter Lane
Nashville, TN 37220
TEL 615-373-3546
FAX 615-370- 8503

Porcelain Tole Treasures
3446 McCutcheon Road
Columbus, OH 43230
TEL 614-471-7407

Priscilla's Little Red Tole House
PO Box 521013
Tulsa, OK 74152
TEL 918-743-6072
FAX 918-743-5075

Rococo Rose
3936 S Semoran Boulevard
Orlando, FL 32822
TEL 407-381-1142
FAX 407-380-9577

Sharon & Gayle Publications
601 Washington Avenue
Newport, KY 41071
TEL 606-655-4700
FAX 606-655-4702

Stan Brown Arts & Crafts
13435 NE Whitaker Way
Portland, OR 97230
TEL 503-257-0559

Steph's Folk Art Studio
2435 Old Philadelphia Park
Smoketown, PA 17576
TEL 717-299-4973

Stone Bridge Collection
RR4
Parkenham, ON K0A 2X0
Canada
TEL 613-624-5080
FAX 613-624-5081

Teaberry Farms
1214 SE 159th Avenue
Vancouver, WA 98684
TEL 360-896-3571

Viking Woodcrafts Inc.
1317 8th Street SE
Waseca, MN 56093
TEL 507-835-8043
FAX 507-835-3895

Wet Paint Inc.
1684 Grand Avenue
Saint Paul, MN 55105
TEL 612-698-6431
FAX 612-698-8041

Woodworks
4521 Anderson Boulevard
Fort Worth, TX 76117
TEL 817-581-5230
FAX 817-581-5235